LANDON

LAN

a memoir

LANDON DONOVAN

written by RYAN BERMAN

DON

PAGE TWO

Cataloguing in publication information
is available from Library and Archives Canada.
ISBN 978-1-77458-691-4 (hardcover)
ISBN 978-1-77458-696-9 (ebook)

Page Two
pagetwo.com

Page Two™ is a trademark owned by Page Two Strategies Inc.,
and is used under license by authorized licensees

Jacket and interior design by Peter Cocking
Front jacket and case photos by Tanya Goehring
Back jacket photo by Kevork Djansezian, Getty Images
courtesy U.S. Soccer
Printed and bound in Canada by Friesens
Distributed in Canada by Raincoast Books
Distributed in the US and internationally by Macmillan

26 27 28 29 30   5 4 3 2 1

landondonovan.com
ryanberman.com

LANDON

CONTENTS

THE ANTHEM

THEY SAY you play the hand you're dealt.

If that's the case, someone decided to play 52-card pickup with my life.

When I brought the deck back together, there was no King.

The Queen was overwhelmed.

And I came out as a pair.

As much as I wish we came out as two aces...

That was the furthest from our truth.

My twin hated soccer for taking her brother away.

I'm Landon.

This is my open book.

WARM-UP

"WHENEVER YOU'RE ready, Landon."

Juliet waits patiently, knowing the hot tea I'm cupping will serve as a magical elixir to calm my mind before her time-traveling couch takes off. We both know it's time to remember. I oblige. I put down the tea and we begin. My eyes shut, memory open, we teleport together to a little-tyke version of me.

I have journeyed back to a rare early moment of serenity.

I am three years old. It is a quiet, sunny day.

I am behind the screen door of my 900-square-foot childhood home, eagerly waiting for someone. The sun glistens brightly through the door. My face is happily warm. I squint as I scan outside through the screen. Outside it is quiet. *Really* quiet.

Out the door to my left is an unassuming tree I like to climb that's just off my mom's property on the neighbors' yard. It's not the tallest tree or the most colorful. If you're not paying attention, you could miss this Douglas fir. But I like everything about this tree. It's sturdy. Stable. Reliable. It isn't going anywhere. It stands tall with great posture, and it's not trying too hard to be anything but what it is: a tree. I imagine this tree, alive and at peace, knows it never has to be anything it isn't.

And underneath that Douglas fir is the someone I have been waiting for.

My eyes light up when I realize . . . *there's my dad.* At three years old, I consider my dad as much a possession as he is a human. He sits cross-legged under the tree with a smile on his face. And he is waiting for just me.

I throw open the porch door and my quick little legs dart me right over to him. I climb into my dad's lap under the tree. When I nestle in, it feels like Christmas morning. No words are said or needed. Safe, enveloped in my dad's arms, we sit together facing the street and life feels complete.

The realness of the moment fades away as I open my eyes and am transported back to Juliet's office. She smiles at me and gives me space to dry my welled-up eyes.

The time machine ride has now ended. I remember why my father was forced to sit off our property in the first place.

The restraining order.

84'

IT'S MAY OF 2014. The song at the top of America's charts is Pharrell Williams's "Happy." I am the opposite of this.

> It might seem crazy what I'm 'bout to say
> Sunshine, she's here, you can take a break

I am 32, and I'm exhausted. I know 32 doesn't sound old—it's not in most professions—but my body feels the aches of a decade-and-a-half-long professional career, one that started when most kids would have been learning how to start a car. But taking a break right now is the furthest thing from my mind. Quite the opposite: My focus is entirely on getting ready for a friendly match against Azerbaijan, a mere four days away. Then we're off to New Jersey for a tune-up against Turkey. This will be followed by a quick jaunt to Jacksonville for one last 90-minute exhibition against Nigeria that should help us mirror our World Cup match next month against Ghana.

> Bring me down
> Can't nothing, bring me down
> My level's too high to, bring me down
> Can't nothing, bring me down, I said

Thirty of America's best soccer players—myself included—have been hammering away in Jurgen Klinsmann's fitness-obsessed routine for a week now. This is our coach's way of getting us ready for the weather we're likely to face at the World Cup in Brazil. It's not pleasant training in this heat, but it's Jurgen's show and I'm lucky to be in it.

I almost wasn't—another reason why I'm not thinking about taking a break just yet. I had a break a year ago when I was on the verge of *broken*. That was a first for me, a three-month sabbatical from soccer that coincided with the early stages of World Cup qualifiers and a serious bout of depression. When I walked away, I knew I might be giving up my fourth consecutive World Cup. And if that's what it meant, I was at peace with it. I took the time I needed to release some of the pressure that comes with being Landon Donovan.

That three-month break saved my life. It almost took my life too.

Jurgen hasn't forgiven me for taking time off as he tends to prefer fanatical devotion—both to the sport and to him. But we've been patching the cracks in our acquaintanceship as best we can. I now have my legs back under me after another season in Major League Soccer. After a couple months' cold shoulder, the wiry German invited me back into the national team for the CONCACAF Gold Cup—the Confederation of North, Central America and Caribbean Association Football—where not only we took home Gold, but I scored five goals and was awarded the tournament's Best Player trophy. Since then, Jurgen's called me in for a couple World Cup qualifiers and the current stretch run to Brazil.

I'm a hot air balloon that could go to space
With the air, like I don't care, baby, by the way

While we're only eight days into our three-week camp, it's been amazing being back with the guys. Michael. Jozy. DaMarcus. Tim. It's just after noon, and we've finished our training session. I stay behind and keep working as the other guys head back to the locker rooms. On this day, I'm the last to escape the field. You think Jurgen's the only one who likes fanatical devotion? So do I. I've always been freakishly obsessive with my training. I learned early on that if you want to be the best, you have to put in the work. *How you do anything is how you do everything.* Today is no different. It doesn't matter if the heat is heavy and the day is muggy. Putting in my work is the box I need to check. So I put in my extra time, and only then do I finally head to join the rest inside.

It's a lengthy walk to the Stanford lockers and I'm almost there, but as I turn the final corner, I'm surprised to see a familiar thin, weathered figure waiting outside. It's Jurgen. His short sandy hair is, as always, ever so nonchalantly tousled and he looks like he hasn't slept. He's fidgety. Looking mischievous. Waiting for something.

As I approach, I realize the wiry German is waiting for me. There are two chairs set out, like in one of those police procedurals where they bring a guy in for questioning. I guess Jurgen's about to hold court and I suddenly feel like maybe I'm the suspect, but I have less than a clue what this meeting could be about. Maybe he wants to talk about managing my minutes? A strategy for mentoring Julian Green? Or could this be another one of his Jurgenesque ideas that never quite seem to amount to a plan? We've only had a week of practice, so I don't connect the dots when he points to the chair and...

Please have a seat, Landon.

Here come bad news, talking this and that (Yeah!)
Well, give me all you got, don't hold it back (Yeah!)

In a direct and swift 15 seconds, Jurgen delivers the crushing news that I won't be heading to Brazil, striking me from my place on the squad. There will be no game for me against Azerbaijan. No quick jaunt to New Jersey to take on Turkey. No Nigeria tune-up to get ready for Ghana.

I try to make my case, but he's made his decision. There is no going back. It's so sudden and random, it hardly makes sense. He's already told us no one would be cut until after the friendlies, and...

frankly, I wasn't really worried about that, much less catching it now in the form of this sudden gut-rattling sucker punch.

Oddly, as Jurgen is verbally cleaning out my Team USA locker, all I can think about is him chalking the national anthem on the wall of the Stanford locker room so the handful of players who had barely set foot on American soil wouldn't look silly for not knowing "The Star-Spangled Banner" on national television.

We sat in those chairs for five minutes total, and in this short evisceration, Jurgen tells me that other players are ahead of me.

Let's agree to disagree, Jurgen.

They weren't ahead of me in knowing what the World Cup was like. I'd been to three. They weren't ahead of me in knowing how to score a goal—or five—in the world's most glorious pressure-cooker tournament that's tuned in to by half the globe's population. That's 3.5 *billion* pairs of eyeballs if you're keeping score. They certainly weren't ahead of me in knowing what it's like to play 150 games for the red, white, and blue. How could some of them, with no true connection to "the land of the free and the home of the brave," be ahead of me in knowing what it's like to be an American?

But in this cold, quick five minutes, I also know Jurgen isn't going to change his mind. I am not going to the World Cup. There will be no last hoorah. It is a shock that sends my system spiraling.

I walk into the locker room, and I can feel 23 pairs of eyes that know what I have just found out. Some look away; some shift downward. The irony of staying on the field and working extra is that I am the last of seven from the squad of 30 to find out that Jurgen has just ended their dream.

I stagger in disbelief to the bathroom and fling open the door to the handicap stall. Quite fitting, as I feel disabled. I've been holding it together but I can't anymore—the full weight of it hits, and I slide to the ground and begin to cry.

There isn't a single part of me that ever felt I would be left behind from this tournament. But I'll be back in the country I love while so many of my brothers I had adoringly fought with before would go to war without me.

This ... this is what I get for caring.

Moments later, where words would fail me, teammates would not.

One by one, they trickled in.

Michael Bradley.

DaMarcus Beasley.

Kyle Beckerman.

They slide to the ground next to me, all of us sitting in silence in the handicapped stall. No one speaks ... besides, what is there to say? We've spent so much time together, these three and me. We've known each other since we were kids. We've come up through the ranks together. Seen the world together. Fought the world together.

If soccer players are good for anything, it's their ability to intuitively see the next play long before it happens. And the longer you take the field together, the more you can correctly anticipate each other's next move. But this was a move none of us saw coming.

They were off to Brazil.

And I was off the roster.

O'

ONCE UPON A TIME, there was a thin, hockey-loving Canadian who had been married once before. In 1980, he made his way to America with nothing more than a backpack and his passport. Now "free" and across the U.S. border, he landed in a familiar-sounding town: Ontario—albeit the one in Southern California—ready to shed his past life and start a new one. This man was Tim Donovan, a take-charge, good-looking kind of guy.

One day, at a pool party in the early '80s, Tim laid eyes on 28-year-old Donna Kenney. She had already been through a divorce of her own and came out the other side with a four-year-old son, who was living nearby with his dad. She was easy on Tim's eyes, a let-life-come-to-her type of gal.

That was fine by Tim, and he pursued her with abandon. The two connected; sparks flew. So much so that for a few small, blissful blinks, things between Tim and Donna settled into a fun and lively honeymoon phase.

But before the California sun could even warm them up to any stated "I do's," the two would get some life-changing news.

Me.

THE BEGINNING

The year was 1981. MTV had just blessed the airwaves for the first time... not like my mom or dad would have known. They were too poor to have that channel. Mom in her pregnant state was almost as wide as she was tall, positively bursting at the belly. If you saw her, you would not have guessed she was only five months into her pregnancy. She and Dad decided they should probably tie the knot. Mom was a special education teacher, and she went forward with the marriage because of the stigma that came with being an unmarried, pregnant teacher.

Sadly, the honeymoon phase didn't last long. And just like that, each one was divorced once again.

Before I even hit the ground running, I was an extremely active baby in the womb, which is kind of the story of my life.

My womb life, for Mom, was quite the experience.

Mom was kicked about in all directions. These tiny super feet on the inside of Donna Kenney had found a way to kick her high and low—almost at the same time. It didn't make sense. She had already brought Joshie into this world during her first marriage and knew baby #2 shouldn't have been *this* big yet. Maybe the doctor had the date wrong.

As much as I wish I could say I was already training to monetize my feet, it turned out that my booties weren't the only ones doing the kicking. When Mom finally went to get a sonogram, the doctor rolled the device over her belly and asked:

Are there twins in your family?

No.

Well, there are now.

Two buns, one oven.

Four feet, one womb.

I shared Mom's stomach with my twin sister, Tristan. My mom was shocked by the news, then in denial. But her third response was . . .

Oh, I'm kind of special.

Although it probably should have been . . .

How is my special education teacher salary going to pay for twins?

Maybe she thought the child support would help. She had no crystal ball to predict that those checks would go as absent as my father was about to.

My mom, 4'11" tall—now feeling 4'11" wide—was ready to be done. So on March 4, 1982, in a Fontana, California hospital, the world welcomed my sister Tristan. A minute later, I emerged. All the warmth and comfort of the last nine months was about to fade away for a while.

Picket fence life didn't last long. There were a lot of verbal spats between my parents. So much so that my mom mustered the courage to break from her usual, submissive character—probably out of necessity—and we bolted an hour north without Dad to Apple Valley to shack up with my Grandma Shirley. It was the first of several separations in my parents' short, volatile relationship.

Eventually, we settled back in Ontario with one of my mom's generous friends. Twins aren't cheap, and Mom needed money and already had a job at a nearby elementary school.

Outside of summers, holidays, and weekends, my half brother Joshie lived with his dad a half mile from our house. With him right down the block, we became inseparable.

Joshie couldn't wait for my sister and me to be born. Actually, he was less excited about Tris and more eager to meet his brother. Joshie was giddy for me to emerge from the womb so we could play soccer together. Happy as he was to learn that one of the twins was a boy who he could teach all he knew about the beautiful game, Joshie was pretty bummed at first at my development.

Well, he just lays there. What good is he?

I mean, I was only a few weeks old. But aiming to please, I thrilled my brother by starting to walk at nine months. And as soon as I could experiment on my own two feet, my training began.

Mom's decision to start Joshie playing soccer is the first big moment of fate that turned me in the direction of becoming a soccer pro. Joshie excelled from the start and fell in love with the game. That devotion transferred to me. Soccer became my love because it was Joshie's love first.

Any time we were together, Joshie put a ball at my feet. Bounced a ball off my head. Rolled it to my left foot. Then my right. Held me up as I dribbled across our tiny apartment, where we'd turn what little furniture we had into goal posts. Joshie never saw himself as my coach. It was just bonding. Sheer playing. Pure fun. It was the only life we knew and we were happy to have each other.

We were all doing our best to live with what we had. And with my dad having removed himself from the picture, my overwhelmed, underwater mother desperately needed a few hours off from juggling twins and her demanding special-needs classroom. As you can imagine, when your dad peaces out and then your mom tries to leave—even for just a few hours—that doesn't sit so well emotionally with two 600-day-olds.

One night, Mom was granted a precious opportunity to blow off some steam when the mother of one of her special-needs students came over to sit for Joshie and us twins. Her mom, who happened to be deaf, was busy in another room with Joshie while she was playing with Tris. When her mother came back out to the main room, she could see—but not hear—my little body pretzeled over, lodged deep between two couch cushions and bawling dramatically more than a normal baby bawls.

Not knowing if I had been stuck in this position for four seconds or four minutes, she did what any reasonable person would do: She panicked. She rushed over and tried to snatch my body up from the couch. Next thing you know... *snap!*

I collapse to the floor. Now, I'm really wailing.

She packed all the kids up and raced us to the hospital. When we arrived, we learned my femur was broken. Fully fractured, two shifting plates going in opposite directions in my thigh. They put my little frame in full-body traction. I was up to my chest in a spica cast, a heinous torture for a hyperactive kid like me. I couldn't stand, much less sit, still. This was a disaster. I was sentenced to serve 11 lockdown days in a full-body cast in a hospital room. Of course, this was also my mother's sentence from me for the crime of going out.

You need a break?

OK. I'll break my femur.

That's what she gets for leaving us for the night.

I ended up celebrating my second birthday in the hospital, but it still delivered one of the best birthday presents I could have asked for. My broken bone ended the break my parents had taken from one another. Over the course of those 11 days, my mom and dad saw each other all the time. It was a rekindling moment for them and they decided to give the marriage one more try.

If you had told me that all I had to do was break the hardest bone in my body to get them back together, I would have done it a thousand times over.

Of course, when you're only two, you need around-the-clock attention of the sort that no one in my family was able to provide. For most of my time in the hospital, I was stuck by myself. Mom and Dad had work. I was left with a television and a few bags of potato chips. My mom would come to the hospital after school let out at 3 p.m. to find me lying in a pile of crumbs.

I healed up. I made it through. But the point is, from a very young age, I was left to power through the gauntlet of these traumatic experiences by myself. I didn't know any different.

Sadly, there'd soon be more traumatic experiences to come.

72'

I SELDOM know where I'm going.

Other times, I rarely know where I am.

I'm not forgetful; it just comes with my profession.

"Landon, there's a ticket waiting for you to Sydney for the Summer Olympics."

"Landon, a car is picking you up at 4 a.m. You're off to Buenos Aires to face Boca Juniors."

"Landon, Coach Ellinger needs you back in the States for U-17 training camp in Bradenton, Florida."

Another day. Another continent. Another adventure. The only constant? A plane ticket to wherever, touching down in a new country bound for the next tournament, match, or friendly. Just yesterday, I was in South Africa. It has been a week since we shocked the world by upsetting Spain 2–0 in the semifinals at the 2009 Confederations Cup. Today, on America Day, I am back in the USA but nowhere near the Pacific Ocean or my home.

When you conquer world-beater Spain, ending their 35-game unbeaten streak, it makes you believe you can achieve unthinkable feats. So on this festive Fourth of July, I'm parlaying my successes looking for another victory: winning back my ex-wife Bianca Kajlich.

As the cab rolls to a halt, its headlights slice through dusk like a spotlight on a bad decision. We are in the middle of nowhere. The driver glances up the long driveway over his shoulder.

"This is it."

"You sure?" I ask, checking my phone. No bars. Of course not. We are miles from anything resembling service or sense.

His silence is my cue to exit. I pay the man, grab my roller bag that has accompanied me from Spain, and step out.

Five hours ago, this felt poetic. Now it feels a bit strange. Earlier that day, I had called my therapist Juliet—my voice of reason, my human reality check. "I want to give it one last try," I said, voice low. "I owe it to her. I still love her. I do."

She was quiet for a beat. "Landon, you've been on this merry-go-round for months. You asked for space, and Bianca gave it to you. Then you realized you liked that space."

She was right. I was a mess.

When I told Bianca I'd had a fling with someone while on loan in Germany, the truth was heavy but necessary. I didn't want to lie. I needed her to know. Our marriage had been cracking, and I think part of me hoped that confession would give me an out. It doesn't make me anything remotely close to a saint, but she deserved the truth. I'm a terrible liar anyway.

Truth is, we had both been trying. Or pretending to try. Our sessions with Juliet had turned into autopsies of our nuptials—we dissected every scene like it was an episode of *Rules of Engagement* (a show you could find Bianca on regularly). Of course, that show came with a laugh track, while this moment in therapy was no laughing matter. I told Juliet I felt trapped in a life that used to be mine. I was always on the road. Bianca, with her acting, was too. When we finally landed in the same place, having to confront each other, all I wanted was peace, solitude, and space.

So I left.

I promised her that if anything happened with anyone else, I'd tell her.

That call, just 24 hours later, shattered what was left of our misaligned marriage.

She moved on. Fast. A new guy. Malibu, of course. I shouldn't have been surprised, but I was gutted. It wasn't even about her being with someone else. It was that she had the nerve to move forward before I was done figuring myself out.

My ego? Obliterated.

I told Juliet, "I can't believe she would do that to me."

My voice of reason calmly looked at me as she delivered the truth. "You slept with someone first, Landon. You're separated. She's allowed to live her life. She's allowed to move on."

Moving on was also the cab I had just pulled up in. I was now alone—now trespassing, trekking up this driveway.

Fireworks crack in the distance, echoing through the valley. Somewhere up ahead, laughter spills out from a party I'm not yet part of.

I reach the house. It looks like something out of a movie—it matches what you'd expect of a modern mountain house found in Aspen. Rustic and regal with cars parked out front. There are shadows dancing behind giant windows, voices lifted in celebration.

I adjust my grip on the handle of my suitcase, take a breath, and ring the bell.

Once. Then again.

The door opens to a man I instantly recognize: Kurt Russell. His beard is wild, but his eyes are kind. I'd met him before through Bianca, and now here he is, confused and a little guarded, staring at me like a misplaced package. "Landon," he says slowly. "What brings you here?"

Before I can respond, Goldie Hawn appears beside him like magic. As she locks her arm around his, you can't help but notice how these two creatures fit together. They forge a bond I'm not used to witnessing in a couple. Not from my parents. And not from my marriage.

Goldie smiles, but it doesn't seem sincere, which is about right with an unannounced guest standing at the door while bombs light up the night behind them. "Bianca didn't say anything about you coming."

"No," I say. "It's a surprise. Is she here?"

They exchange a glance. "Wait here," Goldie says gently.

I'm a feeler. Maybe that's complicated for many men to admit. But the ability to feel is what made me dynamic on a soccer field. I can feel where I need to be and act on those instincts on a regular basis. Now? Here? A thousand miles from my Redondo Beach front door? The feeling I have now is that I shouldn't be here.

Bianca comes to the door and instantly affirms my instincts. Her face—familiar and foreign all at once—tightens the second she sees me.

"You should have called. This... this is inappropriate."

"I'm your husband."

"No, Landon. You're the man who walked away."

I can feel both of us reverting to the roles we often cast for ourselves inside our marriage, maternal Bianca and acquiescing Landon.

"I talked to Juliet, and I told her I wasn't ready to give up. She suggested I share this face to face."

"I'm not sure you crashing my friend's party in Aspen is what she meant." Bianca, even when she was mad or maddening, remained madly attractive. She looks down at my suitcase. "You thought you could just show up and stay?"

While it sounds like a question it really conveys her answer.

"Landon, you need to leave," she continues flatly. "You wanted space. And tonight is not the time. Not the place. We'll talk... just not now."

Before I can say goodbye or anything at all, Bianca serves the role she knows best: making the decision for both of us. I won't be joining Kurt and Goldie or the others. Bianca closes the door—literally and symbolically—right there in my face. A week ago, Landon Donovan was a confident giant killer helping to slay the Spanish dragon. Now, a different, confused Landon is walking back down a driveway in the middle of nowhere with my luggage trailing behind me like shame on wheels.

My phone is still useless. No signal means no taxi. Just me and my roller taking a long walk into town beneath a sky full of stars and a soundtrack of fireworks. With every step, the truth sinks in: This might actually be the end.

It never occurred to me that I would be turned away at the door. Plan A was as far as my mind had taken me—one where I knock on the door, Bianca is happy to see me, and somehow, we find our way back.

The cellular bars on my phone eventually grow, but I have no one waiting for me and nowhere to be. So I just keep walking. Hours later, I make it to the center of just another foreign town. As the stars fade and darkness surrenders to dawn, I put up my hood so that anyone who might come out at this early hour won't bother me. I park myself on an uncomfortable bench and try to work through my confused, scattered thoughts. All that comes to me is that I'm not just lost in a place I don't know; I'm lost in a man I desperately need to find.

1′

MY PARENTS did come back together for a few skittish months, but it once again fell apart.

The end became inevitable. Mom and Dad officially divorced when Tris and I were three and never tried to be together again.

You would think one of the perks of growing up "American poor" is that it would make a divorce and the custody settlement easier. There wasn't much to divvy up. *Mom, you take the Honey Nut Cheerios; Dad gets the Froot Loops.*

My parents shared a lawyer to try and keep costs in check.

At first, the deal was quick, clean, and amicable: one week on and one week off for each of them. But soon things got contentious. A new agreement was reached with the help of the State of California: Mom was supposed to care for us four days a week except Wednesdays, and Dad hosted us three of four weekends every month, a planned break for Mom that never really came to fruition.

Dad was now an electrician in the school district. He earned less than Mom, so he was only on the hook for $150 a month for child support. Raising twins on a special ed teacher's salary is its own kind of special. Those days left us in pure survival mode.

When you have a dad in your life, it's normal to take it for granted. When you don't have a dad in your life, it's normal to feel the effects. I felt and showed many of those effects soon after their divorce.

I had a lot of anger and a bad temper. Who could blame me? I was a three-year-old yearning for his father. The only times I was truly calm were on those rare occasions I was gifted the chance to sit in my dad's lap. The only issue was his sporadic schedule.

The courts had decided that the passing of the twins would happen Friday nights at the McDonald's on Fourth and Cucamonga in the heart of Ontario. Tris and I would be brimming with excitement as we packed up what little we had into our miniature kid-sized suitcases prior to the pickup. When money was tight, which was most times, we would just roll through the Mickey D's drive-thru in Mom's van and order two kids' OJs. Most times, when my father wouldn't show, she'd splurge for the Happy Meal. More often than not, that Happy Meal was an Unhappy Meal.

My mom is an overprotector. As we sat in her van noshing on fries, she would wait for my dad and watch the minutes slip away. Once 45 minutes had passed, she knew there'd be no Friday night transferring of the twins.

Tris and I couldn't spot it until we were much older, but our dad's inability to show up became a depressing, recurring pattern that transformed our mom into an excuse generator who sweetly tried to shield us from the pain.

I bet he's stuck in traffic.

Looks like Dad had to work late.

He probably had car trouble.

Back to our house we'd go with half-full stomachs to match the contents of our suitcases. Whatever plans my mom thought she had would be cancelled. She learned fast that it was better not to make plans on the weekend, because you can cancel only so much. But being the rule follower she was, she'd still go through the motions of packing up those little bags and rolling through that McDonald's drive-thru three out of four Fridays.

Hockey must have gone into overtime.

The car's probably back in the shop.

I'm sure he just forgot it's Friday.

The one excuse Mom didn't generate is the one she didn't have the heart to say—the one Tris and I didn't yet know was the truth: *He doesn't want to see you.*

She always tried to sugarcoat it for us.

Most of the time, Dad didn't show. After eight or nine months, we stopped showing up too.

Mom knew Dad was forgetting us, putting our family behind him like someone else's life. She knew his past and who he was. She was able to move on from him. Me? I didn't have that ability.

As time ticked on, I was turning into a ticking time bomb of a toddler. I got kicked out of two preschools because of behavioral issues. Poor Tris—who was fitting in and faring much better than me—often lost out dealing with the repercussions of my "acting up."

In one preschool, I bit one of the other kids on the nose.

As you can imagine, that was the end of that preschool for Tris and me.

It took multiple tries, but my mom finally found a third preschool that would take us in. As per usual, Tris they had no problem with. Me? I got in under the label of "emotionally disturbed." But we didn't have to switch again, which was church bells to Mom's ears.

When I wasn't getting kicked out of preschools, I was knocking a soccer ball around with Joshie. I remained an intensely active kid and Joshie was the best type of companion. When you're my age, and your older brother isn't giving an inch, you adopt his traits. This tough love wasn't just my play; it was my medicine. He had created a training ground that filled the hours and the void of what I didn't even realize I didn't have. We chalked it up as "play"—and it was. It was the best of times during the worst of times. I was either acting out or active, and there was rarely anything in between.

Dad might not have been too interested in making good on his court-ordered responsibilities, but Mom leaving him hit him hard.

Just because their divorce was behind them didn't mean the problems were.

Mom would be on a date, and suddenly she'd notice... there was Dad in the same place, watching her. Mom had to be constantly on the lookout. And sometimes she would leave the house, and when she came back, Dad had broken in and taken pictures and baby books. The better to remember us by?

Mom went back to court for a restraining order.

After that, I only saw my dad a few times a year.

3′

MAKE YOUR OWN LUCK.

I always loved that saying because I have given up everything I could have been or done for a single purpose: being an exceptional soccer player. I surrendered family occasions, proms, college, friends, girlfriends, time exploring America and other countries I've lived in. I gave up freedom itself—on and off the field—for it. If that's the definition of making your own luck, I agree with that saying most of the time.

As "luck" would have it, I was born with the odds severely stacked against me—in a country called America, where a game that's called "football" all over the world is called something else. Where the sport takes a backseat to basketball and baseball—all the games you don't play with your feet. No organized Germanic soccer academies. No endless replays of the beautiful game. We didn't even have a pro league back then.

When I look back at my life and how it started, knowing where I came from and who I came from, the odds of someone like me making it with no affluence and no father figure? What are the chances?

That brings us to the flip side of the luck equation.

The side of the coin where "luck" is actually luck.

Where I got lucky is that my intense but athletic half brother loved soccer. And not only did Joshie adore the game, but he was damn good. And he wasn't one to do me any favors or take it easy on me because I was younger and smaller. Joshie, who had his own issues with his father, always played tough and made me come up to his level; that's quite a task when your brother is five years older and you're his outlet.

Joshie was a fiercely competitive guy and wanted to play with me all the time. Even when I was five and he was 10, all of that "playing up" against him made it easy for me to match up against more-developed players, even guys who were much bigger than me. I was always smaller, so I never saw my smaller frame as a disadvantage; I could run by most of them, even with the ball at my feet.

So imagine you train with a towering brother who doesn't know the definition of taking it easy on you. And your mom isn't around because she's neck deep in her job scraping together pennies, so you're devouring a continuous stream of soccer techniques from big brother. I had an insatiable knack for learning. I always wanted to conquer the next move. I was fascinated with the technical side of the game. If Joshie studied a move, I wanted to learn how to do it too. But when Joshie moved on to the next idea about how he wanted to score a goal or defend, I obsessed over refining the initial move until I was a machine at it. I would do the same move over and over and over again.

All of that obsessive practice paid off in my very first organized game.

I'm five years old. The other kids are all seven or eight, colossal Californians towering over me on the field. I weave my way through these tall defenders, who are so much shorter and less skilled than Joshie, and score my first goal. The referee blows the whistle. And what comes immediately after the ball hits the back of the net, I cherish . . .

Cheers. Adoration. *Attention.*

Claps on my back from my older teammates. High-fives from parents on the sidelines. A feeling like I have never felt before.

Love and excitement and sheer joy at what I have done, feelings I'm not getting anywhere else outside my intimate inner circle. I feel noticed. I like the feeling so much I proceed to score six more times that game.

Scoring goals became an addiction because it created a contagious new, warm feeling in my life: acceptance. If I was being rejected by a certain male figure, this sensation would be my alternative.

I had found a feeling I wanted to replicate again and again. And if you think I was obsessed (and compulsive) before that game, I was about to take it to a whole new level.

4'

I AM SITTING near the back of the room by a wall of windows in Ms. Goding's fifth grade classroom, and I am not alone. Like most days, I'm accompanied by my best friend and comfort blanket: my soccer ball.

The year is 1992. I am 10 years old at Edison Elementary School, home of the Bobcats. A place that my sister and I have walked to and from, three-quarters of a mile down and three-quarters of a mile back, every single school day for the last six years. Ms. Goding is my favorite teacher, but at the moment I am not particularly interested in the Civil War project she's going on about. It reminds me too much of the uncivil war I've been living with Mom and Dad for 10 years now.

I fade away out the window, dreaming about the recess bell so I can go play soccer with my friends. As my eyes focus on the field, the soccer ball at my feet is put to work. Rolling it back and forth, from heel to toe. Right foot. Then left foot. I do it over and over again, like you'd absently spin a pencil around your fingers—not distracting class or even noticing that I'm doing it, for that matter. But the recess bell doesn't come. Instead, we are all woken up by a sudden and shrill screech from the classroom door.

Creeeeeeeeeeaaaaaak.

In an unsuccessful attempt to be not disruptive, someone has opened the door incredibly slowly.

It's my dad! This is not a dream. *Pinch me.*

We both know he shouldn't be here.

But I don't care. My heart lifts in tandem with my smile, and I sprint over to the door; Ms. Goding doesn't miss a beat. She is quite aware of my troubled childhood and has put in extra time with Mom to get me on track. She knows about my dad, and she knows what his showing up here means to me, so she continues on about crops, cotton, and tobacco.

The encounter with Dad is brief—no words, just the exchange of a rolled-up magazine. Words would have been overrated anyway. My dad got the response he wanted: a happy son thinking his dad's a sneaky hero.

I go back to my desk and unwind my prize: this month's *Hockey Digest* magazine. Brett Hull is on the cover. I wish it were Gretzky. What's not to love about Wayne Gretzky? One of my first heroes. I try to be respectful of Ms. Goding's ongoing lesson, but I can't help but open the magazine to see what's inside. The Great One is now on the L.A. Kings, which I like, although I know my dad's hoping the Edmonton Oilers repeat when the NHL playoffs start in a month.

Like many Canadians, my dad's true love is hockey. *If he only cared about us like he cares about hockey.* Dad was good enough to play a little semi-pro; the game was his escape from reality. I'm sure I benefited from some of those genes.

These spontaneous dad visits to the classroom only happen from time to time. It's one of the perks when you're the son of the school district's electrician. Somehow Dad can figure out how to get to the right classroom to find me anytime he sees fit but couldn't figure out how to get to the McDonald's to pick us up on Friday nights. I'll take what I can get.

When school let out, Tris and I would walk ourselves home. There was a lot of chaos in our world, but there was nothing more comforting than having the relationship I had with Tris.

When we weren't in school, Tris and I were a couple free-range kids climbing trees and jumping off roofs in our neighborhood. Tris was a tomboy, but she was more active and less athletic; she wasn't into sports the way Joshie and I were.

When Joshie came over after school, we could always find a back-yard soccer game to jump into. We played every day. The second we got home, the backpack hit the table and we were running outside to play. We grew up playing with kids from all backgrounds and ethnicities. Latinos, Whites, Blacks, Samoans... we were around a diverse group of people all the time; that was our normal. And when it was game time, it didn't matter what color skin you brought to the field or what language you spoke. If you could play, you could play.

If there was any solace to our youth, this was it. The endless soccer games with Joshie and the neighborhood kids, and a ton of roughhouse playing. It built toughness.

To be real and clear: Joshie built toughness.

With no other male figure providing structure and with Mom starved for time, I didn't have an adult to learn from. There was no nurturing parent's point of view inserting itself into these games or our play. Mom was at work; we were off by ourselves. With no one to watch us, sometimes we'd play eight hours straight in the neighborhood. Being outside every waking moment was the perk of not having daily parental supervision. We always knew exactly what time we needed to be home: when it got dark.

Backyard games with Joshie were starting to get supplemented with organized ones. I tried to once again mirror big brother, but when I was eight years old, there wasn't a team for my age group, so the only way I could play was to make a team playing more than a full year up in age. The local team was Upland Celtic, a team of 10-year-olds in Ontario. A man named Matt McDonough had started the club and was well known in California youth soccer circles. Even though I was underage, he let me have a shot at the tryout.

I was ready. I was beating kids that age anyway and knew I could compete with them.

I thought the tryout went well, but afterwards, Matt pulled me aside and told me I was just too small to play with these older kids. Another sharp dagger of rejection. *Here we go again. Another man not believing in me.*

I went home and didn't leave my room for days. I cried and cried, bawling because I simply wanted to play.

For the next year, all I thought about was making that team. And a year later, I wasn't going to get cut. Another year of developing, growing in all directions, game as much as body. I wasn't going to just make the team—I was ready to show that all those years playing up with Joshie had put me in a position to dominate.

I showed up to the tryout and met Marcel Trincale, the coach of the team. Marcel was the opposite of most men in authority positions I had encountered in my life. For starters he was *nice*. There was a kind and patient streak to my new French coach. Perhaps it was because he was a father of three boys himself, one of whom—Mark—was soon to be my new teammate.

Marcel understood me right away. Over the next few years, he would become more of a trusted confidant than a mere soccer coach. He believed in me. In return, I trusted him. For a boy with a ton of behavior problems, this went such a long way. Marcel was the first man who made me feel accepted, and I adored him for that.

We had quite the year for Upland Celtic. I was scoring goals and triggering adoration from my teammates and their families. So much so that when Mom couldn't get me to a game, one of the other parents would gladly come and pick me up. The joys of being your team's leading goal scorer.

Marcel moved on to coach Cal Heat, a team in Alta Loma, and I moved with him.

This did not sit well with those very same Upland Celtic parents who were singing my praises just a few months prior. Mom got tense calls from other parents telling her she was ruining my life, that the team I was joining didn't compare to Upland Celtic, piling the pressure on the only single mom on the team.

Mom knew I would travel far and wide to play for the right coach. She let me make the call. After all the affection Marcel had shown me, loyalty mattered to me, so I followed him. And unbeknownst to me, my mother paid the consequence. When you're a kid, you can't possibly know how long a day your mom puts in. She would work a full day in her special ed class, then rush home to transform into a taken-for-granted chauffeur, driving me around Southern California. For the next four years, those free rides went wherever Marcel was coaching.

To be fair, Mom could commit only so many afternoons to lugging me around. Lots of people picked up the slack driving me to and from practices and games, Marcel included. Mom did the best she could to drive me when she could. But she was still the only breadwinner in the house ... and in her case, it was more like crumbs.

That was the predictable rhythm of my life: at school or briefly at home, then endless hours unsupervised in the neighborhood with Joshie or in some car heading to or from practice or a game. And lots and lots of soccer. Until one night when Joshie and I made our way back to the house and Mom was waiting to share some surprising news.

Mom was *dating* someone. Paul Cash was his name; he had thick black hair and a thin black mustache. He was funny, although we didn't notice it at first—nothing seems too funny when it's coming from a new guy dating your mom.

When we first met him, we thought Mom said he was a musician. This sounded promising because we were quite the musical family. We sang a lot, and I'd learned a few instruments at school, including piano. I'd even played the violin in front of the entire Edison Elementary School earlier in the year. So, Mom being with a musician sounded like it had some upside to it, but ...

Landon?
Yes, mom.
I didn't say Paul was a musician.
Paul's not a musician?
No, I never said musician ... Paul's a magician.
A magician?
Yes. A magician.
Well. That's ... different.

We started seeing a lot more of the Magician around the house. Unfortunately, we also started hearing a lot more of him, because their love life was ... audible. Mom and her magician friend pulling rabbits out of hats is something you can't unhear, and believe me, if I could have waved a wand and made it disappear, I would have.

And just when we thought we had literally heard everything, the two dropped a bomb on us.

Mom and the Magician—and therefore Tris and I—were all moving in together in Redlands.

What?

Where?

With *him*?

This did not sit well with me.

Goodbye, 622 Fourth Street.

Goodbye, Ms. Goding.

Goodbye, Joshie?!

And if you think *we* weren't happy to be moving in with Paul Cash, you can imagine what it did to my dad when he found out Mom and Paul were getting married. It didn't matter that we had been seeing less of Dad as the years went by; we were still very much stuck in the middle of their contentious relationship, and it only got more awkward when Paul entered our world. Tris and I were already fielding Dad's angry phone calls—playing telephone on an actual telephone to relay heated discussions between my parents.

And once Dad got word of Mom's news? He decided it was time for more serious action.

7'

WHEN YOU'RE 10 years old, Christmas morning is *Christmas morning*. And if there was one thing we adored, it was being together as a family on Christmas.

Every year, Mom saved just enough money to ensure that when December rolled around, not only would there be presents under the tree, but there would be a tree to put them under. She'd do what she could to make sure that Joshie, Tris, and I would light up brighter than any one of the Christmas lights on that hard-earned tree: maxing out credit cards, splurging on gifts, and, without us knowing, plunging herself even further into severe debt. These are the things a mom does for her babies.

Most of the kids I knew wished for soccer cleats.

Some dreamed of Schwinn bikes.

Others coveted Lego sets.

Me?

In 1992, I still just wanted to have a normal family.

With "normal" feeling so far away from attainable, I decided the next best thing was to continue pushing to be an extraordinary soccer player, burying my emotions in endless practice and games. From the outside, it looked like nothing would stop me from playing my way into the spotlight. On the inside, though, I still hoped that spotlight would be bright enough to bring back Dad's attention.

Instead, I received the one gift that this hyperactive, distressed 10-year-old really didn't wish for: moving. At 10, moving to a new city felt like yet another painful training exercise in what I saw as a series of never-ending knocks in my life. To make matters worse, the move happened smack in the middle of the school year. Goodbye, Ontario; hello, Redlands. Halfway through the school year, I found myself in a new town with no friends, no after-school pickup games, and no Joshie. The life I knew was over. And starting over felt like game over.

Redlands had a small-town feel to it. It was only a 30-minute drive from Ontario, but that might as well have been a cross-country flight to a 10-year-old. We were east of Los Angeles and west of Palm Springs, roughly halfway between them, nestled at the foot of the San Bernardino Mountains. On normal days, our weather was a solid 10 degrees hotter than L.A.'s. Come summer, it felt like you were playing in an oven. Temperatures regularly spiked north of 100 degrees.

The predictable free-range evenings and endless soccer games at Edison were replaced by the chaos of a new fifth grade class in a city where I knew no one. Those feelings of anger that had plagued me in my early years were beginning to resurface and the misbehaving came along with it.

To make matters worse, Dad, in another moment of spontaneity, had just remarried too. So, while he and his third wife were settling into Fontana, Mom suggested we go see a counselor to talk through some of my issues. Off we went as a unit. I wouldn't exactly have called us a family at this point; Mom would drag Paul along, which was just another reminder of the problem. But the whole lot of us went—Mom, Paul, Tristan, and me.

We'd sit there together in a compact room with this "counselor," which is a nice word for a "kid shrink." They'd rather not send you to a "therapist" at 10; they're worried it would make a kid like me feel even worse than I already did. I was already angry and isolated, and now—congratulations—I'm also crazy. So no thera-pist... just a counselor.

Bless this counselor's soul, but even as a 10-year-old, I could tell how strange the guy was. A calm, "out there," Bob Ross–looking man. His eyes alternated between looking like they were trying to find a way to escape his head and burning a hole in mine. And no matter what any of us said, however routine, the same cliché follow-up question: *And how did that make you feeeeeeel?*

He'd ask me to discuss moments of my new life in Redlands that I didn't have any interest in talking about, and I'd dutifully recount them—what was happening at school, who I pegged in the head with a dodgeball on the playground... what I'd had for lunch. Nodding slowly, the counselor would then proceed to work his way around the group: *And how did that make you feeeeeeel, Tristan? How did that make you feeeeeeel, Donna? How did that make you feeeeeeel, Paul?*

This was no laughing matter to my mom, but it was sheer comedy to the Magician. He kept it together in the room, but the second we got to the car, he'd pop his eyes out, stare right at me, and snort, "How did that make you *feeeeeeel*, Landon?"

And we'd all crack up at his impression. Talking to the counselor didn't make me feel much beyond annoyed, but laughing about it later with my family... well, that made me feel pretty good. So even though we didn't make it more than a few times to see this kid shrink, that first encounter with therapy did pay off in one way—from that point on, I stopped thinking of Paul as the Magician and just started calling him Paul.

A few weeks into the new neighborhood and I'd yet to find any signs of life, much less anyone to play with. But I was about to be thrown a bone. One crisp California morning I was in the midst of my usual foul-tempered brooding when I heard, somewhere off beyond the back of the house, the unmistakable sound of kids play-ing some kind of sport. When you're a kid desperate for friends, your ears perk up pretty fast when you hear any kind of competition.

I ran out the front door, curled around, and followed the sound to find three boys playing street hockey on roller skates.

The three boys were the Odom brothers. The biggest of the three was Michael, followed by Shawn. The youngest at eight, platooned in goalie gear and taking the brunt of it as his older brothers rifled slap shots at his small frame, was Adam Odom.

The Odoms lived a few houses down off a cul-de-sac. And, as luck would have it, they feasted on sports. Adam was only in third grade, but that was fine by me. He loved sports; I loved sports. Playing anything with anyone beat listening to Tris blast Mariah Carey songs all day.

My friendship with Adam quickly blossomed, a welcome distraction from everything else in my life. And before too long, we were inseparable. If one of us was bored, we'd just walk over to the other one's house in hopes of more playing. If we weren't in school or I wasn't on a field, we were with each other, competing like brothers. And as always, I hated to lose more than I liked to win. We played everything—basketball, hockey, football, soccer, you name it.

Before bed during sleepovers, we'd take to the TV or radio to follow our favorite teams. Being near L.A., we watched a ton of Wayne Gretzky's Kings and Magic Johnson's Lakers. I loved how they scored but also facilitated their respective teams. And I remember vividly how they both spoke and carried themselves—calm, funny, endearing, and comfortably in charge of everything—even off the court. I wanted to be just like them.

Somewhat ironically, Adam and I sponged up every sport *but* soccer. There just wasn't any professional soccer around to watch back then. Living in Southern California, it was all Magic, Valenzuela, and Gretzky, no van Basten, Baggio, or Ronaldo. There was no international soccer available then to American kids. Maybe it was showing on some far reaches of the cable universe, but it certainly was not on the three free channels we could afford.

Adam's mom was a teacher's aid, and Adam's dad was in construction but still made time to coach Shawn's soccer team. Imagine that—playing soccer for your dad? Must be nice. Our families quickly came to trust each other. Many nights, Adam and I would devise our strategy to eat double dinner—starting at either house before working our way to the other. Almost all nights it was mission accomplished.

A year into our life in Redlands, Tris and I had settled in. We were now attending Moore Middle School. While Tris—ever the diligent student—would spend four hours doing her assignments after school, I remained consistent in scribbling out my homework during class. I knew how to game the system and did enough to get solid grades. Mostly, I was just trying to get through my work before I got home, so I could either race out to play with Adam or get to one of my soccer practices.

When I wasn't at school or with Adam, I was relentlessly perfecting my game. I still carried a ball with me every day to school. I didn't realize it at the time, but I was also perfecting my OCD, obsessively trying to control what I could (which was very little). I would spend hours working to master the technical, precise details of a single move over and over and over again until I got it right. My willingness to keep at something until it was second nature was one of the few things I could control.

The rest of my life still felt wildly unpredictable. Actually, one thing had remained predictable: We barely saw Dad. But even there we were in for a few surprises. One of the times we saw him, Dad said something about how Mom was keeping us from him, which, honestly, did not make much sense.

He was quite fluent in persuasion, subtext, and guilt. And I must have known that on some level, but still . . . when Dad starts talking about seeing each other more, that resonates. And it resonates even more, when he goes on to say:

"Why don't you and Tris come move in with me? Get away from your nagging mom? Blow off some steam with your dad? Watch Gretzky all the time?"

Did Dad just say... he wants to watch Gretzky... *with me*? Did dad just say he wants me to *move in* with him?

Hearing these words out of Dad's mouth.... I had never heard dad come close to suggesting something like it before. I didn't even know it was an option. I started thinking about it. And I couldn't get it out of my head.

I want my dad.

I've always wanted my dad.

I think my dad wants *me*.

Until this moment, I had a hard time putting the words together when it came to "how it's been" vs. "how it's going" with Dad. It was simply too painful. In my mind, it shouldn't have been, because we had so much in common. I was supposed to be his apple that didn't fall far from the tree, and we were both deeply into sports. Maybe deep down I always thought that being into sports—or better yet, being good at them—would win over his attention. *If I do this well, he'll be proud of me. He'll love me. He'll show me that affection.* And now here he was saying he wanted *me*.

And whether he really did or not, it turned out he was willing to go back to court to prove it.

9'

HOW DO YOU find it in you to notch up an extra gear in the closing minutes of an already grueling match on a separate continent
against foreign players who are trying to do the same to you? How
do you not only push but press even harder when you've already
run seven miles over 85 minutes in feverish temperatures against
guys who are just as talented as you? What pushes you beyond the
threshold of what most think is possible when you're staring up at
a scoreboard late in a match?

Well, when you feel like you've grown up marinated in pain—
when the first decade of your life is filled with uncertainty, toxicity,
and toil—by the time you get to play a game, you've got this incom-
parable hunger you can tap into to conquer anything you face.
Struggling through and surviving those not-so-beautiful moments
off the field supplied me with grit that, even at age 12, I could channel into a competitive advantage. Add in the endless hours I'd spent
training in the blistering heat of the Southern California desert, and
it's no wonder I can run for days.

I'm not saying it's a great strategy. I wouldn't recommend it. I'm
just telling it like it is.

When I was 12, Marcel became the assistant coach of an elite
travel team called the California Heat, and after a few years running
around in the Redlands heat, I could not have been more fit and

ready to join them. Their coach was Clint Greenwood, a 40-year-old, ahead-of-his-time visionary who was thought of as the top trainer for my age group. Where Joshie had shown me tough love, Clint was less love and more tough across the board; our relationship was transactional at best.

We might not have been best buddies, but Clint was a perfect fit for me. I yearned to be pushed on the field. Clint knew how to push our buttons to get the most out of our team, but he was also way ahead of his time when it came to putting novel ideas in play for how to practice.

Go anywhere kids are playing organized soccer and you'll see teams running laps in warm-ups. Clint didn't see any use for that, so he didn't have us do it. Oh, we still had to run laps—we just had to do it *with the ball*. Other teams end practices with full-field suicides; we finished practice with full-field suicides *with the ball*.

Everything we did—even the fitness work—was with a ball at our feet. It didn't matter what position you played, that was how Clint had us go about our business. Always.

I already carried a ball with me anyway, and Joshie had already pounded this type of footwork into me with our own gazillion hours of backyard training. But practices with Clint and Cal Heat would push me to a new level.

I'm naturally right-footed, so Clint forced me to put in countless reps executing with my left. In finishing exercises, I'd go right, and Clint would shout at me, "If they always know you want to bring it back to your right, you just made yourself less dangerous." He'd give an impassioned soliloquy about how I'd be twice as effective if I could go by someone on my left.

I give Clint a lot of credit for my development. He knew if I worked every moment to get more skilled on the ball, I'd have a leg up on the competition. Clint pushed me to a point that I was, at 12, tiptoeing close to Joshie's skill level, even though he was 17.

It mirrored that precious lesson I still abide by today: *How you do anything is how you do everything.*

Clint's revolutionary practice ideas weren't California Heat's only advantage. We also had a secret weapon: Mike Richardson, Cal Heat's team manager.

Mike would roam far and wide, sifting through all parts of Southern California, looking for little pockets of talented gold that Clint could mold into soccer elite. From Anaheim to Angelus Oaks, Mike would search for kids with unrealized potential from overlooked areas to bring back to Clint. Finding them wasn't just Mike's job; it was his joy. And he didn't just identify the kids—he often picked them up and then drove them home. For some of them, that was the only way they could get to and from practice or games.

If you look at player development in most of America, you'll notice that there are an awful lot of players in the youth system from affluent backgrounds. It takes time to drive players to practices—time that is awfully hard to come by if you're a single parent working multiple jobs. It takes money to join leagues and buy shin guards and cleats. Access to capital churns out a conveyor belt of solid players with a front-row seat to better coaches and elevated training.

Cal Heat was not like that. We weren't made up of the players you'd find at the rich, white clubs in other parts of the state. We were a relatively small club primarily made up of minority and foreign-born players. When you have the luxury of, well, luxury, finding talented kids from rich families isn't the most difficult proposition. When you don't... finding those overlooked, talented kids was Mike's specialty.

Together, we were a strong and cohesive team. Most of that could be credited to the yin/yang of Mike finding kids with potential and Clint helping us maximize it. And when practice was over, Mike would load a bunch of kids into his car and drop them off across the region. With my mom's teaching schedule, there were days when Mike would drop me off in Redlands too.

But usually Mom would be there, finishing up after a long day of work by dutifully shuffling me to practice. We kept the conversation light and pleasant. This wasn't always easy, because Mom was not keen on Clint. For one thing, he swore a lot, and Mom was not a big fan of bad language. For another, it didn't sit well with Mom how Clint lit into us at halftime when we failed to play well. Clint was so loud that the players' mothers on the other side of the field could hear him.

Mom and I were getting pretty good at small talk and not tiptoeing near anything controversial. Neither of us particularly like confrontation. By the time I was playing for Cal Heat, Mom and Dad's renewed custody battle had been going on for quite some time, which made for a fair number of awkward 40-minute car rides. Twice a week, we'd find ourselves stuck in this drive, avoiding talking about what was really on our minds.

That was fine by both of us. Deep down, Mom and I were buckled in for what was looming down this poorly lit highway, the opposite of Easy Street.

10′

_____

10
The highway number was I born next to

622 Fourth Street → 6 + 2 + 2 = 10
My childhood address

10
The age I was when I met my best friend

10
The number of goals I scored in my first Major League Soccer
season with San Jose

10
The number of goals I scored in my last full MLS season with L.A.

'10
The year I scored the Algeria goal

10/10
The date of my final U.S. Men's National Team sendoff game

11'

___

IN MY HEAD, I was dreaming about having a real relationship with Dad. After so many years on the periphery, moving in with Dad might fill and fix my 12-year-old heart. Sharing these thoughts with Mom would be a horrendous idea. I didn't mean to be in the middle of all this, but I was. I was angry, scared, sad, curious, eager, and hesitant all at once. It was a lot for one introvert to handle.

Meanwhile the extrovert of the Donovan twins, Tris, had already put our old neighborhood in her rearview mirror. Tris was happy in Redlands, relying on her new friends and Mom more than me, and had done a much better job putting the trauma of our father behind her. She wasn't looking or planning to go anywhere. This created a big, anxious, damned-if-I-do, damned-if-I-don't dilemma for yours truly. If nothing were to change, I would always wonder what life would be like to live with Dad. If I lived with Dad, I would do so at the expense of breaking up with my twin and my Mom—the two people on the planet I never wanted to hurt or see hurt.

More often than not, when I find myself stuck with a problem or uncomfortable situation, I surrender to my "hold it in" personality. While the court case was going on, I was keeping so much in, I felt like I was running out of space to store it all. When I wasn't thinking about soccer, I was dreaming about the possibility of living with my dad. When I wasn't dreaming about living with Dad, I was compressing all the mixed-up feelings, burying them as far down inside me as I could. Mom believed that when it came to her children, a mother really does know best. But this was a decision she couldn't make; it was going to be made by the courts, which made for an anxious household. My mom started keeping copious notes to prepare for the custody battle. The days when Mom and Dad respectfully shared a lawyer were long gone; this time it was every parent for themselves. If money had been tight before at home, now it was even tighter.

It all was a lot to deal with. And I did it while I zipped past defenders on most weekends. No one was getting in my way—or in my head—but me. And the sound of Dad's voice repeating again and again...

Why don't you come live with me?

It felt like everything that had been brewing for the past 12 years was coming to a head. Mom, to her credit, didn't lay down too many mandates, but one thing she was firm on was that a courtroom was no place for a child. I wanted to go to the courtroom and know what was happening, but I simply wasn't allowed. One morning on the day of that month's court appearance, I got into a shouting match with Mom:

"I want to go! I want to go to the courthouse!"

"You are not going to the courthouse! You need to go to school!"

"*No!*" I snapped, "I'm going! You can't make me *not* go!"

Mom was having no part of it. It was the one subject she was willing to confront, and in true Mom fashion, she made Paul do the dirty work. With me kicking and screaming all the way, Paul did his best to get me into his car and off to school. As hard as it was on me, it was probably even more traumatic for Paul.

The custody battle dragged on for 18 months. It felt like a war. The main reason for the delay? My dad's million excuses for why he couldn't be in court on certain days. I so badly wanted to be wanted by my dad that I lost sight of his excuses. I wanted it to work out. He told me he wanted me to come live with him. He'd taken it to court. That had to mean something. Even with the delays, I believed that if I could will it to work, it would work.

After 18 months of arguments and appearances, we reached an end. On the final day of deliberation, Paul and I waited on the steps outside the Ontario courthouse. With Mom inside, I sat there next to Paul, wearing my lone pink long-sleeve, button-down collared shirt, feverishly scanning the parking lot for Dad's car. It was nowhere to be found. I'd hear a car turn the corner and close in on the parking lot, which brought a burst of excitement, only for it to quickly plummet when it wasn't his.

Mom was inside for well over an hour. She sat and waited, hoping for her version of justice.

A year and a half after my dad had started this custody battle, the judge finally put the nastiness to bed.

The Donovan twins wouldn't be moving in with their father.

Per my mother's wishes, I wasn't in the courtroom the day the judge made this final decision. And neither was my dad. He never bothered to show up.

12′

NOBODY THOUGHT I had a chance.

So much so that if gambling were available, the slender Raul Garcia would have received most of the student body wagers at this locally monumental, once-a-year race at Moore Middle School.

It was no small feat to even be there competing. The top four boys and girls from sixth, seventh, and eighth grade across the A, B, C, and D tracks would qualify for an opportunity to represent their grade in front of the Redlands community in the Moore Mile.

It was the sort of local event where kids made colorful inspirational signs and the route was lined with fire trucks. And an all-out community BBQ where the hearty Coach Hafley himself—our no-nonsense middle school phys ed teacher—would man the grill and cook up hot dogs for anyone who wanted to feast on them.

Hot dogs were the furthest thing from my mind. My only focus was catching up to Raul, who had been leading the field for most of the race. We were approaching the final turn, and you could hear the other students getting louder and rowdier. With the finish line drawing near, I surprised Raul by catching up with him until we were neck and neck.

As we turned the final cone and headed for home, there was no way I was coming in second. Raul was trying to pick it up again, but I had one more gear, waiting for just the right moment. *Not yet...* *3...2...1...*

Like a shot out of a cannon, I kicked in the turbo boost and flew past Raul, opening the space between the two of us as the finish line drew closer to me than it was to him. I crossed it in first place, mobbed by the deafening cheers of my classmates.

Winning the Moore Mile in the last stretch of eighth grade was a typical "me" move—a classic case of using my abilities to get the attention I craved. When it was all said and done, I had won in dramatic fashion: a 5:21 mile to Raul's 5:23, finishing a full two seconds faster.

If Coach Hafley—still grilling dogs and flinging them out to a line of Moore Mile witnesses—could have bet, there's no question he'd have been all in on me with his own money.

Coach was a compact, chummy, and typically no-frills American phys ed teacher. He loved sports like I loved sports, and the two of us bonded for all sorts of reasons. For one, I participated in every intramural after-school activity I could get my hands or feet on. From soccer to Frisbee golf, I was there, and Hafley was overseeing it all. Like me, Hafley was a twin. Being a twin is a bit like being a motorcycle person; when you run into another twin, there's an instant connection.

And there was one other connection Coach Hafley and I shared: He and his twin had tragically lost their father at the age of 14.

I was 14 now. A few years clear of Dad's no-show at the Ontario courthouse, I had similar feelings of fatherlessness and loss. And while my loss had not come from the same sort of tragedy, it still left its mark.

Dad not showing up had told the court all it needed to know. It spoke volumes to me too; it was the McDonald's Unhappy Meal all over again. Clearly, I should have known better than to have been so hopeful. As an introvert, I was used to burying my feelings, shutting them off from everyone. I had had enough of being devastated and having my emotions run through the paper shredder. This was the dawn of a new era of personal compartmentalization and depression. This "new me" would not be so foolish as to be hurt like that again. This new me was just fine with being emotionally walled off.

After his loss in court, it got even harder for Mom to get Dad to pay the child support he owed. He simply didn't want to pony over "his" cash. And after what he'd just put us through, if he wasn't providing us with financial support, Mom wasn't going to let him see us either.

My dad responded by moving further away. The first of several moves took him out of California to a job in New Mexico. He would run from a system that he thought wasn't working for him. I think Dad couldn't get beyond the fact that he had to give money to Mom. And he never connected the dots nor had the awareness to realize that by hurting Mom, he was hurting Tris and me. It wasn't just Mom who suffered; Tris and I were also struggling to survive.

The sun had set on my dream of a real relationship with Dad, and it was also setting on my time at Moore Middle School. At our eighth grade end-of-year banquet, I had an extra-special moment when Coach Hafley awarded me the trophy for Best Male Athlete of the Year. A special way to end the year, made even better by some exciting news: Joshie would be coming to live with us for the summer, which promised all-out play in the neighborhood.

It was the last summer before high school, and roller hockey was a serious neighborhood affair. I would skate with the other kids to the middle school, lugging the goals with us. Adam had the nets and goalie pads, his older brothers right there with him. Each of us brought our gloves, sticks, and helmets, and the battles, bickering, and fights would go on until the sun went down. The joys of summer days with no responsibility.

Soccer was just starting to take off in the United States. The environment was ripe for a kid like me to excel in a game that was experiencing fresh popularity. A new league called Major League

Soccer had been founded in the wake of our hosting—and doing surprisingly well at—the 1994 World Cup. It still felt like more of a minor than a major league, as it tried to convince Americans that soccer deserved to peel some eyeballs away from American football, baseball, and basketball. But for the first time that I could remember, Americans were talking about soccer players like Alexi Lalas, and not just for their crazy red hair or faux denim jerseys. The '94 World Cup had waltzed guys like Lalas, Cobi Jones, and Tony Meola onto American television and into American households and conversations. It wasn't a full roaring buzz of soccer activity, but where there had been silence before, there was now at least a hum. The league wasn't much to write home about, with 10 start-up teams across the nation, but at least it was deemed "professional." If anybody had asked me what I wanted to do with my life, there was no other answer outside of "Play soccer." And for the first time in my life, there was a chance I could actually do that as a job in America.

Not that I had time to watch soccer. When I wasn't partaking in neighborhood hockey games, in the pool with Joshie, or hanging with Adam, I was busy playing as much soccer as I could. Not only was I traveling with Cal Heat, but I was now rotating in with two other teams, and the more games I could squeeze in the better. Some weekends I'd enjoy three games a day.

Adam's dad was still coaching his older brother Shawn's competitive Select team, and when he needed a ringer for tournaments, guess who stepped in? Being two years younger than me, Adam didn't play, but he often came on these tournament trips to watch the games. Having Adam around for the road trip at least gave me someone to hang with.

Thankfully, Mom had grown to love the weekend ritual of watching Joshie and me dart around our respective pitches. The only one who truly was against soccer was Tris; being tugged all over Southern California was her version of hell. You can count on one hand the number of times I can remember Tris at a soccer game without her eyes on a book.

This last summer in Redlands—those moments with Joshie, Tris, Adam, and the rest of the kids in the neighborhood—was the purest of times. Outside of my time on a field, clocks meant nothing, because the sun told us where to be. And the only place we needed to be was on a court, rink, pool, or field. It was a seemingly endless fun ride for a 14-year-old kid looking to stay a kid.

Though I didn't know it, that summer of '96 was one of the last times that my time was . . . my time. My freedom was running out on those carefree days, and my kid card was about to expire.

14'

DING... DING... DONG.

The calm tones of a xylophone chimed over the school speakers for the last time, and for the final time that year I dribbled around, through, or occasionally over my fellow 1,200 froshmates crowding the congested halls of the Redlands freshman campus.

In other schools—or maybe just for other people—playing sports would have given me a little more status. I smugly wore my high-school letterman soccer jacket—a rare feat for a freshman who had to be bused over to the main campus to join his Redlands teammates after school. But I didn't feel like I belonged to any sort of higher echelon reserved for the athletically gifted... nor did anyone else. Near as I can tell, most of my classmates just thought I was really weird.

I didn't have a lot of close friends, nor was I looking for them. I wasn't much of a player anywhere but on the field. Off it, I was more of a loner.

I had been on a serious soccer track now for over a year. My play for Cal Heat had caught the eyes of the Olympic Development Program for the Western Region (which included California), and I'd made the All-CIF (California Interscholastic Federation) team as a ninth-grader. It was a big deal for a freshman to be playing at all, let alone make the All-CIF team. I was already playing against far more physical 17- and 18-year-old high-school juniors and seniors; now it was against the very best of California's high-school teams, each of which had at least somebody considered the state's best young soccer player. And we weren't just playing these guys. Our team got all the way to the CIF semifinals, knocking off Alta Loma High School and their famed upperclassman Carlos Bocanegra on penalty kicks in the quarterfinals. Everyone who followed soccer in the area knew Carlos. I was ready for everyone to know me.

By any measure, on the field that year I had been a rousing success.

And I caught some breaks as a high-school freshman. There was such overcrowding at Redlands High that they decided to split ninth grade off from the main campus, so we had our own school for an entire year with just freshmen. My hallway dribbling might not have flown so well on the main campus, with a bunch of massive varsity linebackers looking to make a statement about the proper place of a freshman playing soccer.

Maybe the ninth grade girls "lost out" on being hit on by those elder high-school statesmen, but it certainly made mingling with them easier for the rest of us freshman boys. I'd never really made girls a priority. I was so in love with soccer, I was late to the girl game. So, when I had met Kelli Rodgers my final year at Moore Middle School, it was new territory for me. We met, of course, playing soccer, which Kelli loved too.

Like me, Kelli had had a tough start in life. Rumor had it that her dad sold drugs out of the garage, while her sister was off partaking in the rave scene. This left Kelli much like me: on her own, left to figure things out for herself. Time with Kelli had become a welcome getaway from both my home life and soccer. We spent endless hours together hanging in her bedroom, most of it accompanied by Boyz II Men songs. Could there be anything better than being 15 years old in your girlfriend's room with "I'll Make Love to You" blaring through her CD boombox?

I wasn't just coasting while kicking it with Kelli. My game continued to progress, and both my Cal Heat teammate Mark Muleady (our keeper) and I ended up making the Cal South state team.

The state team was coached by Luis Balboa, the patriarch of a powerhouse soccer family. Coach Balboa was a big deal. For one thing, he was the first person I met with a direct connection to the U.S. Men's National Soccer Team. Luis's son, Marcelo Balboa, was a stalwart on the team—the first player in U.S. soccer history to reach 100 caps. In soccer, you earn a symbolic "cap" every time you play in a game for your country. No one had played 100 games...*100 caps*...for America before Marcelo. He not only had just earned the respect of his teammates but was also the team's captain.

I was extremely excited for the opportunity to learn from Coach Balboa. The first day of camp, Coach huddles us together. In those first few moments, you can't help but glance around the circle and size up the other players. A lot of us have never seen or heard of one another, but everyone knows that if you have made it this far, you can play. As Coach addresses us for the first time, the eyes of 18 brash 15-year-olds turn as one, hanging on his every word.

And for the first 15 minutes of our first-ever state practice, Coach Balboa gives us an in-depth lecture on *exactly* how he wants us to ... tie our shoes???

"There are no timeouts in soccer. A shoelace coming undone mid-run can be the difference between winning and losing!" Coach Balboa proceeds to go down on one knee and demonstrates: "When you play for me, take your loops into a square knot—not too tightly—because I want you to make a double knot."

We're all looking around at each other. *Is this guy serious?*

"From this day forward, if you choose to go with extra-long laces, criss-cross the loose ends. Not under the arch—behind the heel. Like this. Understand?"

Micromanage much? I find myself thinking of what life must have been like for young Marcelo growing up in the Balboa household.

Though my shoes were now tied according to Luis's precise specifications, the two of us wouldn't exactly get off on the right foot. Luis was a you-do-it-my-way-or-you-don't-do-it type of coach. Whatever he wanted you to do, if you didn't do it exactly, *precisely* his way, you'd be penalized for it.

Mark Muleady and I had a Cal Heat club tournament that was scheduled to happen a few weeks into our practices with the state team. It was a huge deal to both of us; we had been planning to travel as a team to New York for this tournament, and it had been on the schedule for six months prior to either of us making the state team. Mom had saved up paychecks and already paid the deposit so I could attend.

This didn't sit well with Luis.

As a member of the state team, you were training to travel to Bozeman, Montana, to compete against all the other Western Region state teams. We'd heard that players who did well there could be selected to the regional team, which was a portal to the national team. Pretty exciting stuff. Training sessions for the state team were run once a week; the tournament in New York meant we'd be out for one of the weekend practices.

Mark and I went to Coach to make sure he knew about our conflict. "Hey, Coach, just a heads-up. We're going to miss a training session in a couple of weeks because we have a tournament in New York with our club team. We just wanted to let you know."

Luis spent zero time thinking about his response: "If you skip training to go to that tournament, you will be off this state team and placed onto the United team."

Now, I know what you're thinking. That sounds like a promotion to the United States team. It's not. Eleven teams from across the Western Region—including two teams each from California, Utah, Washington, Hawaii, and Alaska—are invited to Bozeman for this tournament. Every one of these teams has a few extra guys on the end of their rosters who are unlikely to actually get much playing time in the games for their state team. Those guys make up the 12th and final team in the tournament: the "United team."

To put it another way: You had to be good to make a state team. But some good is better than other good. While all the state teams were looked at as the Harlem Globetrotters, this final, filler group of spare parts would be deemed the tournament's Washington Generals.

Playing for Southern California meant so much to me. I didn't want to give that up, and neither did Mark. And Coach Balboa was legitimately important. Upsetting him was not something either of us wanted to do. But I also knew Mom had spent money she didn't have to send me to that tournament in New York.

What do you do? Do you piss off the state coach and get relegated to the team of misfits, or do you piss off your mom and piss away the money she spent so you can stick with the state team? Mark and I were devastated. Coach was making two 15-year-olds choose between two things that did not need to be in conflict.

In the end, Mark and I both decided we were going to New York. We'd already committed to it, and it was more important to stand by our commitment than to back out on our word because of this unreasonable demand. And Coach Balboa? Well, he held to his word too. Mark and I were both now relegated to the United team.

From the moment we arrived in Bozeman, all of us who felt unwanted by our state teams—the Rejects of United—banded together to destroy the field. I was driven by an extra dash of vengeance, and Mark was masterful manning our goal. Together, the Rejects of United tore through our pool of six, advanced to the finals, and won the whole damn tournament. Sometimes, the Washington Generals surprise the world and win.

My one disappointment is that we never ended up playing our California team on the way to the championship. I was, however, allowed to tie my shoes however I saw fit. And as the school year and our trip to Montana came to a near-simultaneous conclusion, I received one more piece of fantastic news: I'd earned a spot on the regional team.

16'

___

IT SHOULD come as no surprise that one of Mom's dreams was for her kids to go to college. And while she was now batting 0 for 1 in that category thanks to Joshie, she did successfully convince him to come back to California to live with us after a stint in Idaho. Joshie was now 20. His father's alcoholism had gotten worse over the years and had reached unbearable levels. So Joshie took advantage of his legal independence and moved in with us, although he made Mom promise to stay out of his hair.

Whatever had brought him back, I couldn't wait to spend time with my brother. To share all my news with him, from the Rejects of United to the regional nod and everything in between.

Joshie and I were sitting on a curb one of these summer mornings, when he turned to me and asked me a deep and poignant question: "What do you want to do in life, Landon?"

While I credit Joshie for instilling so much toughness in me, he was, at his core, the family dreamer. And while I'd been too consumed with making it through the present to think too much about the future, these types of questions were not out of the ordinary from him. "What's your dream?" he asked. "What do you want to accomplish?"

My dream? Accomplish? These were foreign ideas to me. I wanted to play soccer, of course, but at best, I thought maybe soccer would help me make Mom happy and I could use it to get into college. Nothing more, nothing less.

Later that summer, my Western Regional coaches took me aside and told me they were sending me to national team camp.

What's my *dream in life? What do I want to accomplish?*

While I didn't have an answer to Joshie's question when he'd asked it earlier that summer, the answer came screaming to the forefront: *I want to play soccer. I want to get paid to play soccer.*

We were playing on an empty field in Ontario, and I had just told Joshie the news.

"A call-up to the national camp?!" Joshie was ecstatic. "Can you believe this?"

We were interrupted by an angry voice and a man running towards us.

"Hey! You two! You can't be here."

"Why not?"

"This is private property. These fields will be occupied soon."

Now, this was a rebellious time for my brother. Joshie snapped back, "But there's nobody here now."

The man aggressively yelled back at us, "You have to go . . . *now*," and stormed off the field. He turned back to bark at us one more time, "You better be gone by the time I get back."

A vein in Joshie's neck bulged out, looking for an escape route. If that vein had its way, it might have taken a run at this man. But it stayed put. The rest of Joshie's head, however . . . well, you could see the wheel of revenge turning in his mind. I didn't like what I was seeing, but as the guy disappeared, Joshie was already in motion, headed directly to one of the goals.

"Fuck this guy."

Notch by notch, Joshie unhinged the net from the posts of the full-sized goal. Removing it completely, he chucked the net on his shoulder. "Let's go." Joshie stormed to his car, and the net and

I both silently followed. He put his car in D and we drove off in silence.

It remained silent until we heard the police siren.

Joshie pulled off to the side of the main road. Looking in the side mirror, I could see two police officers, guns drawn. One of the officers yelled instructions to us. "Get out of the car!"

Joshie looked at me and dropped some quick advice. "Don't fight back. Don't talk back. And don't give them any extra information. This is serious, Landon—you got it? Do everything they tell you to do."

I nodded as I very slowly opened the door. Put up my hands and kept my mouth shut. They grabbed Joshie and me, separated us, and bound our hands behind our backs with handcuffs. They sat us down on the curb and rapid-fired a spray of questions my way. "Where are you coming from? Do you know why I pulled you over? You see that guy? Does he look familiar?"

He did. It was the guy from the field. He was eyeballing Joshie. Josh didn't have it in him to reciprocate the stare. The cops turned to the guy to ask him, "Do you want to press charges?"

The man looked right at Joshie. Then said, "... No."

They took off our handcuffs. No arrest, no warning, we got to leave. We got back in Joshie's car, and I couldn't help but think how this encounter might have gone differently if the color of my skin was black or brown. One minute I'd been telling Joshie about my good fortune and my dreams, the next ... well, sometimes you can't make your own luck. You've just got to catch a break.

We drove our way slowly back home in total silence. It was a stoplight or two before Joshie broke the awkwardness.

"Don't *ever* tell anyone about this."

You think I wanted anyone to find out we nearly got arrested? Hell no.

I was going to camp with the national team.

20′

TRIS AND I were a month away from starting our sophomore year. But that couldn't have been further from my mind because I was a week away from attending my first national team camp. I was giddy one evening when I had a rare opportunity to unveil the big news on the phone to Dad.

It had been quite some time since we had spoken. We had a lot to get caught up on and I knew he'd be eager to hear it. Our conversations were never about Kelli or what Adam and I were up to in the neighborhood. I knew he only really lit up when we talked about my progress in soccer.

I told Dad about everything that had happened with Coach Balboa and the United team and that I was scoring goals and catching people's eyes. That I had done so well at the Western Regionals that I was invited to a camp with the national team. That I had a chance at making the Under-17 National Team squad.

"Now, now. Don't get a big head, Landon."

"I know, Dad."

"No, you *don't* know. That's the problem."

Dad was doing his best to keep me grounded in the face of so many others starting to treat me like I was something special. But I wasn't looking for a dose of negativity to cut through all the positive happenings, and I certainly wasn't looking for a confrontation. All I wanted was for Dad to be proud of me.

"You think you're invincible, Landon. You're not. All those kids are the best of the best."

"I know, Dad."

"Good. Don't get your hopes up. It'll hurt if you don't make that team."

I know a thing or two about hurt. *How about* you *stop hurting me, Dad.*

Twenty-four hours before I was to head to Florida for my first U-17 camp, and I have one last club game to play. It's more a celebration than a game—everyone knows where I'm going after this, and my teammates are excited for me, if, perhaps, a little envious. I'm incredibly amped—running everywhere and even defending. Adrenaline pumping, I chase down a player by the corner flag early in the first half and slide in hard on him near the sideline. Before I can blink, my cleat locks to the grass as my leg gets caught underneath me.

Immediately, I hear...

Pop! Pop!

Like two loud rifle shots.

I'm down on the field and I'm not moving. I'm crying. I'm holding my foot and all the sounds of this soccer field fade away. I don't hear my coach. I don't hear my teammates. I don't hear any of the shocked parents on the sidelines.

All I hear is my father's voice.

Landon, I told you! You are not invincible!

At the hospital, the doctor broke the news that I had broken my right tibia in two places. He said it could have been a lot worse, and I was lucky—no surgery would be needed. But I would be in a cast. And I'd be on crutches for the next five weeks.

That's lucky? It sounded like a death sentence.

I only broke my leg, but the news felt like it broke my soul. I was supposed to be headed to the Under-17 National Team camp. The whole year had been building, one amazing thing after another, and now I couldn't even put weight on my foot.

Everything I thought I was—my identity, my newly discovered dream, my way of escaping from the darker parts of life—was wrapped up in playing soccer. And here I was, my leg wrapped up in a cast, and I couldn't even walk.

Soccer was taken away from me.

This was *my chance*.

Like that... it was gone.

21′

I'M SITTING in a little cube of an office adorned with nothing
but the very basics. A single chair facing a desk, a clunky, beige
'90s cube of a computer, four glaring white walls, a poster of two
high-schoolers holding books and sporting backpacks, and a sign
above them, all in caps, as if to scream the words: COLLEGE &
CAREER READINESS.

My hands are deep in my letterman's jacket and my foot is inces-
santly tapping, waiting for the meeting to start.

A woman I've never seen before finally comes in the door behind
me. She sits at the desk without much of a greeting, grabs a manila
folder, and finds what she is looking for.

"Landon Donovan?"

"That's me."

"Hi, I'm Mary. I'm your guidance counselor."

I'm meeting this woman for the first time, and neither guidance
nor counsel seems likely to be forthcoming from this box of an
office that they're shuffling us sophomores through.

"So, what do you hope to do after high school, Landon?"

"I want to go to UCLA."

"Oh, really?"

"Yes. I want to get a scholarship to play soccer for the Bruins."

"OK. Let's have a look."

My newly acquainted guidance counselor gets up and leaves the room. I sit there and wonder what the computer on her desk is for. Is it just a prop? She's certainly not using it. If all she needs is to pull my GPA, I could have just told her that myself. It's near the end of the first half of sophomore year, a week before Thanksgiving, and to date I'm a 3.6 student. That's pretty darn good for a loner with a habit of doing his homework during class.

I had survived the required five weeks of nothing after my broken tibia. Now, after a month of rehab, I was healed and back on the field playing with the REV—that's Redlands East Valley—varsity team. Things were feeling pretty good with my fixed-up foot. Turns out I am not only a quick learner but a quick healer. The doctor was right; I was lucky.

Mary reenters the room with a disappointed look on her face.

"Do you have a safety school in mind?"

"A what?"

"A safety school. A second, third, or fourth choice."

I put two and two together.

"You don't think I can get into UCLA?"

"I think you should consider something more realistic for you."

My mom had wanted nothing more for us than to go to college and get an education. I could do that for Mom. Soccer could do that for me. I was absolutely and undeniably going to play soccer at UCLA.

My soccer ball and I had heard enough. I was steaming, so I stood up and walked out without another word.

22′

MOST 15-YEAR-OLDS were going to be spending their Thanksgiving break with family and friends; I was getting ready to show my skills against America's best young soccer players in Florida with the Western Region Olympic Development team.

We were headed to the Cocoa Expo Sports Center near Orlando, Florida. The competition was a tournament against the country's three other regional teams. I'd missed my best shot at playing with the Under-17 National Team when I broke my tibia, but bringing the regional teams together for a round-robin was U.S. Soccer's way of making sure they hadn't missed anyone who should be in that now-established pool of American teenagers. It was a second chance—and almost certainly my last chance to catch the eye of someone with the national team.

Multiple age divisions were competing at the same time. My age group was called "the 82s," after the year we were born. We had one training session in Florida to prepare with our regional team, then the round-robin began.

I quickly realized that most of these players weren't going to stay with me because they couldn't run with me. I was blowing past defenders at will. I scored three goals in three games—one against each of the teams in the regional competition.

At the end of the round-robin games, a gruff man in a U.S. Soccer shirt approached me.

"So, you're the monster from the West *everyone* is talking about?"

I didn't really know how to respond outside of an awkward laugh.

He extended me his hand and I shook it, introducing himself as one of the coaches for U.S. Soccer. He said he'd heard about me and my broken leg and was impressed with my speed with the ball and overall play, even coming back from injury. He told me he was looking forward to seeing me play again on the final night of the event, when select players from the regional teams—myself included—would go up against the U-17 National Team.

Going into that nightcap, it was all-or-nothing time. I got there that evening and met a few of the guys I'd be taking the field with. It's a tricky moment. These guys are your teammates, and you're not going to be able to do anything without working together, but you know there are only a few spots—and shots—to make your mark.

As we took the field, it hit me that I wasn't just playing for me. I was playing for Joshie and all that he had taught me. I was playing for Mom and all that she had sacrificed. I was playing for Dad too, and that never-ending quest for his acceptance and approval. But above all—right now—I was playing for me and my dream to be more than an "American poor" kid from Ontario.

When the game kicked off, the opposition showed why they were the national team. They overwhelmed us those first 45 minutes and went into halftime up 2-0.

A team has a palpable swagger coming off the field when they're dominating an opponent. An energy that reads as a heavy pour of confidence mixed with a splash of smugness. The body language of the national team leaving the field was a not-so-subtle message that they—not us—were the best players in America. And after this halftime and 45 more minutes like it, we could just go back to where we came from. They were brash, and rightfully so.

But I didn't have to accept it. I spent halftime committing to myself that I would let nothing get in my way during the next 45. I needed to show that I belonged there, find another gear, and wipe the smug cleanly off these kids' faces.

When the second half started, I was determined to make an impact. The 50th minute turns to the 60th. The 70th. The 75th. In the 75th minute, it happens. I find some space, sprint forward, and receive a pass. With the ball at my feet, there's not much thinking as muscle memory turns me in to the 18-yard box. I am clear and through in space, with nothing left between the goal and me but a charging keeper. He has underestimated my speed and tries to course-correct, but it's too late.

An empty net awaits. My finish doesn't fail.

The whistle blows. There's cheers and taps; we've cut that smug lead in half.

Five minutes later, I kick open the possibility door and run clean through it as my second goal curls in from distance to kiss the back of the net, tying the game at 2.

You'd think I'd just won the World Cup. Screaming. Fist pumping. Running around the field like a madman and a little kid all at the same time. I didn't care that the score was tied, that only 50 people were in the stands, or that most of the national team players were pissed off and wanted to knock my ass back to California. Those goals were my moment—a golden ticket to a life where I could make something of myself.

A few moments after the final whistle blew, I learned that my world was about to get much, much bigger.

Those guys with the swagger that I desperately wanted to annihilate?

I was about to be one of them.

25'

―――――

IT'S BEEN a whirlwind 120 days since I made the national team. Along with 19 other soccer machines just like me, I have begun an intense adventure with monthly training camps all over the USA.

On this day, I am back in California.

I am now 16 and about to experience a new chapter.

A month ago, I was in Pensacola getting my first taste of play against international players. Five games in five days against Mexico, Guatemala, and El Salvador. We won two, drew two, and lost one. My first international game ever was against Mexico, and I did my part to cement my spot as the starting number 10—the team's playmaking, attacking midfielder—by scoring.

It was 1998, and U.S. Soccer had just launched a program called Project 2010, the explicit goal of which was to capture the World Cup within 12 years. We didn't know it, but given our age and talent level, U.S. Soccer believed that the 82s were essential to helping America achieve this goal. They had never fully invested in a team from such a young age or with such a unified purpose. They just needed a coach who could thread the needle on talent and tenacity, working us hard so we could play at the national level without accidentally deflating the egos of twenty 15- and 16-year-old soon-to-be men.

The man U.S. Soccer handed the keys to was John Ellinger, a trusted member of the soccer community for years. It was his first stint with the U-17 National Team. At our first meeting in Florida, one of the kids joked with him, "You know you're our fourth coach, Coach." Ellinger confidently responded, "Yeah, but I'm going to be your last."

Thankfully, he was right.

Coach Ellinger had a way about him. He was cool without trying too hard. But he could be hard on us when he had to be, and usually in just the right amount; he knew what we could handle. We trusted Coach from the start. He was honest but laid back, and he knew how to relate to a bunch of 15- and 16-year-old kids. It made you want to run through walls for him.

I was a late addition to the squad; almost all the other new players had already had some practice time with each other at the end of summer. Coach Ellinger instantly went to work making me feel part of the unit. "Donovan!" he'd yell. "I was reading about this legendary 6′7″ giant who had all these dominant goal-scoring performances—colossal badass! That really you, Donovan?" I stood about 5′8″ at the time and weighed as much as a kite, but what I lacked in size and strength, I made up in speed. You really couldn't do anything but laugh.

"That's me, Coach."

"Alright! Let's see what you got!"

A few months into his stewardship, Coach Ellinger had already put his personal imprint on the team. He was implementing a diamond midfield that included the affable, long-haired midfielder Kyle Beckerman at the top. He also brought in Bobby Convey, a striker who was a year younger than most of us. Both players were Region 1 guys who Ellinger was familiar with, having come out of Maryland himself.

It was also here that I met a lightning-quick midfielder from Fort Wayne, Indiana, named DaMarcus Beasley. Beasley was a smooth, thin, and fearless player who Coach had playing on the left. I learned that Beas had an older brother named Jamar who had also come through the national team system. I knew how important my big brother had been in igniting my competitive fires; big brothers never want to lose to little ones, and little brothers never want to back down to that challenge. We had that shared experience of striving to stick with them while they beat up on us, only to use them as measuring sticks as we got older in our quests to surpass them.

I vividly remembered a dominant Beasley on the field that day during the regional game at the Cocoa Expo. Beasley, of course, mostly remembered my overzealous celebration. However much he might have appreciated my scoring touch, I'm not sure he was so thrilled to have *that* guy as a teammate. To make matters worse, Beasley had been playing in the middle on the 82s as their attacking 10 prior to me showing up. So now the overzealous guy was also taking his position.

I didn't need to worry. Once Beasley and I got on the field together, all that went by the wayside. We both loved soccer. We'd both been the best back home. We both wanted to get better. Here we were, on a dream team of 20 athletic, talented, and confidently competitive kids. Being out there with each other, doing this thing we loved with people as good as we were, was a dream come true.

Coach Ellinger and staff had two years to implement his preferred, proactive style of play in preparation for the next Under-17 World Championships. That would take place at the end of November 1999 in New Zealand, which is about as far away from California as you can get.

One thing that became clear in that first camp was that we either didn't know or didn't believe that America was supposed to be a third-world citizen when it came to competing in the beautiful game. Everywhere I looked, I was surrounded by brash players who knew what they were doing.

There was Jordan Cila, a striker from New York who, like me, made a habit of finding the back of the net. Kenny Cutler from Richmond and my fellow Californian Bryan Jackson would be joined by Beas and Beckerman to form a not-just-competent, but actually dominant midfield. Sandwiched in the back were two 6'2" Twin Tower defenders from Maryland: Oguchi "Gooch" Onyewu at right back and Alex Yi at center back. Next to Yi was Nelson Akwari, an on-field leader out of Houston, Texas. Seth Trembly from Littleton, Colorado, was our speedy and versatile left back; prowling in front of our 6'1" wall of a keeper, D.J. Countess, who hailed from Sacramento.

Coach Ellinger went to work installing an aggressive, attack-oriented system—and we went to town trying to absorb his desired style of play.

Coach made it clear that he expected us to take the game to the opponents. We would press and attack relentlessly. He didn't care what country our opponent hailed from or what flag they waved, and neither did we. Uncharacteristic talk from a bunch of Americans, but we truly didn't know any better.

Coach had a way of making us feel there was always something real behind his words.

We're going to take it to teams.

We're going to press them like hell.

We're going to respect everyone but fear no one.

It's simple, but when you hear it enough and people buy into it, it works. Coach was putting a chip on our shoulders and a swagger in our stride.

We had only a few months to learn how Coach wanted us to play. Just four months removed from my first camp, we were sharing turf with the world's best young players in France. As a kid who'd come from meager beginnings, you can imagine how wild it was to experience Europe for the first time—trying to take in every strange little difference around me. We took two early losses to Germany and Yugoslavia in Mouilleron-le-Captif before getting our legs under us. Then we picked up some much-needed confidence as we rattled off four wins in a row, beating Israel, New Zealand, Austria, and Sweden.

Those first few months were a crazy blur of back and forth, a constant shuffle to and from airports in Florida, Europe, and our homes. We'd fly into a camp for an intense week together before boomeranging back home to the mundanity of high school. A few weeks later, we'd do it again, this time gallivanting off to someplace new in Europe for a tournament against some of the world's finest soccer countries. And then back we'd fly once more for time with our families, club teams, and varsity crews. It was amazing, intoxicating, all-consuming.

As fun as it was playing at this level and traveling on someone else's dime, the fits and starts of the back and forth were tallying up. Even a bunch of teenagers can be only so resilient, bouncing between three different time zones every couple of weeks.

But this pinball lifestyle was about to come to an end.

A month after France, the team was back together near the ankle of Italy's boot in Salerno, when we received some news from Coach. U.S. Soccer had decided that the team needed to be together more, with less-intermittent training, so they were launching an inaugural Residency program in January. The first team to go through it, we would live, train, and go to school together at the IMG Academy in Bradenton, Florida. If we wanted to stick with the team, Coach Ellinger told us, we would have to commit full-time. If not, we were out.

You could hear the wheels turning as teammates were asked to leave their parents, friends, girlfriends, and siblings behind. The first few months with the team had been intense, thrilling, and fun-filled. This was something else—a friendly reminder that winning friendlies wasn't the goal of the program's existence. They were serious about building out a program. And if we were going to be a part of it, it was going to get serious for us too.

Many of my teammates would have to go home and have hard conversations with their parents. Some of them weren't sure this was something they even wanted to do. It's one thing to miss a few weeks of school and spend your weekends flying around to tournaments and training; it's something else entirely to say goodbye to your family and high school as you know it for months on end. But I had no doubts. If they'd passed around the sign-up sheet in Salerno, I would have been the first to sign it. My guess is Beas would have been a close second.

High school was fine, but I didn't exactly have a huge group of friends I was itching to get back to. And if the point of high school is to learn, I'd learned more about the world in four months of traveling than I had in all the years leading up to that combined. And college? I was going to end up at UCLA one way or another, but that dream seemed a little less substantial than the reality of an ancient city in southern Italy. Soccer might still take me to university, but right now, it was taking me almost everywhere else.

Soccer really did give me this gift. While most of my classmates at REV were learning about the world, soccer was my higher education. My postcards home to Mom would become my report cards; my teammates, my new classmates, all of us living the syllabus of an adventure. Soccer had already taken me places I could have never fathomed it would. Imagine being 16 in Kingston, Jamaica, one month, then Bad Waltersdorf, Austria, the next. Playing South Korea in Christchurch, New Zealand, then journeying to Buenos Aires, Argentina, to take on Boca Juniors 40 days later.

I'd miss Tris. I'd miss Kelli and Adam. I'd miss Mom and even Paul. But I couldn't just put this opportunity to the sideline, and I couldn't see myself passing it up.

We would go on to finish 1-1-1 over the course of those four days in Salerno, including a 1-1 tie vs. Italy playing in its home country, a tough 3-2 loss to Russia, a final 1-0 win over Greece on a fantastic finish from Jordan Cila. The more we played together, the more our chemistry and Coach Ellinger's ideas were starting to translate to the box score.

In June 1998, I threw down a hat trick in a 4-1 win against England. In July, we notched two wins against Jamaica in Kingston.

And in August, at a tournament in Austria, I found the net twice to help us beat France 3-0. We had a unified mentality. It had to be that way; when you're playing against the world's best, it takes a full-team effort to be successful.

And when you're playing a team game, it's a little odd to be picked out for individual attention. So it caught me off guard at the Toto Cup in Austria when I was approached by a confident German man who had a presence about him. Named Michael Reschke, he shared that he represented a professional German club called Bayer Leverkusen and point blank said to me, "We are interested in signing you."

My first thought? *What the heck is Bayer Leverkusen?*

But as a lonely, fragile kid with more than a few rejection issues, it was still a new feeling to be *wanted*. I didn't know if Reschke was just feeding me a line. My hunch is he was at the game to scout someone from the French team that we had just torched. Finding an American who could play at this tournament was almost certainly not in his plans.

I'd be lying if I said I wasn't intrigued by the notion of being signed. How could I not be? But I had no idea what the next step might look like. I pulled Coach Ellinger aside the first chance I got and told him what had happened, and he said it was well deserved and that I should find some representation when we got back home. This was way over my head, but at least I knew that if I truly wanted to pursue it, figuring it out would have to be my next task when we got back to the States.

Waiting for me back in California is another surprise from another somewhat foreign man. Flying in fresh from New Mexico, my dad. He says he wants to spend time with me.

And he wants to be my agent.

28′

___

WASHINGTON, D.C., is a spectacular city. The towering Washington Monument. The majestic Lincoln Memorial. The historic Capitol. And of course, the White House, currently occupied by President Bill Clinton, who a few months earlier, had just uttered the sound bite heard around the world, that he "did not have sexual relations with that woman."

I didn't know this would be the first of many treks to D.C. I just knew that on this day—May 30, 1998—my father and I were attending a weekend soiree compliments of U.S. Soccer. We are treated to a perfect, beautiful, three-act play.

Act 1: Dad and I watch the U.S. Men's National Team prep and train at RFK Stadium ahead of their final friendly before they are to leave for the 1998 World Cup in France.

Act 2: The game itself: a goalless tie vs. Scotland. I had heard so much about the USMNT players from Coach Ellinger; here they were now actually playing in front of me and 45,000 others. Kasey Keller in net. Tab Ramos taking corners. The sheer speed of Earnie Stewart, Eddie Pope, and Cobi Jones on display. This is what soccer looks like played at the highest level by fully grown men. I'm still just a boyish-looking 16-year-old, but I can't help but see all of this as a viable future for me now.

Act 3: The postgame presser. Two dozen American sports journalists are looking for answers from U.S. coach Steve Sampson about the team's inability to score against Scotland and its chances in France. My face turns red when Sampson unexpectedly points me out in the front row, telling the gathered media that they'll be writing about this unknown kid someday. I awkwardly half stand and give a sheepish wave to the grizzled throng of sports reporters staring back at me, wondering what this baby-faced 5'8" kid had done to make Coach think he could help the country beat Mexico or anyone else in the world.

It was the first time I felt that boulder of pressure laid on my back by the federation or had a glimpse of just how big the mountain was that U.S. Soccer wanted us to shoulder. It was just a little shout-out on a different team's day, but the weight of it lay heavy on my impressionable teenage mind.

30′

———

WE'RE BACK in Europe on another business trip. Coach Ellinger is showing us tape of Brazilian sensation Ronaldo. He's running away from people at ease until he finds himself in a showdown with a goalkeeper.

Coach Ellinger pauses the tape to tell us what he wants us to see. "Look—right here. He's watching the goalie and waiting for him to set his feet. And when he does…." Coach presses Play again. "Bam. Then into the empty net for an easy goal."

Ronaldo would accelerate at the exact moment the keeper's feet had set—a split-second moment of seemingly instinctive greatness from one of the world's best. In a fraction of a blink, he's darted past the frozen keeper before effortlessly rolling the ball into the open net.

The next day we play against Austria, and I'm running at full speed past their backline with the ball at my feet. Waiting for me is a showdown with the Austrian keeper, desperately rushing out of the goal towards me to try and cut off my scoring angle.

It happens fast but my instincts see what they were hoping for.

His feet set.

I dribble past him.

I effortlessly roll the ball into the open net.

This is what I love most about soccer. Once I see it, I can do it. Once I do it, I can get it down, and once I get it down… it's committed. Your game is your own, but it's made up of pieces from everyone else you've ever played against, or with, or just watched enough. I can see bits of my game in the games of the guys playing now, like a chef using a familiar spice. The dish might come out in their own unique way, but you know how they used the ingredients.

We lost that game to Austria 4–2, but Michael Reschke from Bayer Leverkusen was there again in the stands, watching me work my improvised magic from the night before. And this time, he was undeniably there to see me.

While my showdown with the goalie had come to a quick and satisfying resolution, there was a pricklier showdown coming back in America when Mom heard the news about Bayer Leverkusen. It only got pricklier when she learned of Dad's reappearance in California and his sudden desire to represent me in that negotiation. While it was exciting to be wanted by a German club, Mom still wanted me to go to college. And as fate would have it, I received a piece of news that only complicated matters more: If I was still interested in attending UCLA, they were prepared to offer me a full-ride scholarship to play for them. So much for needing a safety school.

It was a choice that weighed heavily on a 16-year-old. Mom was clear about her preference. She had always wanted her children to go to college, and she still wanted me to get an actual education. But to her credit, she sought out the names of a few agents to ensure we had a knowledgeable voice to help us make this huge decision.

I had just returned home from a week of training at the IMG Academy in Bradenton, my future home for Residency. The team and I had been getting acquainted with the facilities, a multisport facility and prep school that, prior to our arrival, was primarily being used for tennis players.

With Residency not starting until January, I was getting ready to play a fall afternoon varsity away game with REV at Yucaipa High when Mom told me that an L.A.-based agent named Richard

Motzkin was coming to watch me play. She had received the names of two potential agents and spoken to both on the phone; Richard was the one she was leaning towards. It wasn't just that they'd had an easy conversation that left her feeling good about him. Richard Motzkin had actual experience representing American soccer players overseas; his clients included World Cup star Alexi Lalas, who had gone on to play in professional leagues in both Italy and Ecuador. But what really sealed the deal was that Rich had something else in common with Tris and me; he was a twin. It was a helpful similarity, and it helped Mom get comfortable with Rich coming into our lives at such an important time.

I don't know if I was nervous or just jet-lagged, but I didn't play well. At one point, I missed an absolute sitter from inside the 18-yard box, and didn't do much else to make myself known over the 90 minutes. So, while the game came and went without much to write home about on the field, walking towards me was the agent—with my Mom *and my Dad*. I couldn't tell you how many years it had been since I'd seen my parents together in the same place.

Rich Motzkin held out his hand and introduced himself. He was not much taller than I was and dressed casually, with short, dark hair, a slender build, and a solid handshake. Rich was in his early 30s, around twice my age, but when you're 16 all grown-ups look the same: grown up.

"Hey, Landon. Nice to meet you."

"Thanks. You too."

"Sounds like we're all heading to Applebee's together. Want to ride with me so you can show me where we're going?"

"Sure."

We peeled off from the rest of the group to Rich's car, a black Jeep Cherokee, as the small talk continued.

"Mom says you're a twin?"

"I am. My sister is the sweet one and I'm the competitive one."

That sounded familiar.

"What's her name?"

"Lisa. I'd do anything for her, and she would do anything for me. It's a pretty special relationship. She is so selfless and generous... she has this massive heart and always sees the positive."

"Is she your only sibling?"

"Oh no, there are six of us."

"There are only two of us, although my half brother Josh basically lives with us half the time. Tris—my twin—she would also do anything for me."

He smiled. "That's what twin sisters are for."

There's a lot of instinct in soccer. And my instinct was telling me that Rich was genuine. He wasn't trying too hard and there seemed to be something inherently good about this guy. And yes, it didn't hurt that he had a twin.

At dinner, talk turned to soccer and the options on the table. Mom shared she was thrilled that soccer had landed me a scholarship at UCLA, while Dad loved the idea of his son being a professional. In his view, I should take an offer ASAP before the team came to their senses, changed its mind, and pulled the offer.

You could feel the tension between my parents, who hadn't broken bread together at the same table since I could remember. Yet, here we all were, all together in the middle of the restaurant, having a spirited and emotionally charged debate about yours truly. Mom thought "going pro" could wait—that I should take advantage of my full ride to college. Dad thought she was naive to expect that the opportunity would remain open. I could get hurt or fail to live up to expectations. Other kids were going to catch the eye of these pro teams. There was an offer on the table now. To his way of thinking, I needed to take it or risk losing the opportunity completely.

Not wanting to hurt anyone's feelings, and hoping to avoid confrontation, I remained silent. So did Rich, who sat there taking it all in. He eventually suggested we go around the table and have everyone say what they thought I should do. We already knew where Mom and Dad stood on the issue; what was everyone else thinking?

Tris had remained pin-drop quiet through most of dinner, and when it was her turn to speak, there was a little moment where time stopped while she tried to find the words she was looking for. Then she smiled at me like she always did. "I just want my brother to be happy. Whatever he thinks will make him happiest will make me happiest."

Tris didn't see me as a soccer player. I was the other half of the Donovan twins, and all she wanted for me was my unadulterated happiness.

The dinner ended without resolution. As we exited the restaurant, Rich asked if he could speak to me one-on-one for a second.

We went to talk near Rich's car for some privacy, and what was supposed to be "a second" turned into 45 minutes of Rich giving it to me straight.

"I know you are trying to please both of your parents, Landon. I respect that and I appreciate that. And I know that it's extra hard given the differences between them and all the issues that already exist there. But put that aside for a second. What I want you to really think about is what *you* want to do. Not what you think you should do. Not what you think your dad wants you to do or your mom wants you to do. What *you* want to do. This is your life. No one else gets to live it but you. Take all that other stuff away—what is it that *you* truly want to do?"

I told Rich I didn't want to upset Mom. And that we didn't have a lot of money. I told him I liked the idea of going to UCLA on a full ride thanks to soccer—that when you have a teacher for a mom, getting an education is important. But I also didn't want to upset Dad, and I thought he had a good point about taking opportunities when they came, and that the money of a professional contract was something to seriously consider. There might not be another chance to go pro.

Rich nodded and listened. He understood why I was so conflicted. And I liked how grounded he seemed. He was like a detective putting the pieces of the last 16 years of my life together, puzzling out the whole of the mystery so he could look at it all and make a clear decision. It was new territory to me to have a grown man really listen to what I had to say.

And with all the convoluted pieces of my family puzzle and two possibilities out on the table, Rich made sure I knew the decision was mine. "I can't answer this one for you, Landon. It really does come down to what you want. Between us, if you had to say, deep down, are you leaning one way more than the other?"

I didn't feel like I was talking to someone I had just met a few hours earlier. I didn't feel like I was confiding in an agent. I'd never met one before, but I didn't feel like I was talking to one now. I felt like I was sharing with someone who was genuinely looking out for my best interests and centering the conversation on who I was and what I wanted. He was just trying to help me make sense of it all. So I answered as honestly as I could.

"Well... I think the truth is... in my heart, I really want to see how far I can go in soccer?"

Rich nodded. He understood.

"Then my advice is to talk to your mom and let her know how you feel. If it's what you want, Landon, I really think she'll understand. Again, if I can be a bit forward: I know you want to please everyone, but you have to figure out what you want and how to speak openly and honestly about it to both your parents."

He was making a lot of sense.

"One other thing: Do not feel any pressure about needing to make a decision now. That's simply not the case. It's in the club's self-interest to make you think you need to quickly make a decision because they're striving to lock you in. They want you to think they're the only offer and that their offer might go away. If something is here today, it'll be here next week or a month after. And if not this offer, there will be others. If you can play, you can play, and some team is going to want to have you."

Rich gave me his number and, just before stepping into his Jeep, said one more thing. "If you want my advice or counsel, call me. But I'm the wrong guy if you're looking for someone to pressure you into a decision. That's not needed at this time, and that's not my personality. Nice meeting you, Landon—and good luck."

A week or so later, I called Rich and we spoke for an hour, me mostly asking questions and him answering them. A few weeks after that, I rang him again for another conversation. Mom felt comfortable with him. I trusted him.

Over the next few months there would be lots of these conversations. It soon became clear that we were going to have a business relationship, but it also felt like the beginning of something more.

85'

I'M BACK in Southern California a mere 48 hours after Jurgen Klinsmann's Germanic axe cut me from the National Team. Bruce Arena, Rich Motzkin, and I have gathered in Bruce's office at the L.A. Galaxy complex in Carson to digest the news.

While I'm in a strange space mentally in May 2014, tomorrow is game day for my Galaxy team, albeit a match I never imagined I'd be playing in. Rich thinks I should get back on the field in front of Galaxy fans as quickly as possible. In a truly ridiculous bit of timing, I am a mere goal away from tying the all-time scoring record in Major League Soccer history. How weird a celebration would that be, putting my name atop the list just days after having the dream of a final World Cup yanked out from under me? Nothing makes me want to celebrate more than a reunion with my old childhood friend, rejection.

Rich is well aware I'd be hardest on myself. "Landon, look... This was clearly personal. Jurgen didn't tell anybody in advance. He knew it was an off day for the media and U.S. Soccer. He'd clearly planned it out and wanted to show everyone it was his team by clearing you out. Sunil is livid."

Sunil Gulati, the president of U.S. Soccer, had been far away from Stanford yesterday. According to Rich, Sunil and the U.S. Soccer board were in the air on their way to an international meeting when Jurgen started cutting players, and they found out about it only after they had touched down overseas. It was a deliberate, pre-meditated decision by Jurgen to wait for them to be out of pocket so the blindsided board wouldn't be able to deal with the news. Not that any of that matters now.

The three of us continue this way in the safe confines of Bruce's office, spit-balling ideas for what I should profess to the media. Rich's phone rings—his wife, Randee. He picks up.

"Hi honey... Yes, I'm with him now." He looked up at me. "Randee asks if you're OK."

"I'm OK."

"He's OK."

Of course, I'm not OK. How could I be fuckin' OK?

Rich's call ends, and he rejoins us in our half war room / half therapy session.

"Randee's going to prep the guest room, in case you want to stay the night."

I nod. I'm planning to stay at Rich and Randee's instead of Hannah's tonight. One upside of being in a relationship with someone who doesn't really understand soccer is you don't have to deal with another coach on the home front. But it does have its drawbacks when you need a little soccer consolation. Hannah and I have been together just over a year now, and while she is now my biggest cheerleader, she doesn't really know the intricacies of soccer. I kind of like having that respite. Of course, she knows enough to ask why someone wouldn't take one of his best players to the biggest competition in the world. And she knows that I'd need the space to talk out the nuance of it with Rich, who has now been with me for 16 years. You hear all these brutal stories of player-agent matches gone wrong, and I was so lucky to get it right. I'm 32 years old and he still calls me his "practice child."

Bruce, on the other hand, would sarcastically describe me as his problem child. He chimes in as only he can. "Landon, if there are

23 players in America ahead of you, the USA should have no problem winning the World Cup."

That should make me feel better, but it doesn't. I've done this long enough to know that a huge public shitstorm is coming. Jurgen and I are going to be answering questions about this—separately—for a long while. And it hasn't even started. I'm still trying to navigate my emotions, toggling between the pain and a self-pitying anger.

In my venting, I know we have to come up with an actual statement. And in my mind, I'm thinking something like: *Jurgen is taking a handful of players who really think of themselves as German, some of whom wouldn't give a fuck if we go out in three games and they never stepped foot in America again.* I've been criticized in the past for being truthful, and this thought is nothing but my truth. Rich and Bruce talk me off that ledge, calling it the "light things even more on fire" response. So I decide to keep that sound bite to myself.

But we know it's only a matter of time before I have to face the media. A few hours from now will be that moment.

32′

TRIS HAD a lot to look forward to in the second half of sophomore year: choir, school, time with Mom and her friends. One thing she didn't have to look forward to? Me.

I knew what she was thinking. Your twin doesn't really need to tell you. The sport I loved was officially taking her brother away. And while all she wanted was for me to be happy, soccer continued to be something she downright resented. Never more so than now, because soccer was officially splitting up the Donovan twins.

There would be no more back and forth across the country. My bags were packed fuller this time for the IMG Academy. We were sitting together one last moment on the floor of Tristan's bedroom. However much she wanted me to do whatever made me happy, she didn't want me to go. She wanted her brother to *want* to stay at home. But the decision had already been made. I didn't want to stay home. I was heading east to Bradenton...then further east than that. Bradenton would be but a few months' rest stop before trekking to Germany under my new four-year contract with Bayer Leverkusen.

Leaving Tris and my other loved ones behind was the cost of chasing my dream. I now realize the choice was never between UCLA and a pro team in Europe. It was between staying in Redlands with my family or going all in with soccer. Realistically, did I have another choice? Did I choose soccer or did soccer choose me?

Mom was equally conflicted that I was giving up a full scholarship to UCLA and, in many ways, breaking up the family. But once I made up my mind, I was relentless about it. I knew college for Tris and me was Mom's dream, not mine. So I took to the task as hard as any other training exercise and begged her to let me go. I wore her down; I can be convincing. And when she saw how Rich had structured my contract, she reluctantly accepted.

Rich had included in the contract that Bayer Leverkusen would cover the full cost of UCLA, just in case. Plan A was now Plan B, fully covered, compliments of Bayer Leverkusen. UCLA was officially my safety school. We were still working out the final details of the contract, but no matter what happened next, soccer had already exceeded the bar. And as much as I wished Tris could have come with me, I knew this was something I had to do on my own. I would have to leave behind my family and the only country I knew. I would have to learn a new language, a new set of rules, and a new culture.

I did make one promise to Mom, Rich, and Coach Ellinger: We agreed I'd knock out my GED, a high-school equivalency test, prior to starting my crash course in independence. And so one Saturday morning, mom dropped me and a #2 pencil off at a high school in one of the tougher parts of San Bernardino. I'm pretty sure I was the only person there with a signed six-digit professional contract. Three hours later, I had earned my GED and locked in the opportunity to go to college ... if ever I chose to do so.

Amazingly, this made me a free man for the few months I was in the Residency program before I had to report to Germany. IMG Academy was established to replicate a professional setting for amateur high-school athletes, providing them with a healthy diet, rigorous daily training, and proper physical therapy, all while making sure those athletically gifted high-school kids were still attending school.

This west Florida system had already helped produce several world-class tennis pros, like Andre Agassi, Jim Courier, and Monica

Seles. U.S. Soccer hoped to replicate this approach in soccer—bring their best young players together early enough to develop them and produce a winning national team.

With a $1.5 million investment split between U.S. Soccer, Nike, and the IMG Academy, the 82s would become the lab rats in the experiment. We would train, play, and stay together every day, preparing for the U-17 World Cup. If no parents and all the soccer you can eat sounds like a dream life, well... it was, and it was a great way to build camaraderie between a bunch of incredibly talented teenagers.

Even dreamier: Thanks to Mom and the GED test, I didn't have to go to school anymore. I could focus solely on training and sleeping, two things I loved to do. I even made the hard decision to break up with Kelli. It was one of the toughest phone calls I've ever had to make, but I knew it was the right move.

The day had come to finally sign my contract with Bayer Leverkusen. And while you'd think this would put me in an even better mood, I had to admit I was conflicted anew. We had just come home from competing in the World Championship qualifiers in Kingston, Jamaica, and we'd created a conundrum for ourselves. While we didn't lose a game, we'd still only gone 1-0-2, and Jamaica had sealed the top spot by securing two wins and a tie. Mexico had qualified by winning the other division, which meant we were in a playoff for the final slot with El Salvador, the other second-place finisher, with the two-game series scheduled for May. The Residency experiment would be deemed a failure if we didn't even finish in the top three of our CONCACAF region to make it to New Zealand. We had no choice but to play El Salvador in a home-and-away aggregate, with the first game taking place in Central America.

To make matters worse, at the end of our last game against Jamaica, with the Reggae Boyz only needing to tie to advance, I got so frustrated that I kicked the goalie on a ball I knew I wouldn't get to. It was a deserved, instant red card—the only red card I would

ABOVE: SoCal Babies: me in the middle surrounded by Mom and Dad, twin sister Tristan, and big brother Joshie, 1981

LEFT: With Dad, growing fast; I'm on the left

BELOW: Me and Tris, Ontario, California

With my best friend
and comfort blanket, a
soccer ball ...

... Or sometimes, a
baseball mitt

ABOVE: With my first real team, California Heat, age 10

LEFT: Our place in Redlands, California, had a pool— perfect for soccer practice

ABOVE: At the Under-17 World Championships in New Zealand, November 1999
Phil Walter, Getty Images · courtesy U.S. Soccer

FACING PAGE, TOP: Proudest moment
so far: playing for Team USA at the 2002
World Cup in Japan and South Korea
*Henri Szwarc, Bongarts, Getty Images
courtesy U.S. Soccer*

FACING PAGE, BOTTOM: In my comfort
zone, with Tris and Mom

The youngest player on
the U.S. team at the 2000
Summer Olympics in
Australia—we finished fourth
Darrin Braybrook, Getty Images
courtesy U.S. Soccer

RIGHT: On the cover of *Soccer America*, 2001, the year after my senior team debut

BELOW: Poster boy for the San Jose Earthquakes, underdog winners of the MLS Cup in 2001

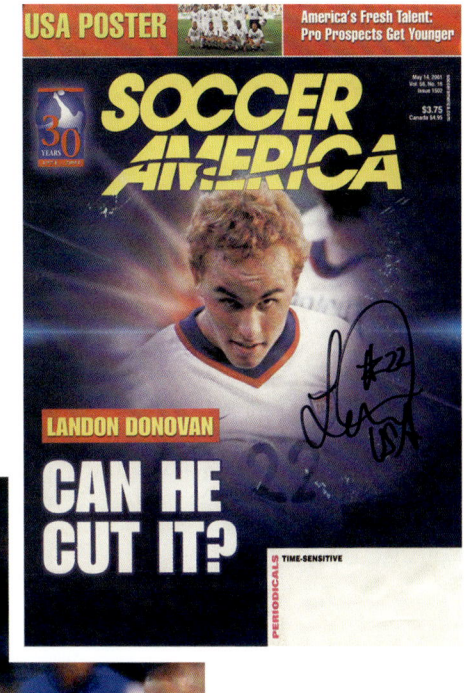

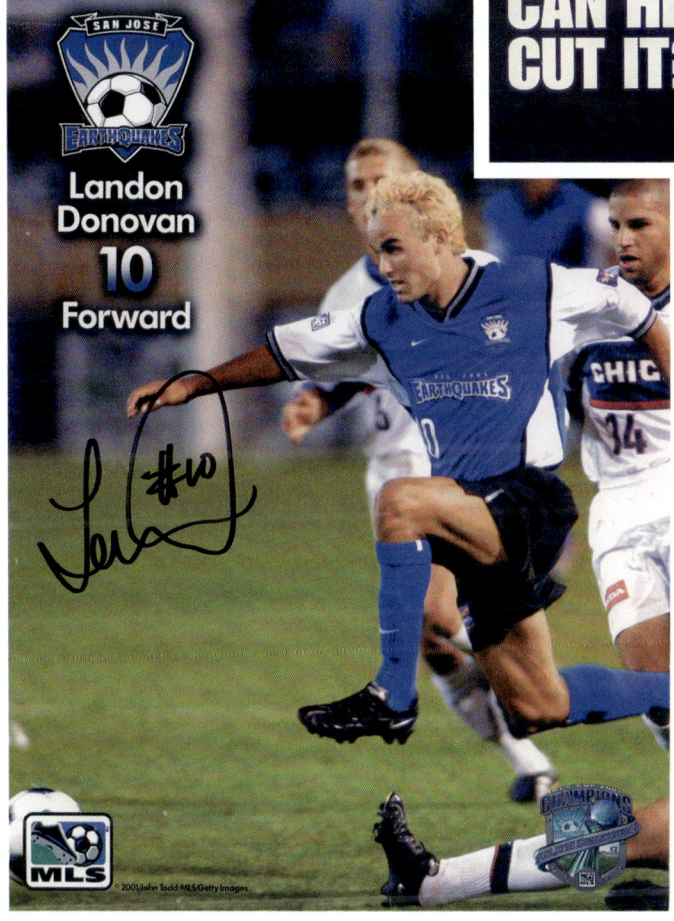

With my agent of 27 years and counting,
Richard Motzkin, in 2003 and 2025
Bottom photo by Tanya Goehring

receive in my entire career. And while I was immediately remorseful, it didn't occur to me until considerably later that I might have also screwed up our chances of making it to New Zealand. I was now faced with a one-game suspension to be served during our first game against El Salvador. I pride myself on wanting to be a great teammate, and when I realized I'd hurt the team by taking myself off the field for one of our most important games, it hit me hard. I'd have to hope for the best while I watched the first game from the sidelines.

So I was feeling mixed emotions signing my first official contract. I was about to turn 17, and I was also about to be transformed into a professional soccer player. Rich had flown in for the signing. With a few flicks of the pen on my new four-year, $400,000 deal, it was done. As nervous as I was about finally settling it, I was also undeniably giddy. I didn't know what exactly was ahead of me, but money—for the first time in my life—wasn't going to be a problem.

Amazingly, this was already the second deal Rich had pulled together for me. In 1999, the most gifted U.S. soccer stars were earning $1,000 annual allotments from Nike. In a tremendous leap of faith that I might be going places, Nike had signed me to a four-year endorsement deal that would pay $25,000 annually the first two years, then bump up to $35,000 in years three and four. Having the swoosh commit to me as a 16-year-old was something special.

When Rich wasn't working on these deals, he made damn sure my newfound finances and visibility didn't inflate my ego. Rich was good like that. He never looked to advance me just as a player or a client—he always wanted to make sure I was a good human being. His job included everything from being an agent and financial planner to providing fatherly advice and serving as the best life insurance policy a neophyte kid could ask for. Rich took control of establishing my assets, setting me up with financial managers, accountants, and retirement specialists—a world of people

I'd never known I could have needed in my dribble-through-the-high-school-hallway days.

I wasn't just getting a crash course on money, I was also getting a rapid tutorial on the fundamentals of being a man. Having inked my deal with Bayer Leverkusen, my remaining California time was dwindling. I flew into LAX late one night and stayed overnight at Rich's place, in a spare bedroom they kept for me for whenever I didn't feel up to making the drive to Redlands. On this particular evening, Rich let me borrow his Jeep to go out and see friends in Los Angeles.

I got my first real lesson in "Man" from Rich the next morning. He had an early-morning meeting, and I had emptied out his gas tank driving around L.A. the night before. Rich had to stop to fill up, which made him late for his meeting. Something that I found out about when Randee Motzkin, Rich's wife, woke me up and handed me a phone. I groggily held it to my ear . . .

". . . Hello?"

"Landon!"

". . . Yes?"

"Have you ever heard the expression, 'Leave things in better conditions than you found them'?"

I had not, actually.

"Uh . . . no?"

"Landon, I don't care if you're a soccer star. You bring my car back with gas in it, certainly not with a red line on empty. Has no one ever taught you this?"

Given my extended silence, Rich quickly figured out that no, in fact, no one had ever taught me this. So he continued . . .

"If you ever borrow my car again and return it empty, it'll be the absolute last time you take the car out. You borrow something from somebody, you bring it back in better condition than you found it. Someone lends you their car, you fill it up. Got it?"

I got it.

Is this what it's like to have a dad around? I wasn't used to anyone chewing me out about stuff, at least stuff off of the soccer field. So yeah, I might be an entitled 17-year-old, but I was embarrassed.

Rich's wife, Randee, was another woman in my corner. Randee was a lawyer with an impressive résumé of her own, but to me she was the Motzkin Chief Home Officer. She was motherly by nature, which isn't usually what you think of when you hear the word "lawyer." I felt an instant connection to Randee. She never cared about how I did on the field, just how I was doing when I stepped off it. It was as if they had adopted me into their family when Rich started representing me—which in a way, they had. In so many ways, I was still just a kid. When I'd stay with them, Randee would make meals, do my laundry, and just allow me to be me. I really was their practice child. There were no catches and no obligations; I was just an honorary member of the Motzkins.

I still had a lot to learn about life, and Rich took me under his wing. Where guys like Coach Ellinger and Clint Greenwood had made a huge impact on my professional development, Rich was making an immediate difference on my personal development.

Perhaps he felt the obligation to live up to my mom's trust in putting her child in his hands. Rich had plenty of other things to deal with; he didn't need to take responsibility for instilling sense into someone else's teenage boy. But Rich took me under his wing anyway. And because of that, our relationship grew to encompass everything: trusted confidant, masterful agent, and father figure. Rich took to calling me "Pibe"—Spanish slang for "kid."

There would be many late-night conversations where Rich would nudge me in the right direction. He took it upon himself to teach me about the world and the difference between right and wrong. When I had questions about things, Rich would encourage me to put down the remote control and pick up a book to expand my mind. And he often ended his emails to me with the same sign-off: TRTTD.

The Right Thing to Do.

I learned from Rich to take care of the people you love, that you're only as good as your reputation, and that you should never, *ever* do something that goes against who you are just to earn an easy dollar. At the 2000 Summer Olympics in Australia, a company called Golden Palace—they ran one of the first gambling sites on the internet—would offer me $50,000 to have "Golden Palace" temporarily tattooed on my chest. More if I scored and showed it off. Rich's email to me about it was short and to the point:

Pibe,
As much as nothing says "America loves gambling" like "Golden Palace" inked across your chest for 50K+, this is a hard no. TRTTD!—Rich

May 1999 arrived before we knew it; it was time to head to El Salvador. The U-17s had trained and played for a year and a half to get to this moment. In the final run-up to leaving, we'd even conducted the strangest training session I'd ever been part of, to help prepare us for what it might be like in El Salvador, with coaches chucking water balloons at us while we tried to play. Why water balloons? To stand in for the bags of urine that El Salvador's supporters had been known to throw at opposing players. We all laughed until we realized the coaches were serious. We head to Central America prepared for the worst.

As we enter our locker room in a foreign land, we can feel the whole place shaking above us. We're just kids, but the stands are packed full of passionate fans of all ages. The energy is incredible. And as the team takes the field, I go my own shade of crazy because I can't be out there to help my teammates. I feel helpless on the bench watching. Twenty-five minutes in, it gets worse, as we give up an own goal off Nelson Akwari's foot. Up 1-0 on an own goal against America, the stadium is pulsing with an almost maniacal glee.

A few moments later, we earn a corner and as Beas trots over to take it, from out of the throng of screaming fans standing seemingly right on top of him comes the cut-off head of an unplucked chicken, landing right at his feet. Beas jumps back, startled, staring at this beheaded chicken and it staring back at him.

It turns out that you can't prepare for this type of chaos with a couple of water balloons, but that doesn't mean you can't pull it together and fight back. Maybe the El Salvadorians didn't think a bunch of kids could take it and respond like men, but we aren't fazed by their antics or by being down a goal. The 82s have given up enough first goals in enough games; we've probably already given Coach Ellinger an ulcer. But that also means we know we are equipped to come back. So just before halftime, Jordan Cila quiets the madness with an equalizer. And when we come out tied in the second, we steamroll them.

By the time the final whistle blows, we have scored the next six. USA: 6–El Salvador: 1. Jordan Cila was unstoppable with a hat trick and a few assists. A few weeks later we met again on our home soil, this time with me happily back on the pitch, and dominated El Salvador again, winning 4–0. On an aggregate score of 10–1, the U.S. U-17 team was going to the World Championships come November.

After all the travel, the sacrifices, the hard work… it had all been for something. Residency brought a 20-match unbeaten international streak across a 14-month period. We'd beaten teams in England, across Europe, and down in South America. We'd played Manchester United's U-19s in England. We were kids, and we were beating men. We'd shocked these teams, putting them on the wrong side of the hyphen. We were *that* good at this age. On a roll.

While New Zealand was on the minds of the entire U-17 squad, I had more pressing matters. The championship wouldn't be until late fall. For now, summertime was here, and for most, a well-earned break.

For me, there'd be no time off or summer break—just the opposite. A new life lesson awaited me in Deutschland.

33'

LOTS OF FOLKS go to business school for two years, but they usually go to college first. I was skipping the college part and about to earn my MBA in International Soccer. If every domestic league has its own variations in style, then the Bundesliga is exactly what you'd expect from the German one: The clubs are prepared, rigid, and excellent at execution. Bayer Leverkusen is one of the top clubs in the Bundesliga, a consistent podium team where every staff member, trainer, and player knows their place and role.

I had my own apartment less than a mile away from the training facility. If I needed anything at all, the club had paid a family on the top floor to be available to me. I wasn't itching to have a lot to do with them—I was almost as excited about being on my own as I was about the soccer experience—but they were there if I needed them. I also got the keys to a new Audi, to get me to and from training. And while this was more an Audi of the utility kind than the luxury variety, it was still an Audi, and more than exciting enough for a kid who'd only just gotten his driver's license.

As generous as Bayer Leverkusen was in gifting me keys to the apartment and car, no one would be gifting me the keys to their soccer empire. The investments the Germans were making in their newly acquired asset—me—were intended solely to ensure I could fully focus on what they were paying me to do: get better at soccer.

The first time I walked into the massive Leverkusen facility was nothing less than mind-blowing. The facility was masterfully thought out, every detail carefully designed to nurture and develop players. A huge equipment room and state-of-the-art medical treatment facility. A quiet lounge room. Hangout areas intended to encourage mingling and team bonding. And multiple, spacious locker rooms for the different tiers of the team. I'd never been exposed to anything like it. I'd signed my contract without ever visiting, and this was before the internet—I couldn't just google "Bayer Leverkusen" and see what I was walking into. The facilities at Bradenton had been nicer than anything I'd seen before, but this... this was professional soccer.

The facilities Leverkusen's players had available to them made IMG Academy look like a sideshow. To go from there to this well-oiled international machine, with its layers of thoughtful planning and well-established legacy of developing potential, was eye-opening. We definitely had some catching up to do back in the States.

Of course, this was catnip to me. Now at my disposal was the biggest buffet I could ask for to maximize my game. The flip side, though, is that none of this was done just for me. Quite the opposite—I was now just one of 50 talented teenagers in Leverkusen's elite program. Gifted soccer players from across the globe, all busting their asses to make the first team. And while I had been the star everywhere I'd been in America, that held no weight in my new club's deliberate and unemotional conveyor belt development process. From their perspective, I was just one of many kids with the potential to become a cog in their machine. From quantity comes quality. They didn't really care who I was or where I came from.

The club machine was a pyramid: the youth kids, then the Amateur Mannschaft, and finally, the cherry on top, the main Bundesliga team. I was immediately put in with their other 16s, some of whom had been training in the program for years already.

Joining Leverkusen was the most adult thing I had ever done, but you never feel more like a kid than when you are the new kid. And believe me—I did. As a natural loner and the sole American in a group of kids throwing inside jokes in German slang at each other, I already felt like an outsider looking to prove myself and earn a way in. Increasing my awkward kid feelings was a surprise guest who'd decided to accompany me for my first two weeks in Germany: my dad.

I'd craved the opportunity to connect with Dad my whole life. And here at long last it was, shipped straight from the be-careful-what-you-wish-for department. As a pro—and on my dime—that day had come. I had always hoped my success in soccer would make him proud and here he was watching me play—really, intently watching me play, for the first time. But he was also trying to tell me how he thought I should be acting around other players, trainers, and coaches. For two weeks straight, Dad was suddenly... *trying to be my dad*. Out of nowhere, telling me how to act, how to respond, how to play.

All this commentary did not sit well with me. When I was a kid who could have used advice, he was nowhere to be found. I'd made it here without his advice, and now he's trying to tell me what to do, how to act and how to be? Who is this guy? Why is he now joining me in the winner's circle without running the race? And the answer to that seemed clear.

With the endless unsolicited advice, having Dad there made this feel like the longest two weeks of my life. Years of neglect had been boiling under the surface and I finally let it all out.

Why do you think you can tell me what to do? You don't *know me. You* were *never* around.

He was shocked. It was the first time I had ever really confronted my dad about, well, anything. I was an angry kid, but until this moment, I'd always held back and allowed him to keep the upper hand in our minimal, transactional relationship. He had walked all over me for a decade and a half, and I was done with it. I was done with him. My anger at my abandonment, his disappearances and continuous excuses, the court cases and missed payments, and everything else he'd put us through—it all came pouring out.

My dad left a few days later. I was, at long last, officially on my own. With nothing left to distract me, I could once again be singularly focused on the one thing I could count on in life: soccer.

Once Dad was gone, it didn't take more than a couple days to get acclimated. The 16s trained on an orange clay-like substance— some strange kind of dirt—and as I got my feet under me, I quickly realized I could more than hold my own at this level. I started to see the process the German machine was running. Leverkusen had many players train up a level, but play down with their actual age group, and I was soon bumped up to train with the 18s while competing with the 16s. The next goal was to train with the reserves and play with the 18s.

I'd arrive at the facility 15 to 30 minutes before training each day and practice with the 18s from 10 to noon. Then a shower and lunch at the newly built Lindner Hotel BayArena connected to Leverkusen stadium, and by 1 p.m. I was free to do as I wished. On afternoons when I didn't have German lessons, I would stroll around the quaint village community around my apartment, exploring. There was a bakery, a pharmacy, and a cute Italian restaurant that became a favorite of mine for takeout.

Saturday was game day, but some of my largest lessons that first year came on Sunday, our one day off. I learned exactly how much the weather dictated whether I left my apartment or not. And when the weather was miserable—which it often was—it meant more to my temperament than just having to deal with cold, rain, sleet, or snow. It often dictated my mood. When it's dark and ominous for three weeks straight, a California kid used to sunshine and endless outdoor running can start to feel down. It was brutal.

Outside the morbid weather, there was so much about German life I simply didn't know. I didn't know the language. I didn't know you were supposed to bag your own groceries. And I really didn't know that absolutely everything is closed on Sundays. On my first Sunday off, I woke up starving around 10 a.m. With my refrigerator empty, I went down from my flat to grab anything to eat. The bakery? *Geschlossen*. Italian place? *Geschlossen*. Grocery store? *Geschlossen*. Are you kidding me? Can you imagine every store in a California town being closed just because it's Sunday? I knew that I had the day off; I didn't know that *everybody* had that day off too.

Thank god for Mom's quarterly care packages. They were a lifeline from home that helped keep me sane, though I know they were expensive to send. There were letters from Mom, Tris, and Joshie, and a whole bunch of things I couldn't get in Germany. Snacks, books, and all my favorite cereals: Honey Bunches of Oats, Honey Nut Cheerios, Life. These letters and food were treasured connections devoured at the oddest hours of the night. A literal taste of home.

And while I was getting homesick off the field, as the months went on, I was getting frustrated on it. I was excelling on the field with the 16s, but I wasn't here to play tiers down from the main team. I was here to compete at the highest level, and as near as I could tell... right now, I wasn't. I was just another kid in the system to be brought along at someone else's pace.

I didn't get much out of the Two-Week Dad Experience, but one thing he had said kept coming unpleasantly back to me. I'd complained about feeling frozen out that first week there, that the other kids wouldn't pass me the ball. And he just laughed in his typical manner and said, "Why would they? They aren't interested in *you* succeeding." It was cynical, but it also wasn't wrong. The other players were only interested in passing me on their quest up to the next tier. Helping someone else get there instead didn't interest them.

This was a sad realization for me. Is that what it's like to be a professional? Was it really every man for himself from here on out?

This was not soccer as I knew it and not the way to build a team. I was keeping tabs on my American comrades in Residency who were prepping and training without me for the World Championships. I'd only been in Germany for four months, but I was missing their support and camaraderie. They probably thought I was living the sweet life as a well-paid soccer professional. Truth is, I was frustrated, lonely, and getting a little bored with the monotony of German life.

My most direct line back to the States was the original social media: AOL Instant Messenger. This was before the days where cell phones, texting, and lazy emojis would shrink the world and make keeping up a breeze. And while I was living nine hours ahead of Mom and Rich and six ahead of Beas and the boys, I was lonely and would stay up all hours of the night just to connect. I'd reach out to anyone I knew on AOL. I'd chat with Beas to see how Residency was. I'd IM with U.S. Soccer brass Sunil Gulati, who I'd only really met at RFK on the D.C. trip. If Rich were up, I'd tell him my truth—that being a professional soccer player wasn't all it was cracked up to be.

It was amazing how quickly something that felt like freedom could turn into a straitjacket holding you in place. Here I was on my own and independent. I could stay up all night if I wanted to. I could eat Frosted Flakes for dinner. And for the first time in my life, money was not an issue. But I was an outsider. I may have been a loner, but even a loner longs for connection. I had no real friends on the team. I barely spoke the language. And in the one thing I cared about—soccer—I was starting to miss playing in meaningful games like I missed being wanted by coaches and teammates.

It wasn't all bad, of course. While I didn't know if or when I'd jump up another level, I was improving a lot as a player. I'd go out twice a week to train individually with one of the U-18 coaches and a goalkeeper. At first, it was literally a foreign affair. No one had ever worked with me like this before—pure one-on-one coaching to target a weakness and make it a strength. It wasn't long before I knew the pattern of the finishing drills and had gotten proficient at them. By the fourth session, it was... bang! *Tor!* Bang! *Tor!* Bang! *Tor!* I would score, over and over again, until finishing became second nature.

While I wasn't seeing the field outside my time with the 16s, they were developing me, as promised. I just didn't understand why they weren't letting me compete in games that were equal to my level. I'd been playing meaningful minutes for my country for almost two years. But I was a 16 to the Germans. It made no sense to me. Why would you pay six digits over four years to stick a kid three tiers down in the club and let him waste away? It made me really appreciate being called up to play meaningful games for the USA.

Almost six months into my time in Germany, and now a month out from the World Championships, I was given the green light to head back to Bradenton to train with my U.S. teammates. I was ready to take my pent-up aggression and put it to use on the field in a game that mattered. It felt like more than an opportunity to play; it felt like an opportunity to prove to the club that I should be playing. I would be going to Bradenton to train for the final four-week stretch with the U-17s before we headed off to New Zealand.

It was amazing to be back on the fields in Bradenton. I'd missed the guys—I'd missed *Americans*—and just being out there again felt freeing. But I hadn't just been away from them for six months; they'd been away from me. I noticed right away that my technical capabilities had noticeably improved by comparison. It made sense: In Germany, I was somewhere between a boy and a man training with professionals. The level of intensity in Germany was top-notch—every man for himself—and it had started to rub off on me. I was learning a physical game and toughening up. And when I felt us lacking that in Bradenton, I let my teammates know about it. There was an edge I had grown from my time at Leverkusen that I didn't have before. When you're playing with grown-ass millionaires who demand the ball, you give it to them. I brought that newly learned but unliked behavior back to the States and was now considerably more vocal about what I thought was the right way to do things. Which led to another noticeable new trait: I had become a bit of an asshole.

You can run for the full 90 minutes, but you can't hide from what your mind is coping with. I felt anonymous in Germany. I felt replaceable—one cog in a whole pile of them in the cog factory of the 16s. Like many others in that German environment, I was solely focused on my performance on the field and not on making relationships off it. That sadly translated back home. Maybe there was just too much of a chasm between the reality of my solitary life abroad as a 17-year-old professional and my teammates' boarding school existence in Florida. Whatever the reason, without really meaning to, I kept my teammates at arm's length. I was friendly but incapable of being their friend. These should have been some of the best times of my life. Instead, I was so focused on being successful, I didn't take time to appreciate the ride or the people I was on it with. I still wish I could go back to those epic times with those guys and fully live in those moments with them.

We had a month together before the U-17 World Championships. Off the field, it gave me time to try to catch up on the bond others had continued forging while I was away in Germany. On the field, we were already there, clicking almost seamlessly. We were a confident group, and we knew we had the mentality, chemistry, and proficiency to make a major run down in New Zealand.

A year earlier, we had ventured to Christchurch, New Zealand, to get familiar with the temperature and terrain of Kiwi country. In five games over a week, we'd gone 4-0-1, scoring 25 goals and giving up zero. Our one tie? A scrappy 0-0 match against New Zealand, the team we'd face a month from now in our first match.

Coach Ellinger knew the host nation would want to show well in front of their fans and this game would be an all-out battle.

Toughness became an integral part of our training. Did we have the legs to compete late into games? Could we outscrap, outrun, and outplay these guys for 90 minutes on their home soil?

Early one morning, Coach Ellinger took us to the IMG Academy track. A stopwatch dangled from his neck.

"Welcome to the first half of your first World Championship game. Think you have what it takes to go the distance with the host country? Yes, you're talented; but do you have the mindset and mettle? Fitness will matter! Give me two miles as fast as you can. Yes, there will be training after this. Goalies... *you're running too.*"

D.J. Countess and Steve Cronin were less than thrilled to be included in the exercise. As for the rest of us, whether we liked it or not, it was "go" time. Coach Ellinger blew his whistle, and we were off. Lap by lap, around the track we ran. It takes eight laps to go two miles, and I want to be the first one through the eight. By the third lap, fatigue starts setting in with many of our defenders. By the fifth lap, a handful of us lap the goalies. And by the eighth and final lap, I've found another gear. My cross-country days on top of my training in Germany help me cross the finish line first in 10 minutes, 30 seconds, well ahead of everyone else.

One by one, huffing teammates find the finish line, and you see a bit of everything. Walk it out. Hands on knees. A few of our big guys have to sit down. When the last of our teammates, one of the goalies, crosses the finish line, Coach Ellinger stops his watch.

"Halftime is 12 minutes. Then we're onto your second half... one more mile to add to your time. Your goal? Under 17 minutes and 30 seconds."

Moans across the track. The goalies aren't even standing. When the 12 minutes are up... second half.

Coach knew talent without effort would be a recipe for failure in this tournament. These final four laps were his way of reminding us we were going to have to fight. He blew his whistle, punched his stopwatch, and we were off and running again.

I imagined myself back in the Moore Mile, chasing Raul Garcia. For those four laps, Coach Ellinger might as well have been Coach Hafley as I flew around the track—running my last mile in just over five minutes. Three miles in just over 15 minutes—the best time on the team.

With preparations done, it was finally time to fly down to New Zealand. Training was over. The World Championships lay ahead. With first-round matches against the host country, Poland, and Uruguay, it would be no easy lap around the track.

36′ GOAL!

AT LONG LAST, the thing we've been training for these last 18 months is here: the 1999 Under-17 FIFA World Championships in New Zealand. It's the first tournament of the international football federation for which players born after January 1, 1982, are eligible to compete. Sixteen nations—including Germany, Brazil, Spain, Ghana, and Mexico, our CONCACAF nemesis—have gathered to show each other and the world their next generation of stars.

We'd landed in Auckland a few days earlier, many of us accompanied by loved ones. With a trip to New Zealand requiring so much time away, it was out of the question for my mom or Tris to come, but Rich and Randee, my fill-in parents, had made it in support. As for fan support… we knew supporters in this faraway land were going to be few and far between, but that was OK by us. We were a battle-tested unit now, used to going into other countries and taking care of business.

We were on a mission. Could we put American men's soccer on the map in a real way? The U.S. Women's National Team was already the belle of the ball after winning the World Cup on our home soil earlier in the year, but the U.S. Men's National Team had finished dead last in the 1998 World Cup in France the summer before. As far as the rest of the soccer world was concerned, the Stars and Stripes were an afterthought in the men's game—a first-round speed bump to be driven over on the way to the real tests of the tournament. In the seven World Championships that had been held since its founding in 1985, the U.S. had yet to get even a sniff of a medal round.

Our laughably low status was on full display in the pretournament press conferences. Coach Ellinger was asked what the goal was for the U.S. team, and he'd responded that he'd consider anything short of a run to the semis a disappointment. Later that day, a reporter asked Kevin Fallon, New Zealand's head coach, if he had any thoughts on Coach Ellinger's statement, and he laughed and dismissively responded that he wasn't sure what Ellinger was smoking but thought he should set a more realistic goal.

Maybe Coach Fallon was just so used to overlooking the U.S. team that he hadn't done his homework on us: We came into New Zealand riding a 21-game international unbeaten streak, unheard of for the U.S. We hadn't lost an international match in 15 months. We appreciated him gifting us such great bulletin-board material and couldn't wait to smoke his All Whites on the field.

We had swagger, a shared goal, and shrunken egos across the team. Our motto: WIT. *Whatever it takes*. We took the field in the opening match of the tournament against New Zealand, ready to show them and the world who we were. What better way to make a point than to take it to the home team in front of 14,000 screaming Kiwi fans in their brand-new North Harbour Stadium?

So naturally, 16 minutes in, we found ourselves down 1-0. I'm sure Fallon had a good chuckle with his team at halftime about Coach's semifinals prediction. But in the second half, Abe Thompson tied the game for us in the 69th minute. Six minutes later, I put the Kiwis in our rearview mirror for good. *Thanks for the motivation, Coach Fallon.*

Uruguay and Poland drew 1-1 in their first match, so we are at the top of the table going into Game 2. We again live up to our reputation for conceding the first goal and are down 1-0 after an ugly first half against Poland, conceding a goal on a penalty kick just after the 40th minute. But... *WIT!* In the 89th minute, we manage to draw a PK of our own. All that is standing between us and the crucial fourth point in pool play is towering 6'11" Polish keeper Tomasz Kuszczak. I prepare inside the penalty box, the ref blows his whistle, and I target a space low and to the corner that I hope will be just out of his giant reach. It's a race to the bottom between the ball and him, and the ball just wins out. Minutes away from a loss that would drop us to third in the group, it's a huge swing of momentum. When the game is blown final a few seconds later, we are sitting atop Group A, locked with Uruguay, each of us with four points going into our third and final pool match against one another.

Most of the drama of this third game faded moments before kickoff when New Zealand knocked off Poland 2–1, sending both Uruguay and us through to the quarterfinals. Knowing we had made it through, the biggest pressure was off... but we had no time to celebrate. Still at stake was winning our group to matador a likely showdown with Spain, who were atop Group B before their final match with Mexico.

It took until the 90th minute, when the towering Oguchi "Gooch" Onyewu's late header found the back of the net, sending us to the top of Group A. Our eyes turned towards the mighty Spaniards' final match to see what was coming our way... but landed somewhere considerably closer to home when Mexico, shockingly, beat Spain 1–0, knocking them out of the World Championships. The team now standing between us and our semifinals goal was a team we knew all too well: Mexico.

With four days until our quarterfinal match against Mexico, Coach Ellinger granted us a day off to explore New Zealand's North Island. Rich, Randee, and I took advantage of the day to get our first real view of Auckland. It's a storybook backdrop, gorgeously nestled within two large harbors, its iconic sky tower and beautiful cityscape hovering over the Hauraki Gulf. Beautiful though it is, my mind was only half on the boat tour we chose; half remained fixated on the games still to come.

I couldn't help but think about how the rest of the world was learning what my teammates and I already knew: that the Americans are for real. We were well coached and hard to play against. With Beas and me both competing at such a high level, the international media was starting to cover us. We were proving on the field we weren't just good for an American soccer team—we were good for any team in the world.

It was a special time for a special group—we were announcing to the world that America was joining the party. And while it felt good to be noticed, I also knew that we had reached the end of Residency. We'd spent 18 months building to this moment, and soon it would be over. And when it was, no matter the result, a ticket back to Germany was awaiting me on the other side, along with everything that went with it.

Four days can go by fast.

As we took the field against Mexico, our too-regular CONCACAF foes, we knew one thing: We were a good team, and we were ready to play *El Tri*.

Unfortunately, maybe we weren't ready enough.

Just two minutes into a swirling quarterfinal, we again pulled an "us." Hector Vallejo, the striker who'd scored the game winner to put Mexico through over Spain, capitalized on a cross we didn't clear. Just like that, we had served up a serious confidence boost to Mexico along with an early 1-0 lead. Mexico knew us well and jumped on us early. To make matters worse for me, I wasn't just marked—I was double-teamed from the get-go. Their game plan was to take me out of *our* game plan, and I was afraid it might be working.

In the 20th minute, things took a turn for the worse, as Ricardo Sanchez went down while entering our penalty area and drew a penalty. Barring a miracle, it looked like I would be on a flight back to Leverkusen sooner than I had hoped. But instead of staring at a 0-2 hole on the scoreboard, we got to watch the miracle: D.J. Countess made an epic save to turn Sanchez's PK away. It was a huge adrenaline boost that turned both momentum and our play around.

We started putting Mexico's defense under pressure and peppering shots at Adolfo Cabrera, Mexico's keeper. Fifteen minutes after D.J.'s save, and 38 minutes in, Beasley took a long ball off his chest from Seth Trembly and dipped a left-footer past a helpless Cabrera. You could feel Mexico get tight as we started to find pockets of space. Five minutes after Beasley's goal, Jordan Cila put in another one. For the first time in this tournament, we'd enter halftime with a lead. The energy carried over to the second half, and when Kyle Beckerman put away a Gooch cross with a header from six yards out, we'd extended our lead to 3-1. Sitting on a two-goal lead is never easy, and sure enough we ended up giving one back, but there wasn't much doubt we were holding onto this one. With a 3-2 victory, for the first time ever, America was through to the medal rounds.

Hello, semifinals. We had cleared Coach Ellinger's pretournament bar. Not so laughable anymore.

And we still wanted more.

A sound Australia team awaited us. They'd topped Group C, outclassing both Brazil and Germany in the early rounds. In one of the worst halves we'd played in 18 months, they badly outclassed us, and we found ourselves down 2-0. But there's something to be said for training against grown men and building up toughness. Just one minute after we'd fallen behind 2-0, I found the back of the net to cut the Socceroos' lead in half. A much better second half and a 52nd-minute equalizer by Gooch had us locked in a 2-2 thriller by the end of regulation and still there at the end of overtime. The semifinal match would be decided in the worst possible way: a shootout. We'd each get five penalty kicks; whichever team scored the most would advance to the finals.

I had the honor of taking the first kick, and with the opportunity to set the tone, I put it home, scoring our first goal.

Mark Byrnes, who had scored Australia's first goal of the game, answered, hammering home his PK too.

All we both could do now was watch and hope for the best.

After five rounds, we'd both have to watch a little longer. Both teams had made four of five. We were into the even-more-dreaded round-by-round kickoff. Tied after six kicks. Still equal after seven.

And then... it happened. Our eighth do-or-die shooter sailed a ball high and off target.

Australia made us pay.

As the Aussies celebrated—piling on top of Josh Kennedy, the forward who'd made the deciding kick—we were left with our hands on our heads and a whole lot of tears.

It was a gut punch. To come so far and lose on PKs... We all thought we had the chops and talent to win it all. Snapping the streak and losing like that took a little something out of us. No one wanted to talk. No one wanted to eat. And in our last-ever practice as a team, with the third-place game to play, we were simply a mess. With our heads still stuck on penalty kicks and missed opportunities, we lost to Ghana 2–0 in the third-place game; we just weren't fully there. No bronze medal to take home.

Still, no U.S. U-17 team had ever gone further or achieved more than the 82s; our fourth-place finish was unprecedented territory for the program. And while we didn't make it through to the finals, we'd clearly made a mark. Even FIFA recognized the quality of our play, honoring Beasley with the Silver Boot, awarded to the second-best all-around player of the tournament. And me? After tallying three goals as a heavily marked man, I was named the top player of the World Championships—the first American to ever win the FIFA Golden Ball. Beas and I did have something to take home after all.

We all did. I can't fully articulate the transformation we had undergone as individuals and as a team. We had come a long way, from assembling to learn about Residency in Salerno, to that incredible winning streak, to the World Championships. It happened in incremental moments, a subtle maturation process that took a bunch of high-school kids from just playing a game to competing for something more. We'd each come in used to being the best back home and wanting to prove ourselves to each other and the world. The U.S. Under-17 Men's Team may have gone home fourth out of 16 in the world, but we were undeniably good enough to have been in contention for first. Every one of us went home bitter... but better, knowing we'd done something no one outside of America thought we could do—even if precious few back home knew what we had accomplished.

It was hard to pack my bag and harder to say goodbye to my coaches and teammates. The boys—men now, really—were headed back to scatter to homes across the States. And I was headed back to Germany. It wasn't lost on me that, while America had made a deep run in the tournament, the Germans hadn't made it out of pool play. Between the success of my team and my new Golden Ball, I was curious to see if there would be any change in my status or playing time upon my return to Leverkusen. I had seen firsthand what playing up could do. And if they weren't going to play me up where I felt I deserved to be, I didn't know if it was worth being there.

I remember messaging with Rich about it one night shortly after my return.

ME: I don't really want to be here if I'm not playing.
RICH: You're coming back for the holidays, yes?
ME: Yes.
RICH: We can talk about it then.
ME: I'm beyond bored.
RICH: Landon, you have to give it a shot. And you signed a contract. TRTTD.

There it was. *The Right Thing to Do.*

With three and a half years to go on my contract, it was time to buckle up and power through. I hoped they had taken notice of my success in New Zealand. If they hadn't... I was in for a long, cold time in Germany.

37′

IT HAD BEEN a year since New Zealand and the World Championships. Some aspects of my tournament play there must have caught someone's eye at Bayer Leverkusen, because upon my return I was finally moved up to play with the reserve team. It's a whole lot better than being stuck with the 16s or 18s. In August, with a new season upon us, I was officially called up for the first time to the first team along with my fellow reserve teammate Anel Dzaka, a Turkish center midfielder and overall good dude. But even with this call-up, it seemed like I was going nowhere fast—it was right back to the reserves after that. It felt like being an American was working against me.

Even worse, I still hadn't made any real connections in Germany, on or off the pitch. Almost all the other teenage players were either German or Eastern European, and almost all of them had their family with them to keep them happy and occupied. The older players were mostly seasoned professionals with lives of their own outside of soccer and weren't interested in babysitting some 18-year-old American, particularly not one who was still stuck on the reserve team. With no one there to just be with, I was up all hours of the night either messaging with people back home and dreading the next day and its inevitably dreary weather. Sometimes I was depressed because I was lonely. Sometimes I was lonely because

I was depressed. If I were playing meaningful minutes in actual games, maybe it would be better, but the gray cloud over Germany and my mood didn't seem like they would be lifting.

A month later, though, a ray of sunshine breaks through: I'm given my dream opportunity when I'm invited to join the U.S. team for the 2000 Olympics in Sydney, Australia. At only 18, I am the youngest on the squad by five years, although Beas is also along as an alternate. The bulk of the team are 23s, but each nation can include three players over the age of 23 on its roster. Joining us are stalwart keeper Brad Friedel (29), vocal veteran D.C. United defender Jeff Agoos (32), and fellow Bayer Leverkusen and Californian Frankie Hejduk (26). It's been a dream of mine to represent the country at the Olympics... and it's another chance to temporarily leave my Leverkusen purgatory for more meaningful games and experience.

Our first game was scheduled deep in the southeast corner of Australia in a city called Canberra, which unfortunately required us to miss the opening ceremonies in Sydney. Mom and Dad missed the World Championships a year ago; I was not going to let them miss another trip Down Under. As special as it was to have them both in the stands, though, Dad and I were not on great terms after our German showdown, and he didn't do me any favors here. I was the youngest player on the U.S. team and was only used as a substitute early on. Dad wanted me to play and was highly vocal about it—so much so that he openly criticized our coach, an Englishman named Clive Charles, in an online soccer forum. Of course, that got back to the team, which didn't help me feel any less like a kid or an outsider. And can you imagine what the outcry would be like today if the father of a player went after a coach on social media?

I approached Coach Ellinger, who was there as an assistant on Coach Charles's staff; I knew I could trust him and talk openly about both my dad's comments and my lack of playing time. He understood that my dad didn't speak for me and reminded me to keep going and stay patient; my time would come. I was new to this team, and I knew that Coach Charles had to manage personalities as well as minutes. But Coach Ellinger knew what I could do, and I had the sense that he would be in Coach Charles's ear.

I'd eventually come off the bench as a "super-sub" in our final pool match against Kuwait, and in the waning five minutes, I played a nice one-two with forward Josh Wolff. I found him on the right side in space and he rolled it back across to me, where I had nothing but an open net. It felt good to contribute to our 3-1 victory, which helped put us ahead of Cameroon, the other team coming out of our pool, allowing us to avoid Brazil in the quarterfinals.

Facing Japan in the quarters, we got a 90th-minute PK goal by Peter Vagenas to tie the game in regulation and won in a shootout, 5-4. We were on to the medal rounds and the bustling Olympic Village in Sydney, with two chances to make the podium.

The only problem was that waiting for us in Sydney was Spain, who handily dominated us in an annoying and highly Spanish possession match 3-1. The third-place game against Chile was even more frustrating, because we played some of the best soccer of the entire tournament only to surrender a tough penalty in the 69th minute and then concede a late goal to lose 2-0.

Coach Ellinger, Beas, and I had once again found ourselves on the other side of the world and just off the podium in fourth place. Cameroon, who we had tied earlier in the tournament, ended up taking Gold, while Spain was left with Silver, and Chile the Bronze. And while we felt disappointed, it was the furthest the USA had ever gone in the Olympics, and I thought I had shown enough to get another shot with the first team back at my dreary German home away from home.

A month later, that long awaited shot finally came ... just not in Germany. It turns out my stint with the U.S. Olympic squad caught the eye of the powers that be with the U.S. Men's National Team. The L.A. Coliseum is calling my name as I earn my first official call-up in a true I'm-proud-to-be-an-American moment. I'm sitting in the very best seat money can't buy keeping the very end of the bench warm during a not-so-friendly "friendly" against our rival Mexico. My cleats aren't even tied and I'm not expecting to see the field. But when Chris Henderson goes down injured in the 30th minute against *El Tri*, down past the veterans on the bench comes Coach Bruce Arena. Surprisingly, he says to the teenager wearing number 13...

"Landon, warm up."

I follow the boss's order and sure enough, I'll earn my first cap on this day because Hendo can't continue. Being so close to home, I know I have friends and family as part of the minority in the stands rooting for America (back then, Mexican fans always outnumbered Americans).

The final 15 of a scoreless first half are a blur. To start the second half, I make a blur of a run towards the box as Clint Mathis somehow slips a ball through a Mexican defender's legs towards the center of the 18-yard box, where I break away to a one-on-one with the Mexican goalkeeper. And with *El Tri*'s goalie charging, the move I learned from Coach Ellinger and would do many more times in the future, presents itself:

Wait for his feet to set...

And when they do...

Quick cut to the right... goalie left behind... and instinct does the rest as I tap the ball into the net.

Goaaaaaaaaal! 1–0 *USA!*

I untuck my shirt, throw my jersey over my head and sprint to the midfield line. I'm so excited, but there's no time to celebrate as we now have a lead to hold. We keep it going later in the half when I get a ball on the left side and clip it centrally to a cutting Josh Wolff. Wolfie runs onto it perfectly and finds the back of the net. We take down Mexico 2–0 in Los Angeles—an iconic score that will mean more in the years to come.

Most of the fanatic American Outlaws will tell you that the legend of *Dos a Cero* started on February 28, 2001, at a World Cup qualifier at Columbus Crew Stadium. Wolfie and Earnie Stewart scored two goals for America that day, in our first win against Mexico in a World Cup qualifier since 1980. And while that game meant so much more than this one, *Dos a Cero* started for me here, on October 25, 2000, the day I notched my first goal and first assist for the U.S. Men's National Team, in my first game with the squad.

Is anyone paying attention back in Leverkusen?

I shared a room with Chris Klein during the week of this game. Chris was an all-American kid—older, grounded, big brother material. It was his first cap opportunity as well. One night he asked me how Germany was going, and I just gave it to him raw.

"I've only got two hours of training a day and some German classes. Outside of that... I sit at my computer all... day... long. I don't have any friends on the team. I don't know anyone off it. I've never been anywhere so gray and dreary. They don't play me in the games. I don't go out. I'm so, *so* lonely all the time."

It was emotional. It was the truth. I was in a foreign land where I felt American players were either looked at with great disdain or overlooked altogether. No one took me out to make me feel like a part of the team or a valued coworker—I was just some kid from America taking up a spot my German teammates probably thought should be theirs. I believed I had done enough to get a sustained opportunity to play with the first team.

I had let Rich know that I wanted to feel like a valued member of Leverkusen. But Leverkusen continued to stymie me. I was just another teen in their machine, and an American at that. They felt I hadn't done enough to prove I deserved the minutes. They valued me so little that, in 16 months, I hadn't played a single minute in the Bundesliga.

Closing in on my 19th birthday, Germany felt like more of a trap than ever. The few joyous moments I'd had in my year and a half as a professional had all come with American players playing meaningful minutes for American teams. Back in Germany in the rain, I called Rich frustrated, overwhelmed, and crying. I told him, I can't take this anymore. I feel like I'm wasting away. None of it is working: The people. The food. The playing time. "Rich... The right thing to do is for you to get me out of here."

Rich cleared his schedule and the next morning was on his way to Leverkusen.

39'

AFTER 16 depressed and lonely months in Germany, I could see that the choice I'd made to sign with Bayer Leverkusen had dragged me too far away from everyone I cared for back home. I felt lost without Mom, Tris, and Joshie and their easy support, and no one at Leverkusen had stepped in to provide something similar. To them, I was just one piece on the board, full of potential but also easily replaceable. They would train me in soccer, but in life, I was on my own. As the lone American teen among dozens of German professionals, I'd never really become part of the team on or off the field. I had been so bored that one long weekend I'd jumped on a 12-hour flight from Cologne to Frankfurt, then Frankfurt to Los Angeles, just to spend 16 hours soaking up the sun in L.A. before flying back to Germany.

Now I'd finally found a way out. Rich had arrived in Germany and pulled some TRTTD magic, convincing the Leverkusen management that I had a real shot to make the 2002 U.S. World Cup team, but only if I was regularly playing meaningful games. Leverkusen made it clear that playing with the main team wasn't in my near future. So Rich convinced Bayer Leverkusen to accept a two-year loan to Major League Soccer, which, at the time, had never paid big money for a player.

It was a win for both sides. For Leverkusen, at the very least, they were free of someone they were starting to view as a problem child and getting cash for it. Best-case scenario, they'd get a player back in two years who was more developed, more accomplished, and more mature. And MLS was desperately seeking marketable players for the league; they were getting an *American* soccer player with serious star potential. It was not lost on me that the thing holding Leverkusen back from giving me that shot in the Bundesliga was part of why MLS wanted to bring me in.

Many of my teammates from Residency were now peppered across MLS, and I had grown more and more curious about what it would be like to play in the league. I'd had more than a few 2 a.m. marathon conversations with Beas on IM about how much he liked playing for Bob Bradley's Chicago Fire, where he was now racking up meaningful minutes alongside Josh Wolff. Chris Armas—U.S. Soccer's Athlete of the Year in 2000—told me the league had been great for him too, and that it was a lot more competitive than people gave it credit for. They were both convinced that MLS was improving and was only going to get better.

The only drawback to heading to MLS was the allocation system: When a player who is not from college enters the league for the first time through the transfer window rather than the draft, he goes to the first team on the allocation order list. That would have me landing with the team at the bottom of the Western Conference: the San Jose Earthquakes. They weren't just bad now—in their first five seasons in MLS, the Earthquakes had never finished higher than fourth place. And they had fired their coach in the off-season and brought on a first-time manager with no professional experience outside of two years as an assistant coach in the league.

Only one part of all that mattered to me: I could get paid to play professional soccer *in California* for the next two years. I'd rather play for the last-place team in the pro league in America than be stuck with a reserve team in Germany. Far better to go where I was wanted and, more importantly, where they would let me play. Rich wasn't lying when he said I needed to be on the field if I wanted to make the 2002 World Cup team. Watching one of the world's top clubs in Bayer Leverkusen is an amazing experience for a 19-year-old, but I wasn't going to break into Bruce Arena's World Cup plans partaking in reserve matches for the next year.

California meant playing. California also meant sunshine. Best of all, California meant home. San Jose might not be Los Angeles, but I would be *close enough* to Mom, Tris, Rich, and Adam. A mere 400 miles to Redlands beats being on another continent with an ocean between us.

On March 30, 2001, it became official—the breaking news scrolled across the ESPN2 ticker, that I had been loaned to Major League Soccer's San Jose Earthquakes. Tom Neale, the Earthquakes GM, called it a colossal move, saying, "The acquisition of Landon is an extremely positive step for the Earthquakes, MLS, and U.S. soccer. This signing represents another example of MLS's ability to bring the top, young American players into the league."

Between that statement and MLS blaring that I was the "quintessential future of American soccer," the stakes were high from the get-go.

I wasn't that worried about the pressure. Between the Under-17 World Championships, playing in the Olympics, and the rigor of German practices, I felt battle-tested for what was in front of me. Maybe Leverkusen thought I was too inexperienced or immature to play in the Bundesliga, but I was just ready to play again and eager to join my San Jose teammates and Frank Yallop, their first-time coach. I knew coming in that there would be expectations. I was prepared for that.

What I wasn't prepared for were the facilities. The Quakes played at Spartan Stadium, an apt name for a grungy facility at San Jose State University. Going from the world-class, professional comforts of Leverkusen to the rundown college athletic center of the Quakes was quite a shock.

And while I might have needed a little time to adjust, none of what we had—or did not have—seemed to deter Coach Yallop, who didn't complain about how there's no real locker room or on-premises masseuse. We latched onto his positivity and personality. My training camp began just a week before the start of the season, but that one week of camp was telling. In that short time, you could see that Frank had put together a roster that was better than most league pundits thought.

There was El Salvadoran national team standout and striker Ronald Cerritos, who spoke better-than-average broken English and had a knack for scoring big goals. There was midfield goal scorer Manny Lagos, who, prior to joining the Quakes, had a run of tough-luck injuries and had moved from team to team in seasons past. There was seasoned defender Troy Dayak and the high-energy Jimmy Conrad. And there was another new player Yallop had signed, Canadian Dwayne De Rosario, who you could tell in practice had the potential to light up a scoreboard.

Our keeper was Joe Cannon; like me, he was new to MLS. Joe ended up being my roommate, and he was nothing short of hilarious. He was a great guy off the field and a great goalkeeper on it.

One of Coach Yallop's other newly acquired players was veteran defender Jeff Agoos. Coach Yallop had traded two first-round picks for Agoos; slated to be our clubhouse leader and captain, he seemed less than pleased about moving to a perpetual last-place team on the left coast after years of consistent winning and three championships with D.C. United.

Picking Goose up from a championship-caliber organization like D.C. United was a huge coup. Goose might not have wanted to be there, but he had no intention of losing—he wanted to make me and everyone around him better so we could all help our team win. So he'd bark at me, "You need to score goals. Finish... the fucking... ball!"

Fourteen years older than me, long-haired Goose was a gruff, intense veteran presence who looked like he had walked off the set of *Game of Thrones* and straight onto our soccer field. His tough-love, no-nonsense attitude reminded me a bit of Joshie, albeit a little scarier. I do well with tough love so long as it's not just tough with no love; with Goose, I could tell that he was taking care of all of us in his own way. And while Frank was the coach off the field, Goose was always our leader and coach on it.

When the season arrived, I was on the bench for our first match in Los Angeles against the Galaxy. Here we go again, I thought. And when I found myself still riding the pine in our second game against Dallas, I could feel the frustration rising.

Maybe Coach didn't play me because I was still recovering from two fractured ribs I had suffered two weeks prior in a match with the U-20s in Trinidad. Whatever it was, Frank could sense my pissed-offness. Part of the deal with being the manager is managing the personalities of your players. For Frank, that included a snotty, know-nothing 19-year-old who thought he knew everything. Ego came with the territory. Even though Frank was in his first year as the head man, he handled the situation like a caring pro, telling me to stay patient and that my time would come sooner than I thought.

Apparently he meant it, because in the third game he started me. We both knew I wasn't a great player yet, but he let me loose, which built trust in both directions. And when I play for a coach where I can feel the trust, I always reward him with my play. I finally had my chance to start, and . . .

. . . proceeded to score zero goals across the next four matches.

By Game 7 of my inaugural MLS season, I was starting to get itchy. The team was doing well. We'd won two in a row, but I had yet to get on the scoresheet and didn't feel like I had done much. And while I was getting used to being a pro, I'm a striker, and strikers want to score goals. In my mind, that is what I was being paid to do and I still had nothing to show for it.

Coach saw it differently—or at least, that's what he kept telling me: "Landon, I don't care if you score. Just keep playing the way you're playing. I'm not worried about it."

We're in front of 7,000 Quake fans at home. There's less than five minutes left and we're clinging to a 1–0 lead against the Metro-Stars when, in the 86th minute, we float a ball over the top of the defense. I see the defender throw his hand up and glance over at the ref hoping for an offside call, but when no flag goes up, I know it's on. I bring the ball down with my knee and as the goalie guesses to his left, with one touch, I send it right and into the back of the net.

Baaaam!

MLS *goal #1!*

You never forget your first.

And I'll always cherish the goalie I beat to give us a 2–0 win on the day...

The legend himself, Tim Howard.

While it felt incredible to finally get that first tally, it more importantly helped secure a three-game winning streak that turned into something even more. From April 28 to July 4, now just over halfway through the season, we rattled off 12 games unbeaten. This is what confidence feels like.

The Quakes were clicking. We believed in each other and had become a tight-knit group. Already I was brash, vocal, and cocky; three clear signs that I felt comfortable in San Jose. Besides, Agoos knew how to knock me off my pedestal whenever my head got too big, and Coach played the right notes to make me feel like an important piece of the team. I could feel their acceptance. It meant a lot to me. When I'm playing for an organization that wants me, I thrive. After my Leverkusen experience, it was so refreshing to feel like I was part of the team.

MLS was proving to be the opposite of the league Rich had rescued me from. Where Leverkusen had been distant, large, and machine-like, keeping players at arm's length, San Jose was tight and familial, with an us-against-the-world mentality. Where the Bundesliga was a professional league with eons of history and heaps of red tape,

MLS was still working out its kinks. Where fans were showing up to pack modern stadiums in droves in Germany, in MLS you could find yourself playing a game in a crumbling high-school stadium and pinpoint the exact fan yelling at you from the stands. *Hey, Landon, nice hair line!*

MLS was still in the foundational, brick-by-brick days of building a league, and it often felt like it might not get past the brink of collapse. But the leaders were pleased with the direction the league was headed, and from what I gathered, they were also satisfied with my performance to date. I wasn't just a big investment for them. I was more like a big gamble—a kid entering MLS in the last year of my teens but counted on to help carry and support an entire league. While I had chafed at the lack of playing time in Germany and was thrilled at receiving it in the USA, the demands of having to act like an adult at age 19 weighed on me. Most kids my age are not working a professional job until 9 p.m. every day, then waking up the next morning to do it again in the most public of forums.

It caught up to me one morning, when I acted my age and missed the team's flight to Tampa.

I had to hitch a later flight to the east coast, and as you can imagine, Goose was all over me...

Where have you been?

I was so embarrassed. Coach was not happy and did what any coach would do by benching me. But what I remember most about it is how he told me. Coach said, "You can't get away with not turning up, missing a flight and expect to play. You're not starting... sorry." It was classic Frank. He was saying sorry *to me* for benching me, even though I was the one who had missed the flight. And he was right not to start me. I didn't enjoy sitting there watching our team lose to the Mutiny 2-0, but I was sitting there because I had let the team down. And I knew it.

I promised myself this would be the last time I'd hurt my team like that, and I came out blazing in our next game against the

New England Revolution. Forty minutes in, I'd already found the net twice.

The team already had amazing camaraderie and chemistry. We now knew we had a serious squad that could keep winning. Playing and earning three points every time we hit the field would have been enough, but it was also so much fun to be around each other.

I was learning—sometimes slowly—how to be an adult and a professional. On the road, I roomed with Richard Mulrooney, a midfielder who was six years my elder. The way Richard came to work every day was an example of the consistent level of preparation needed to succeed in the league. I'd always put in the time for training, doing extra after, but there was more to it than that. He was the perfect on-the-road roommate for a kid like me still trying to figure it out; aside from the fact that he couldn't help himself from grabbing a chocolate chip cookie after every pregame meal. I credit him with really teaching me how to grow into a pro.

At 19, I was still a baby-faced kid with a big poof of bleach-blond hair who looked more like I belonged at a Green Day concert than on a soccer field. And while I put on a hard shell and exhibited all the swaggering confidence of youth, like any teenager, I was still a jumble of emotions inside and working through life as I lived it. I'm sure it made me a pain in the ass to everyone around me, but it made me a bit of a dream for the few reporters covering the MLS beat. I'd had some introduction to the press before through my U.S. youth duties, but this was the first time I was really getting asked the questions, and I didn't think anyone cared what I had to say. So... if something popped into my head, I'd throw it out there. If a defender was popping off on the field, I'd nonchalantly share it with the press. I was becoming a popular interview, but possibly a less popular teammate. No one really likes you giving the other team bulletin-board material. The press liked how unguarded I was, and I must admit: After a lifetime of disregard from Dad and my monk-like existence in Germany, I liked the attention.

The deeper we got into the season, the more confident I became. I wasn't just seeing minutes on the field; I was contributing and scoring. And when I was invited to be part of the East vs. West MLS All-Star Game, hosted in San Jose at the end of July, I scored four times in a 6–6 barn burner.

My game felt like a snowball rolling downhill over the course of that first season, gathering more and more snow as it went. My finishing sharpened. My mental toughness grew. My play brimmed with confidence. This is why I'd needed to be somewhere I could play: I was learning on the run in real time. When practice was over, goalie Joe Cannon and I would stay late and practice more. I was grasping that being in the right place at the right time was only occasionally about luck and frequently about instinct and knowledge and endless repetition. Joe and I practiced any situation we could think of so our bodies would know where to be at exactly the right time.

That meant simulating all types of scenarios in front of the net, where I made my living. Learning how to time runs when someone has the ball out wide and is looking to cross. Learning how to hold off a defender and how to run into the box. All the individual things mattered; they added up to something bigger as part of a team game.

With the end of my first MLS season in sight, we were blazing towards the playoffs, and I could feel my play accelerating at exactly the right time. We had come fully out of last year's cellar to hold down one of the top seeds in the West. Our first-round opponent was the Columbus Crew.

I came out like a man possessed, putting us up 1–0 in the first five minutes of the game, then notching a second on our way to a 3–1 victory.

After taking down the Crew, we were on to the conference finals, and a bloody back-and-forth best-of-three series against the Miami Fusion. With the teams tied one game apiece and still tied late in the third and deciding game, Troy Dayak scored a sudden-death winner on a set play in the 94th minute to send us past them, and we found ourselves in a position to take home San Jose's first-ever MLS Championship. At age 19, coming this far with a team that finished dead last the year before was beyond a victory. But with that championship in sight, all we could think of was finishing the fight.

The team standing in our path? San Jose's California nemesis, the team we'd been chasing all year: the L.A. Galaxy. The championship game took place at Columbus Crew Stadium in Columbus, Ohio, the rare soccer-specific stadium that the league had built in 2001. Leave it to two California teams to have to fly east and layer up for the October Ohio chill as they try and win an MLS Cup.

The day of the game came, and it was a gorgeous morning for a championship fight. The Galaxy's roster was a laundry list of well-known players, including expensive Mexican stud Luis Hernandez and U.S. National Team players Cobi Jones, Paul Caligiuri, and Alexi Lalas, plus two of my Olympic teammates, Peter Vagenas and Sasha Victorine. The Galaxy had won the Western Conference ahead of us, but only by two points. Their offense was more potent on paper, but our defense had given up the fewest goals in the conference. And we had played L.A. twice this season and won both games. We liked our chances.

Still, we knew L.A. was as hungry to hoist the cup as we were—possibly even more. They had lost in the championship game twice now, the latest just two years ago. If three times is the charm, then this should be their year. We knew they would be ready. Manning L.A.'s sideline was legendary coach Sigi Schmid, one of the most successful soccer coaches the U.S. had ever seen. Sigi consistently made good teams great and great teams better; beating him here would be no easy feat, and a real feather in the cap for Frank as a first-year coach.

It had been a little over a month since 9/11. Captain Agoos had the honor of joining representatives of the New York City police and fire departments for the coin toss of the MLS Championship.

I may have been only 19, but I appreciated the rightful standing ovation from the Ohio fans for the New York men and women in uniform who stood before us. It was an emotional few moments that I would need to pack away, something I was an expert at. With the coin toss now behind us, it was time to do what we'd come here for.

We came out confident in the first half, unafraid of a team we had swept during the season. While we dominated possession and looked for holes in their defense, it was proving difficult to secure any chances.

The few times they transitioned and counterattacked, they put us on our heels. And in the 21st minute, their speed and pace broke through our defense. A Greg Vanney long ball from 40 yards away took two bounces before Luis Hernandez lit into it, dipping a volley from just inside the 18-yard box that darted high and left past my roommate.

Quakes: 0–Galaxy: 1.

The next 20 minutes were frustrating. The Galaxy seemed content to stay compact and go into the half up a goal, and I started to feel the minutes slip away. But in the 43rd, with halftime almost upon us, Ian Russell played a quick one-two with Richie Mulrooney deep on the right sideline, and Richie turned on a dime and whipped a curling ball from the corner behind the backs of a couple defenders facing their own goal and directly into my path. It bounced once near the penalty spot, and I pounced with a one-touch strike up and to the right corner, easily past Kevin Hartman, L.A.'s diving keeper. I ran downfield with my fists in the air, as my teammates gathered round for a celebratory hug. Halftime... and a whole new ballgame.

In the second half, we wore out their penalty area with quality chances but couldn't finish, missing the target often. When we did put a shot on frame, like Ronnie Ekelund did with a bending strike, Hartman would gather it. Deadlocked at one apiece at the end of regulation, overtime beckoned.

We were quite comfortable with extended games; we'd played seven this season and lost none of them. We didn't intend this to be the first one, not with the championship on the line by sudden death and with both teams hoping for a golden goal.

Each team had made late subs, with Coach Yallop putting in Dwayne De Rosario at the other forward spot in the 85th minute for Ronald Cerritos. Four minutes into overtime, a 40-yard-long ball landed right at Dwayne's feet. He collected the ball on the left, then suddenly shifted two gears up and sped into the box with a light touch to the right. He was now isolated against L.A.'s exhausted center back, Danny Califf. Dwayne hits a curling shot off his right foot...

... clipping off Califf's not-far-enough extended foot...

... touching off the hand of the horizontal, diving Hartman...

... clanging off the inside of the far post...

... and...

Goaaaaaaaaaaal!

The Quakes take down the mighty Galaxy!

Let the celebration begin.

It was a celebration as joyful and honest as any I have ever had. Dwayne Franken-struts, jersey over head, across the field to be mobbed by our fellow Quakes. I run at Joe Cannon—himself running full speed towards me—and we tackle each other to the ground at midfield, rolling around like little kids. The laughingstock San Jose Earthquakes were now the champions. I looked at my teammates, and the stadium and the American fans and the trophy, and tried to sponge it all in.

That's when it hit me: The kid who wasn't good enough to get on the field in Germany was now a champion in America. Out from under the dreary cloud of Bayer Leverkusen, I was playing soccer, hoisting cups, having fun, and only getting better.

40'

_____

"I GOT the tree. The ornaments. The wrapping paper. The gifts. The ham... Consider me your little helper, Mom."

Rich laughed.

"That must have made her day."

"It made all of our days."

Rich and I are resting in a first-class lounge in the Vancouver airport as we await our flight back to Los Angeles. I am sitting back and reminiscing about the festive events of last month: a now-rare, in-person American Christmas, where boardgames flourished and Mom's debt, for once, did not. The biggest perk of my contract.

Spending the holiday on American soil with Tris, Joshie, Mom, and Paul was an unparalleled treasure. I was even able to enjoy genuine quality time with Adam, who I had missed dearly. A lot had changed for both of us, but not so much that we couldn't still pick up as if we had never left off. And now that I was a mere road trip away, I was hoping there'd be more of this kind of friend time together, aided by my gift of an unlimited gas card—as much a gift to myself as to him. Now, whenever Adam wanted to bolt up to San Jose, he'd have the means. Although if all goes according to plan, I wouldn't be in the States much this summer.

I was having fun filling in the guy I called Boss. It had been nearly six months since I had really seen Rich, although we talked all the time. Rich's hands had been especially full during our run to the MLS Championship, as just three months prior he and Randee had given birth to their first not-practice child. Eden Ilana Motzkin came into the world on July 16, 2001, and when Rich and Randee had asked me if I would be Eden's godfather, I felt like I had turned in my temporary practice family card for a lifetime Motzkin Membership. It was always about family with Rich and Randee, and this was no different. I was still just an overgrown kid myself and lacking much by way of an actual father. I wasn't entirely familiar with the job description, but playing the role of godfather to their daughter was an honor I took to heart.

Rich and I had traveled to Vancouver to Electronic Arts Canada, where the video game maker was developing their second official EA Sports FIFA World Cup game. They brought me there to cover me in motion capture sensors that looked like little balls to mimic my movement. According to them, I was likely to make the U.S. team for the World Cup in Korea this summer. And while nothing was settled yet, if EA Sports was going to all this trouble to get me in the game... I guess Rich telling Leverkusen that I had a shot at the team, but needed to be playing to do it, was spot on.

Outside of the running, jumping, crouching, kicking, and awkward posing in this skintight "suit," the rest of the trip had been pretty cool. We got to tour the facility and see how they created video games. And they were paying me for this! I couldn't wait to tell Adam about it.

As we continued to chat, someone from across the business class lounge caught Rich's attention. He turned to me and said, "Hey, who is that girl over there, she looks so familiar. Do you know who that is?" I turned to see who was sitting in the lounge with us, and a switch in my body immediately flipped into nervous awkward teen meltdown mode.

Denise Richards?! The girl from Wild Things!

She was sitting with someone who appeared to be her agent. Though she needed no introduction to any teenager, I failed to coolly explain who she was to Rich, who nonchalantly suggested we go over and say hi.

"Are you crazy? We are *not* saying hi to Denise Richards."

"Come on, let's go."

This is not happening.

This is *not* happening.

This *is* now happening...

Rich drags me over to her and calmly interjects into their conversation as only an agent can.

"Hi, Denise? We were just sitting over there, and Landon recognized you and wanted to say hi."

All three of them turn my way, and it's clearly my turn to say something. Except I'm suddenly *so* nervous. Denise Richards is staring nicely at me, and I, in turn, am staring at my Nikes, which are pretty nice, but not exactly Denise Richards nice. My hands have now somehow made a mad dash into my pockets, and oh god, it's quiet in here. Shouldn't somebody say something? Rich looks at me to do it... and, when I don't, keeps going...

"Landon is a really big fan of your movies."

Again, all eyes on me. My mind is racing but my mouth remains frozen. Come on, man! Say something! Finally, I look up, and spit out the first thing that comes to mind:

"Especially *Wild Things*."

My god. You *idiot*.

How can I be so sharp on the pitch, the supposed new face of American soccer, an instinctive finisher, who then meets a famous person and can only contribute "Especially *Wild Things*" to the conversation?

Denise politely smiles at me and says, "OK. Thanks for saying hi—have a safe flight."

As Rich and I walk away, my inner self screams *fuuuuuuuuuck*.

Despite my #WildThingsFail, my trip north to work on the FIFA World Cup game had only gotten me giddier about the actual

2002 World Cup. All signs were pointing to me being selected to the U.S. team heading to South Korea, and I couldn't wait to share the news with my family. Playing back in California had made seeing everyone in my inner circle considerably easier, but it was also about to give me another unexpected lesson in the careful-what-you-wish-for column when it came to my relationship with my dad.

Dad was now living a thousand miles away in Lincoln, Nebraska. It had been a while since I'd finally reached the breaking point with him in Germany, but the way things had ended still left me uneasy. When we had a chance to catch up over the holidays, he'd hit me with a classic guilt trip. "How come you never come visit me? You can't get on a plane to see your dad?"

What I wanted to say was, "Dad . . . you're the one who keeps moving further away from California. *You* left." But I held my tongue. We agreed that we would meet early in the next MLS season, when the Quakes would be at Arrowhead Stadium in Kansas City to take on the Wizards. My hope was that, come April, Germany would just be water under the bridge for both of us.

A week out from the game, Dad called me to confirm he was still planning to make the drive, only he wasn't coming alone. And he had a favor to ask: "You're making all this money now. Can you grab tickets for me and a few of your relatives?" Relatives was an interesting word choice, since, relatively speaking, I didn't know hardly any of them. But I obliged.

April 13 arrived, and I had a chance to see Dad and his brother pregame, along with meeting a few members of the extended family he'd invited to join us, including folks who had made the trek in from Michigan, Tennessee, and Kentucky. It was strange but nice seeing so many people from his side of the family. And it was good catching up with Dad and talking about the previous year and winning a championship. Dad was more curious about what I thought would happen the next month with the World Cup camp, and I told him that all signs were pointing to both Beas and me making the team, a pair of 82s on the brink of competing together again. That made him quite happy.

Sharing the news with Dad and having him see me on the field should have been a highlight. Instead, it was a disaster. It was a shit game, a 2-1 loss that truly irked Coach. I was wiped. After most games, especially at home, I sign autographs for fans, sometimes for up to two hours. After this game, exhausted and feeling lousy, I wanted nothing more than to get back to the hotel and sleep. I got on the team bus and headed out.

My dad was livid. He couldn't believe I hadn't come back out afterwards to say hello again to the members of his family who had been waiting with the other fans by the players' gate. How ironic: After all these years of him standing me up and not feeling a bit apologetic about it, I stand him up one time and I'm supposed to care that he feels truly hurt.

Twenty-four hours later, Dad sent me an email saying he couldn't believe I didn't make the time to sign autographs for those fans. That I broke their hearts. That I was obnoxious for doing so. He cc'd his brother on the email, and—the real kicker—ended it by asking, "How could you do this to me?"

I'd wanted to have a real relationship with my dad my entire life. Every time he showed back up after one of his disappearing tricks, I welcomed him back into my life, believing that this time he was there because he wanted to be my father. I so wanted him to be there that I was willing to ignore that he rarely showed up for two decades. Maybe it had been the two weeks in Germany. Maybe it had been the slow buildup of all that had come before. But waking up to this email—his "I'm the victim" accusations and blindly hypocritical anger over *me* not being there for *him*—enraged me.

Dad didn't care about his son, Landon. Dad didn't care about Landon Donovan the human being. Dad only cared about Landon Donovan, soccer star, and what our association could do for him.

This was breaking news to no one else but me. Mom knew. Rich knew. Joshie knew. It took an email for the tinting to fade enough from my rose-colored glasses to let Dad's true colors come through. I spent a healthy 15 seconds on my response.

Dad—Who the fuck are you to tell me what to do? You have no idea about my life. You haven't been around. How would you know what I do or don't do? Don't fucking reach out to me again.

I didn't sign it. I simply clicked Send.

41'

BRUCE ARENA had a plan: The young guys can tag along. Get a taste of the global stage. Not really play any meaningful minutes but soak it up and learn so that they could lead the way come the '06 World Cup.

DaMarcus Beasley and I saw it differently. We had something to prove.

In May 2002, at our pre–World Cup camp in Cary, North Carolina, Beas and I took our relationship to an entirely new level. The youngest in camp by a landslide, we were naturally roommates. Who else would want to stay with the two underage kids anyway? Five of our 21 USMNT teammates were born in the *sixties*. If you added Beas's and my age together, we would still be only five years older than team captain Agoos and two of our goalies.

When it came to our far-more-adult teammates, we kept our mouths shut and went to work trying to earn their respect. In training, we'd get kicked, jump back up, and go in again. We'd get pushed down by an older body, then push that older body back.

Training for the World Cup was no laughing matter to me in 2002; I was determined to make my mark. I'd had one full professional season under my belt in MLS and part of another one, and almost no experience on the field at the top level of international soccer—I was still a kid to these guys, and I knew it. I wanted to let them know I took this seriously; I wanted to stand out for doing things well, not for being a punk who messed around or didn't listen.

If I got a "Pretty good, Landon" from Bruce, I knew I was doing alright. "Pretty good" was the pinnacle of Arena compliments, the most his dry humor would allow. As camp went on, and the "pretty goods" built up, it started becoming clear that I wasn't just going to be on the team but would perhaps even play significant minutes. Beas too—after he took fire at the 2001 Gold Cup, it was clear he had shown enough to belong on the roster.

The bar couldn't have been lower for Team America. Despite entering the 1998 World Cup in France ranked 11th in the world, the U.S. men's team had floundered to finish 32nd out of 32 teams, behind Tunisia, Bulgaria, Scotland, and our CONCACAF friend Jamaica. To make matters worse, at the draw in December, a little over a month after we had knocked off Jamaica to qualify for the World Cup, we learned we'd be part of the dreaded Group D, including a world-class side in Portugal, the host nation in South Korea, and a tough, veteran team in Poland. Outside of the 23 players who made the roster and the handful of coaches who had seen our daily progress, there were not many people who believed we had what it took to finish much higher than we had in France.

That's just how we liked it.

When camp opened, we were 19 strong with four on the roster still playing overseas. By the end of Cary, with the full crew, you could tell this was a special group. Competing every day with the best players in the country is only going to make you better. All of this talent didn't mean we were going to win the World Cup in South Korea, but we knew Bruce had built a team that could compete at that level, full of people committed to raising the profile of soccer in the United States.

It had been less than a year since 9/11; we had just gone to war in Afghanistan. And while I was just a kid who didn't really follow politics, it started to click that our performance at the World Cup

A TROPHY WEEK

Sports Illustrated

STANLEY CUP
RED WINGS RULE

U.S. OPEN
TIGER ROARS

NBA FINALS
LAKERS PARTY ON

WORLD CUP

The U.S. Steps Up

Americans Win Big for First Time Since 1930

20-Year-Old Striker Landon Donovan Against Mexico

JUNE 24, 2002 www.cnnsi.com
AOL Keyword: Sports Illustrated

Sports Illustrated cover, weeks before the 2002 World Cup kicked off in South Korea

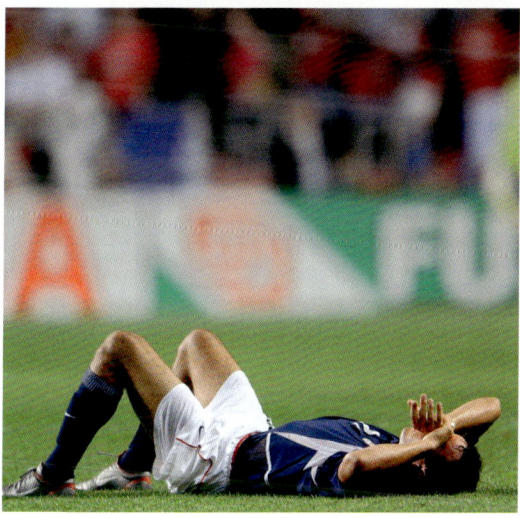

ABOVE: In our third 2002 pool game, Poland beat us to a pulp, 3–1, but I did score my first World Cup goal · *Simon Bruty, Sports Illustrated, Getty Images*

LEFT: Down but proud after giving it all in a heart-breaking 1–0 loss to Germany in the 2002 World Cup quarterfinal · *Emmanuel Dunand, AFP, Getty Images*

FACING PAGE: Grappling against South Korea in the 2002 Gold Cup, ahead of the summer's World Cup *V.J. Lovero, Sports Illustrated, Getty Images · All photos courtesy U.S. Soccer*

ABOVE: Celebrating at
the 2002 World Cup
*The Asahi Shimbun, Getty
Images · courtesy U.S. Soccer*

FACING PAGE: The second
official EA Sports FIFA
World Cup game

ABOVE AND RIGHT: Flying
high with the Los Angeles
Galaxy: Over the next 14 years,
I would play 317 games and
score 141 goals for the Galaxy,
winning four MLS Cups
courtesy the LA Galaxy

FACING PAGE, TOP: With Rich
on the day I signed with LA,
March 31, 2005

With Galaxy teammate
David Beckham in 2009
courtesy the LA Galaxy

was going to mean more than just soccer matches and that there were questions of national pride and international standing and, yes, politics wrapped up in these seemingly neutral games. As a team, we had a handful of discussions about what it meant to be an American and what the American spirit was.

We weren't just asking big questions—we were also playing some decent soccer. In the two weeks after camp, we racked up a 2-1 victory in a friendly against Uruguay and followed it with a 5-0 thumping of Jamaica. And while we dropped our third and final pretournament friendly to the Netherlands 2-0, we left America sensing we were ready.

Of course, in a reminder that representing America in the international game is as much about America as it is about the game, we were greeted before takeoff by a police chief letting us know that they had received information suggesting we were a potential target for terrorism. As if competing against Portugal and the world's best player Luis Figo wasn't enough, now we had to up the ante with anxiety and extra security measures.

We touched down in South Korea tailed by helicopters in an otherwise shut-down airport. There's nothing quite as welcoming as tanks on a tarmac. And this was to be the norm for us in Korea. Our team bus was surrounded by soldiers. We were sandwiched between multiple SUVs for extra protection. There were even air-quality tests at the fields because of rumors of potential chemical attacks. So much for just going out and playing.

We put it out of our minds as best we could when we finally got down to opening our 2002 World Cup campaign against Euro 2000 semi-finalists and heavy favorite Portugal. My status for the game had become clear about four days out in our "phantom" game—a walkthrough where our U.S. team was broken into two teams, with the subs acting as the opponent against the starters. Beas and I were both included with the starters, and on Wednesday, June 5, four days later, we were phantoms no more: The two of us were now standing in the tunnel of the colossal Suwon World Cup Stadium as part of our starting 11.

You can study an opponent on TV and in film sessions, but when their players make the leap from two dimensions to standing directly next to you in line for your World Cup match against them, your heart starts racing and the reality of it sinks in quickly. As Portugal's starting 11 stood beside us in their distinctive burgundy and green kit, they had every right to feel confidently dismissive of us.

That's exactly how I felt about them. I'd come into camp assuming I wasn't likely to play much, and here I stood, about to start in our first game on the world stage.

There was no pressure on us whatsoever. It was all on Portugal. They were expected to compete for the World Cup. Us? We'd flunked out of this thing four years earlier. I knew for a fact these guys were overlooking us. We were a warm-up game. An afterthought on the road to the real tournament.

Just a few feet away were striker Luis Figo, midfielder Rui Costa, and defender Jorge Costa. All of them seasoned all-stars in international and professional play, household names to every citizen tuning in from Portugal and most of the rest of Europe. In Portugal, the game would be treated as a national holiday—stores shut, TVs on, broadcast to millions of fans on giant screens set up for a party in their old central squares. Not in America. While we knew there would be more eyeballs than usual tuning in to see what we could do out here, for the most part back home, it was just another hump day.

But when Beas's eyes met mine, it was like the switch flipped. They say a picture is worth a thousand words... well, then a look is worth twice that. *Look at us, man—a couple 82s getting ready to go play against the world. Respect everyone. Fear no one.*

And after everything we had already been through together, we *were* ready. We took the field, and you felt the energy of 37,000 rabid fans. I was surprised to see how well American fans had traveled, as our flag flew widely about the stadium during the playing of our national anthem. This is what pride felt like.

We were without our usual captain, Claudio Reyna, who was still recovering from a hamstring injury, so Earnie Stewart wore the armband. I was starting up top with Brian McBride. I felt every bit the confident 20-year-old, sporting #21 on the team's white jersey with red and blue trim. I wanted a World Cup goal so badly. I had dreamed of scoring one as far back as I could remember.

My dream is swiftly replaced by an even dreamier start. We earn a corner after a free kick is redirected out of bounds, and we run a set piece that Bruce has had us practice relentlessly. Earnie Stewart is to serve the ball into the box in hopes of finding Brian McBride's head in the middle of the 12-yard box. Defender Tony Sanneh will open up space running to the near post while John O'Brien will head for the far post. My job is to take up space right in front of keeper Vitor Baia, so I'm on the goal line looking to clean up any trash.

Earnie's ball lands on the head of a streaking McBride, who puts it on frame, only to have it kept out by the left hand of a diving Baia. But while he dives for the ball, the Portuguese keeper also wipes out the defender just behind me on the goal line. They crumple to the ground, and the ball lands behind me, suddenly exposed on the doorstep of an empty net. I turn to track it, but before I can do anything, in comes a streaking John O'Brien to take this gift and pound it home. We are instantly transformed into a chaotic celebratory swarm of white jerseys, surprised and ecstatic, with a sudden 1-0 lead a mere four minutes into the game.

With that one strike, we have officially equaled the total number of goals the U.S. team scored four years prior in France. In four minutes! It's an absolute dream start, and Portugal looks dazed by their misfortune. But they're a veteran team, and we know they are a dangerous one. The last thing we want to do now is let up, stop attacking, and let them get back in it.

So we don't.

In the 29th minute, an Agoos free kick lands at the feet of a Portugal defender, but he misplays his clearance and the ball serendipitously lands on my foot deep in their territory, in the right corner. I look up and spy McBride running clear in the middle of the box and attempt to curl a cross around defender Jorge Costa and onto McBride's head, but the ball clips Costa's head and curves towards the goal. Baia is now going in the wrong direction, and as he attempts to come back left for this sudden ricochet, he once again manages to get that left hand on the ball, and once again it is not enough, as the ball bounces off his hand and hits the inside of the post before settling deep into the net.

2–0 America.

Is this really happening right now?

I throw my hands up in disbelief. I was looking to make the right play, crossing it in for McBride, and suddenly I have an insane gift of a World Cup goal… which moments later is ruled an own goal on account of the ricochet off Costa.

But I don't care who gets the credit. We now have a two-goal lead on Portugal.

Seven minutes later, McBride finally gets what he deserves. I collect a ball near the half line from central midfielder Pablo Mastroeni and feed Sanneh deep down the right touchline. Sanneh chases it down, surveys the field, and serves a ball centrally between two defenders and onto the waiting head of McBride. Baia's left hand is nowhere close enough this time, as McBride punches it home off his head into the right side of the net.

America: 3–Portugal: 0.

Thirty-six minutes into our first game and we have matched America's total goals at the 1994 World Cup.

We give one back on a corner kick rebound a few moments later, and the end of the first half is a testy few minutes, but we leave the field at halftime up 3–1.

WTF. What do we do now?

The answer, or course, is you do everything in your power to hold on for dear life, because Portugal is still Portugal, and they are as pissed as you are shocked. Portugal shows up for the second half; lucky for us, our keeper Brad Friedel does too, making stop after stop. Then halfway through the second half, a Pauleta cross from the left side turns into an own goal of our own—an unlucky mistake off the shin of Goose that reduces our lead to a gut-sinking 3-2. And with that bit of bad, but admittedly equal, fortune, Portugal is but one goal away from tying things up.

Bruce subs me off in the 75th minute, and I am left to chew my nails with the rest of America for the last 15. Portugal is attacking, knowing their title hopes might rest on turning this around and securing at least a tie. And we defend and defend, delay and delay, and hope, desperately, for that final whistle to lock this in. When the fourth official holds up the sign signaling there are just two minutes of extra time, and we're still clinging to a 3-2 lead, I think: *This is the American spirit.*

Those two minutes feel like two hours. At last, each minute comes and goes. The referee blows the match complete, and a huge wave of accomplishment crashes over us as we storm the field. Mighty Portugal has fallen; the United States has won.

America isn't finishing in 32nd place this time.

With three points secured, we sit in a first-place tie with host South Korea at the top of Group D. And the World Cup has only just begun.

42' GOAL!

WHEN YOU play soccer for a living, you always get quite a bit of downtime. A heavy security detail locking us down in Korea meant a lot of waiting around at the towering JW Marriott Hotel, in the bustling Gangnam District in Seoul. While Rich was adamant that I should use that free time to read books, he also approved of the new hobby I had recently picked up from some of my elder statesman teammates: crossword puzzles. Gregg Berhalter and Frankie Hejduk were always fiddling with crosswords, which I soon discovered was the perfect type of challenge for an introvert like me.

I have always enjoyed dabbling in solo intellectual activities. Whether it was learning the violin in my school days or taking on these crossword puzzles in South Korea, I've always gained energy from hobbies that let me take some time alone to focus on something outside of me. A dedicated task like that helps recharge my batteries so I'm ready to go when it's time to be with other people. Of course, it would also be nice to be able to break up the inside activities by taking in some of the city, seeing as we're here and all.

I had been to Asia for the first time a year earlier for a friendly with South Korea, intended to help the team get the lay of the land for the World Cup. We played South Korea again in the Gold Cup at the beginning of 2002, beating them 2–1 thanks to a game-winning scorcher of a goal by Beas in the 93rd minute. It was an incredible coincidence to have been drawn into the same group with them come the actual tournament.

It helped us quite a bit to have played them twice already; it's hard enough to fight an opponent in front of 70,000 of their own fans. Coming out for warm-ups 90 minutes before the game, there was already a wave rushing like a red Korean ocean around the packed stadium. There wasn't an empty seat in the house, and every filled one seemed to be taken up by someone in the same red jersey, a mass of people chanting from start to finish.

We knew Korea would be tough and well coached; their coach was respected Dutch football manager Guus Hiddink, who knew what was at stake for the host nation. The Red Devils had made the previous five World Cups but had never won a match prior to their 2-0 win over Poland in their first game of pool play. With that momentum and the crowd behind them, there were high expectations for South Korea to advance to the second round.

We started in a 4-4-2 lineup with Brian McBride and Clint Mathis up top. John O'Brien remained in the middle with our captain Claudio Reyna, now back from injury. Beasley and I were set free to run the wings. In the back were the same five from the Portugal win, with Eddie Pope, Jeff Agoos, Tony Sanneh, and Frankie Hejduk spread across the defense and Friedel between the posts.

It was a beautiful sunny day, and in the 23rd minute, we silenced that sea of Red Devils fans thanks to a pinpoint perfect ball from John O'Brien to Clint Mathis, who let his instinct do the rest. The celebration lasted for only eight minutes, however, as the Red Devils capitalized on a foul, called against yours truly, roughly 40 yards from the net—sending a free kick into the box and connecting for a header to score, triggering a seismic eruption across the country. For the rest of the game, it felt like we were fighting off both the team on the field and the 70,000 in the stands, but we muscled out a 1-1 tie, keeping us even with South Korea atop the pool. All that stood between us making it to the final 16 was an already eliminated Poland team. We knew very little about them outside of the fact that they had dropped their first two matches and that a win or a tie would put us through.

And yet, with nothing to play for but national pride, Poland beat us to a pulp, and the score could have been worse if it weren't for Brad Friedel making his second penalty shot save of the tournament. Down 3–0 late in the game, I tallied my first World Cup goal to cut the lead to two, but it felt anticlimactic coming in such an inexplicable thrashing. Having needed only a tie, we found ourselves now watching both the clock and the score of South Korea vs. Portugal, desperate for help from the host nation to put us through.

There's nothing like letting destiny fall into the hands of another. You often need a lucky bounce or two to go your way in competitions like these, and that lifeline came when the Red Devils went up 1–0 on Portugal in the 70th minute. If they could hold their result for the remaining 20 minutes, we'd be through to the final 16. It was a lead that you'd think wouldn't be tested, as Portugal was now playing down *two* men. Yet, here Portugal was dinging the post twice, the second one off the inside of the post with just two minutes remaining. We were waiting by our bench as Michael Kammarman, the U.S. National Team press officer, relayed that the game was now in added time, South Korea still clinging to their lead. Finally, he shared the result was final! Thanks to our gracious hosts, our disaster play against Poland had not knocked us out—we were officially on to the Round of 16 as the second-place finisher in Group D.

Awaiting us there? The first-place finisher from Group G: Mexico.

Facing an unfamiliar opponent like Spain, Brazil, Italy, or England in the Round of 16 would be one thing—world-class teams with whom we had no firsthand familiarity. Facing an all-too-familiar foe like Mexico, however? This was the universe hurling us lifeline #2, just about the best-case scenario.

No one expected us to win, of course. For far too long, we couldn't beat Mexico anywhere. But in 2001, we had finally flipped the script and knocked them off on American soil. Confidence came with that. We now had the opportunity to face them on a neutral field, and we knew from our matches that more American fans had traveled here than Mexican fans. Without the altitude, smog, and crazed support of a game in Mexico City to give them an edge, we knew we could beat them.

We also knew it wouldn't be easy. Mexico hadn't dropped a match in pool play, giving up only two goals and topping their group above Croatia, Ecuador, and Italy. This was a quality Mexico team. They didn't just think they could beat the United States—they expected to. And as with any USA vs. Mexico match, we knew it would be an all-out bloodbath. Things are never gentle when we get together.

While Mexico has the pressure of being the favorite, we have pressure of our own. We aren't just facing Mexico; we are facing ghosts. No U.S. men's team has progressed past the Round of 16 in 72 years. No wonder the world has a low opinion of U.S. soccer players—they've barely seen us play, and for 72 years on the world's biggest stage, we've barely shown we can.

But getting here has raised our profile, and people back home are starting to pay attention, including in the highest places. President George W. Bush phones us just before the match. You always remember your first presidential pep talk. And when the president takes the time to call you, you really feel that America is paying attention and pulling for you.

Our chat with 43 in the rearview mirror, we take the field in Jeonju—a word which translates to "perfect region"—and prepare to face our regional nemesis.

We're down two of our regular back-four starters, as Goose is out with an injury and Frankie Hejduk's two pool play yellows has him suspended for the game. So Bruce turns to a fully capable Gregg Berhalter and Pablo Mastroeni.

With the personnel changes, we pivot from our usual formation and employ a 3-5-2 lineup. The deep greens of Mexico control possession for the first seven or so minutes of the game, but when our first counter opportunity comes, it unfolds in a blur, Captain Claudio Reyna taking the ball in a burst down the right sideline, dancing through and past two Mexican defenders, then crossing a low ball from the end line to an oncoming Josh Wolff. Wolfie sends a quick one-touch flick back towards the penalty spot to an unmarked Brian McBride, who uncorks a one-touch right-foot finish into the back of the left side of the goal. Eight minutes in and America's on top.

It is an absurdly hot day, but the heat is the last thing on my mind in the 65th minute, when John O'Brien sends a ball down the left wing to a streaking Eddie Lewis. I'm running a 60-yard sprint parallel to Eddie straight down the middle of the field, calling for a cross as I enter the penalty box a step ahead of a defender. Suddenly Lewis crosses it and it's tracking perfectly towards me a few feet off the goal line.

A second later, I *track...tuck...then...bang!*

Off the left side of my head, past Mexico's diving keeper, I curl to the corner before it even hits the net as the crowd erupts. Shirt now off, I slide to my knees, and am greeted by Beas and a slew of teammates on and off the field.

Twenty-five minutes away from the quarterfinals. Up *Dos a Cero* against our rival. The moment feels big—and it is.

Time is ticking away, and it gets dirty, because of course it does. Hard-slide tackles, jersey tugs, deliberate stomps, and excessive pushes. Mexico attacks but never really threatens. Waves of cheers from the crowd pushing us onward and celebrating what we've already done. And as Friedel makes yet another save, the final whistle brings a clean sheet. It's over. We have done the unthinkable.

For the first time in 72 years, America is going to the Final 8 in the World Cup. No previous U.S. men's team has even won two games in a single World Cup before. The throng of Sam's Army that made the trek to South Korea sings and cheers victoriously in the stands, raining sweet sounds down upon us. We take it in. We're moving on.

Who will be awaiting us?

Ze Germans.

45'

IT'S BEEN three weeks since we all returned to our regularly scheduled lives in an America that suddenly cared considerably more
about soccer than it had a month earlier. Rich and Lewis Kay, who
is now my publicist, have me running the talk show circuit, cul-
minating in an appearance on the *Late Show with David Letterman*.
And if Letterman is talking to soccer players, the American public
is starting to take notice.

The bright lights of celebrity have been shining on me a lot
suddenly, and it's been a wild three-week ride for this 20-year-
old. Being recognized for my play on the field, having people
take an interest in soccer *and* in me—it hits all my Abandoned
Landon, need-for-attention buttons. But Uncomfortable Introvert
me hasn't miraculously gone away. Having to suddenly be on—like,
on on—all the time is a different feeling. And while we're all getting attention, it seems the lion's share is coming my way. I came
home from the World Cup with FIFA's award for the Best Young
Player in the tournament—another first for an American soccer
player. And now? I'm about to walk the red carpet of Los Angeles's
Kodak Theatre.

The ESPYs annually recognize excellence in sports performance.
Hosted by Samuel L. Jackson, the event will see 34 pieces of iron
presented, including one to Best Female Athlete of the Year Serena

Williams and the Best Breakthrough Athlete award to some new NFL quarterback named Tom Brady. I'm no expert on American football, but I think he's got a chance to be pretty good. It's the 10th anniversary of the ESPYs, but this will be my first appearance.

I am one of three nominees for Best Soccer Player, along with Alex Pineda Chacon—who led MLS in scoring last season—and stalwart goalie Zach Thornton. Between this, the interviews, and being recognized by more people coming off our World Cup run, it sure feels like the American public is taking to me, and Rich has locked in a handful of new endorsements, including Gatorade.

While I really want to win an ESPY, it's not because I want more awards, and it's not because everyone from Barry Bonds to Kobe Bryant to Snoop Dogg are in the building... it's because I hope it will impress my date for the night.

In a true sign that soccer's gone Hollywood, Lewis Kay thought it would make a good show to have me walk the red carpet with another one of his clients, an actress named Bianca Kajlich. Lewis's original plan was for me to be Bianca's date at the upcoming premier of her slasher flick *Halloween: Resurrection*, in which she plays the lead role. That sounded like a lot of fun, but my schedule didn't allow it. Instead, we met for the first time after the Earthquakes vs. Galaxy Fourth of July fireworks game at the Rose Bowl.

I learned afterwards that Bianca and Lewis ended up doing one too many beer bongs out of a vuvuzela and almost got kicked out of the stadium. I was still one year away from getting into bars and wasn't into partying, so... maybe this should have been a sign that pairing up with a 25-year-old girl who liked to have a drink or few wasn't going to be the world's most perfect match. But at the time, it felt a lot more like a sign that Bianca was going to be someone fun to be with. Given my tendency towards lonerism, being paired with an extrovert seemed like it might be helpful. Later that evening, after the fireworks, a few of my teammates and I ended up meeting up with Bianca at a house party in Long Beach.

I learned that she, like me, had decided college wasn't for her, preferring to focus on a professional career. While she did like being social, Bianca was serious when it came to her acting career: She was focused on acting like I was focused on soccer and wasn't planning to forget that her work came first. We ended up having a great time hanging out together at the party house.

I was hoping that the night of our first official date would also be the night I won my first ESPY. If I ever needed a reminder that soccer was still not football, basketball, or baseball, I needed look no further than our designated seats at the Kodak Theatre. We were tucked away in the balcony, laughing and making the most of it, while gawking at America's finest sports stars as they took their seats far below.

Our conversation was nothing short of easy. You would think a 25-year-old woman might not want to be out and about with a 20-year-old man, but I wasn't your normal 20-year-old. I'd been a professional for over three years now. Mix in the living abroad and all the international travel my U.S. team duties had exposed me to and I was very worldly for a 20-year-old.

And as easy as Bianca was to get along with, it didn't hurt that she had long hair and a great smile and was stunningly attractive.

The date was going well, and then it went better: All eyes flipped towards me when I was called to the ESPY stage to accept the award for Best Soccer Player. You could feel a palpable admiration from the crowd that seemed to care more about soccer than they were originally letting on. Perhaps many of them had even watched us outplay eventual World Cup runner-up Germany just a few weeks prior in the quarterfinal. We had peppered their keeper with an arsenal of shots, outshooting the heavily favored Germans 11–6, but goalie Oliver Kahn played lights out, and none of us could crack him. I had my chances—I didn't want my Leverkusen friends to forget me—but when Reyna played me into space for my best one, my touch was sloppy and left me with a bad angle for my shot. I might have scored if I was just a little more experienced—and got a little cleaner touch on it. It would have been no small joy—and no small irony—to send the Germans home unhappy. They hadn't made me very happy there; it would have been nice to return the favor.

As it is, we lost 1–0 thanks to Kahn's outstanding keeping, Michael Ballack's highly skilled header, and some hard-to-swallow reffing: a controversial no-call on a clear goal-line handball. Would we miss a penalty kick to tie when we'd had such quality all game? Would Germany keep it together if we got that call and the pressure was now squarely on them? Unfortunately, we'll never know: No call was made, and the game moved on.

Even so, it was clear that we'd played them to a standstill, clearer still that we belonged on the main stage and could have gone through if the ball had bounced just a bit more our way and the refs hadn't given them a hand. I'd rather have gotten further on the world stage than stand on this stage at the ESPYs, but winning this award in front of such a talented group of athletes, and in front of my date, wasn't such a bad consolation.

After the ceremony, we decided to go back to Bianca's place instead of my hotel room at the Mondrian. We stayed up all night talking. She was getting ready to head to North Carolina to start taping the sixth season of *Dawson's Creek*. I was heading back north to San Jose for the MLS season. That was another thing we had in common: We were both professionals in the public eye, and the constant travel to be where our jobs required was just part of our status quo.

What started as a Lewis Kay publicity set-up would turn into something more. For the first few years of our relationship, we grabbed little moments where they presented themselves in between the requirements of our top priorities: our careers. In the beginning, we really didn't label the relationship—we just knew we liked each other and were both willing to find those pockets to be together.

Bianca and I were two people still new in the public eye trying to find our voices. But even then, we knew we were quite different. You don't go into soccer to become a celebrity, although celebrity might find you. But acting? Well, Bianca enjoyed that attention. She wanted to be in the public eye. In fact, her whole career depended on it.

I was a lot more private. But it was getting harder to remain that way. The World Cup had boosted me to an entirely different level of soccer-playing fame, unique for an American soccer player. I was becoming a household name. That was good for soccer and great for my bottom line—but the more attention I was receiving, the more I was starting to realize that I didn't really want it.

45'+1' EXTRA TIME

BIANCA AND I were starting to get more serious. In the first few years we were together, I didn't sense that either of us really thought our relationship would go anywhere because of the constant physical distance our jobs put between us. And there were a handful of times in the early years where it seemed we were breaking up. I was never a fan that Bianca smoked. It's her body and she can do what she wants, but I make my living outrunning people on a field, and the last thing I need is to be inhaling someone else's nicotine cloud.

Bianca tried to quit multiple times. But whenever our work schedules would take us in separate directions, she would slip back to her easy companion. There were evenings when I'd snuck into town and left a voicemail for her—*Surprise! I'm back and on my way to your place*—and she would race to her apartment to try and wash off the smoke.

There was a lot in our relationship that wasn't perfect, but we both kept trying to make it work. Deep down, we were two wounded people still wrestling with fragments of our childhood. Why do pain and trauma bring people closer together? Yet, here the two of us were, finding common ground in our shared understanding of coping with unpredictability. For me, it was with my father who could never be counted on. Bianca had her own father issues. Her father was a strict perfectionist who had defected from

Czechoslovakia in the late '60s. Her childhood was spent alternately coping with and caring for her dad; he had a heart condition that put him on the brink of death on several occasions. Bianca was always trying to find a sense of security and, even with the repeatedly-breaking-up-then-getting-back-together nature of our relationship, she felt secure with me. The fact that I was private, committed to what I did, and, well, financially stable all played a role.

I visited Bianca once while she was filming *Dawson's Creek* in North Carolina. We were on a beautiful walk, and I don't know why I felt compelled to share it, but in mid-conversation, I blurted out my fear about the relationship, that it would end poorly because of me.

I feel so bad because I know I'm going to end up hurting you.

I could always create a little space between me and an opponent. I was doing the same in my personal life, something I now know I had done many times before. Maybe I justified it by thinking I felt too committed to my career or too young to be in a serious relationship, but it doesn't matter—we ended up taking time off after that, each of us throwing ourselves back into our overloaded work schedules in our separate cities. But we still talked. It was five months before we were together again in person. I was in L.A. for the 2003 MLS All-Star Game, and Bianca joined me at the historic floating hotel, the Queen Mary, we were all staying in. It was great to see her, and almost equally great to see who she had brought with her: her dog Thor, a 20-pound golden shepherd mix, who was equally thrilled to see me. Before long, we'd slipped right back to where we'd been before my subconscious had tried to push her away.

I liked Bianca. She was curious about the world in the same way I was. And she had a way about her that helped me let go and have fun. I was always so serious about soccer; she was able to take some of the air out of that balloon and get me to relax and think about other things. She'd show up for a weekend in San Jose, blast music, and get me dancing—something nobody else could do. It felt good to have someone bring out my goofy side.

As our relationship started to grow, so did our dog count. Thor was soon joined—at Bianca's request—by another mutt, a Lab mix aptly named Loki, as he was a tricky fella and not a fan of men. Every time he'd see a man—mailman, UPS driver, visiting teammate—he'd just bark and bark until we finally got him to calm down. Loki had been abused at a young age by his owner, and there was enough that was familiar about his behavior that it made me wonder if I was barking at the sight of other men myself.

While I was ready to call it quits on the dog count, the boss of our relationship was not.

After Loki, Bianca rescued two more dogs: Luna, a Boston terrier, then Santiago, a vizsla/pit bull mix.

The fact is that Bianca, now 26 to my 21, was calling the shots. If she wanted to get another dog, we were getting another dog. If she wanted us to get back together, we were going to try and make it work. I was serious for a 21-year-old, but still a go-with-the-flow type, avoiding confrontation off the pitch. I didn't know how to say no, and I didn't have much backbone.

The little backbone I did have was bracing for the next serious weight about to land on my shoulders. My loan to MLS was up. I was headed back to Leverkusen.

46'

___

MY LUGGAGE is packed and here with me. The non-refundable, one-way ticket is still in my backpack. But I am not in Leverkusen—I am in Birmingham, Alabama.

It's been four months since I returned to the just-as-dour-as-I-remembered-it climate of Leverkusen, and an additional three days since the U.S. National Team ended up on the wrong side of a World Cup qualifier, losing 2-1 at Azteca. But right now, on March 30, 2005, I am pacing around a hotel room in the Magic City hoping Rich can work his magic again. While the U.S. team has a winnable match this evening, my current state of agitation has little to do with facing Guatemala tonight and everything to do with an anxious off-field battle that has once again erupted.

Rich is furiously working a phone conversation; it's like watching a baseball pitcher unleash every pitch in his arsenal. But time is not on our side. The ticking clock of the MLS deadline is inching closer to 12. If it doesn't happen today, the period for transfers will be closed for the next six months. Rich hangs up the phone and turns to me.

"That was Don Garber. It's possible."

"How possible?"

"I'm going to need some space, Pibe. Listen: If we do this, you can't undo it."

Rich is staring at me looking for double confirmation... *Are you sure?*

"Rich, I packed my shit, took it with me to Mexico, and left nothing behind."

He understands: I've never been surer of anything in my life.

"Come back in an hour."

Rich goes back to work doing Rich things, and I head to my room.

I'd gone back to Germany ready to get to work. Leverkusen might have been the same dreary place with the same dreary clouds, but I was a different player than when I left four years ago. I'd played four seasons in MLS where I won two championships, started five World Cup games, been named FIFA's Best Young Player of the World Cup, and in 2004, become the first American named U.S. Soccer Athlete of the Year three years in a row. If I was too young and inexperienced when I left, I am now young but experienced. If you play me, there's a solid track record that I'm going to produce.

Beyond all that, thanks to my time with Frank in San Jose, I've developed as a man. I loved my time, my teammates, and the trophies we hoisted together. I'm not a teen anymore—I'm turning 23. But I was always in San Jose on a loan. So, when it was finally time to return to Leverkusen to finish out the remaining two years of my contract, I was ready to do that. It's not like I was excited to get back to gray weather, Sunday closures, and that warm German demeanor. I'd had four great years playing in America, but a contract is a contract and a deal is a deal.

Only maybe it isn't in Germany. I'd been told I'd finally have my chance to play with the first team—that all that collected experience meant something. I arrived in Germany with two years left on my original six-year deal to play for a new Leverkusen coach who had no preconceived notions from my previous stint.

None of that mattered. Since I went back, I'd had seven games with the senior team at Leverkusen, only two of them starts. They hadn't played me in a game in the two weeks since the last one. This is giving me a chance? How am I supposed to get better *not* playing? I was downright livid. If the Germans won't give me time on the field, why am I here?

I don't need to prove to the Germans that I can play soccer. I just want to play.

I'm at my happiest when I'm playing. I'm at my happiest being an ambassador for MLS, a league I believe in. I'm at my happiest competing for America and for Americans. And being back in Germany again for a few months made me realize that I'm at my happiest competing in the States. It's a country that is both good enough and big enough for me.

I finally figured out what I want to do. Not what other people think I should do. Not what media pundits think I should do. Not what a coach or someone in Leverkusen or some anonymous fan on a website thinks I should do. The only "should do" I need to listen to right now is the voice in my head saying, *Landon, you do you.*

Is it wrong to want to be happy?

If Rich can get me home, it will make *me* happier. It is also clearly in the best interest of the league.

So, what are the complications?

Number one, MLS will have to buy me from Leverkusen. In its nine years of existence, MLS has yet to buy a player. With the run-up to the 2006 World Cup fully underway, Rich thinks it's a prime opportunity for MLS to attract Americans to the sport by bringing me back home.

There's a second issue. Alexi Lalas is now the general manager in San Jose, and he's traded away San Jose's rights to me in exchange for Ricardo Clark. In his defense, I had just left California when he did it, and I was supposed to be in Leverkusen for two years. Literally everyone thinks I'm going to be playing for Leverkusen for the rest of my contract... except, apparently, Leverkusen. Regardless, there's no way Alexi could have known I'd be trying to boomerang back to MLS so quickly or he would probably have held onto my rights. My bon voyage is going to feel like whiplash to San Jose fans.

Coming back to MLS now means going back through allocation, and the top slot is held, once again, by a last-place team: the newly renamed FC Dallas (formerly the Dallas Burn). When I came to MLS four years ago, I was just happy to be clear of Germany and with a chance to play; I didn't care that San Jose wasn't a historically good team. Now? I want to be close to home. So Rich doesn't just need Leverkusen to want to dance, he needs to find a way to make a deal work with MLS and, hopefully, a team willing to make a deal with Dallas for that allocation slot.

An hour feels like an eternity when I come back to Rich's room to see where things stand.

"Leverkusen wants $5 million for you."

"Five million?! Holy crap. Does any of that come to me?"

"No. It's a transfer fee. And it's not going to happen. Too expensive. I'm working on chopping it down. It's good: They're open to the move."

"So now what?"

"Any interest in playing in the Premier League?"

This is the last thing I thought I'd hear in Birmingham.

"Just had an interesting call with Portsmouth. It's an option."

I am suddenly a deer and Rich is the headlights. Do I want to play in the Premier League? Heck yes. It's a last-minute curveball and… it's intriguing. But I've just spent days dreaming of coming home. Would England really be that different from Germany? Another new country where I know precious few people, another new league with no real reason to give me a chance, another two years away from home with more rain… no. The Gold Medal option is still getting me back to the States. The Silver Medal, crazy as this sounds, is a trek to EPL's Portsmouth.

But where would I land in the States? San Jose's unlikely—the moves necessary to get me back are simply too prohibitive with them having already given up my rights. But the most obvious landing spot won't sit well with San Jose's fans. Where would it make the most sense to both the league *and* me to end up? How about a marquee team in California, in the league's second-largest city: the L.A. Galaxy. San Jose's biggest rival. But after eight long years away from the people I adored the most—mom, Tris, Bianca, Joshie, Adam, Rich, Randee—I must confess that the opportunity to live and play at my actual home in front of my family and friends would be a dream come true.

"I need another hour, Pibe."

So off I go again, my future hanging somewhere in league limbo while Rich works the phones to try and make something work between Bayer Leverkusen and MLS. While he's doing that, Rich is also now negotiating with the Hunt family, the owners of FC Dallas. The good news, at least according to Rich, is that the Hunts realize that the league will be better off having me and are willing to work something out to help do that. But they're making a big ask: They're willing to trade my rights to Los Angeles, but in return they want *El Pescadito* ... a.k.a. Carlos Ruiz, L.A.'s top striker, a former Major League Soccer MVP. Carlos helped deliver the Galaxy its first title in 2002—getting them over the hump with a golden goal in overtime to erase three previous championship game failures—and he remains hugely popular in L.A. It's an extra twist in what's already a tangled saga, because it just so happens that Rich also represents Carlos ... and I'm going to be facing him here in Birmingham in just a few hours, since he's the star of the Guatemalan national team.

Rich is negotiating with Bayer Leverkusen on behalf of Major League Soccer, with the owners of MLS about pooling to pay a rights fee for an international acquisition for the first time ever and about how they'll handle my allocation, with the Hunt family at FC Dallas and the Anschutzes at the Galaxy about trading my rights and what's in it for Carlos, and with the Premier League just in case all that falls through. All while juggling a new deal with the Galaxy on my behalf if any of it *does* go through.

I may be Rich's practice child, but thankfully, he's a serious professional when it comes to his craft.

It feels like another six hours has passed when I return to Rich's room.

"This might get done, Pibe."

Rich can't disclose details, but it seems like Carlos will be seeing a significant raise if the deal goes through; Carlos loves playing in L.A., but he loves significant pay raises more and isn't instinctively opposed to moving to Texas. And while Carlos will have his salary rocket up, Bayer is inching down from their original $5 million transfer request. And MLS is clearly now open to paying *a* fee, so the Leverkusen/MLS back-and-forth tennis match has become more a game of chicken over numbers and who will blink first. With the ask now around $3.6 million, Rich thinks we are now in striking distance.

Rich and MLS commissioner Garber arrange a quick phone huddle with the MLS owners, and the 12 MLS teams agree to pony up $300,000 each to cover this unheard-of-for-MLS $3.6 million transfer fee. It is the first time ever that MLS has paid a multi-million-dollar transfer for anyone. MLS believes in me, and they've found a way to get me back. After this, I know I will always want to make MLS proud.

There's only one negotiation left on the table: my contract with Los Angeles.

MLS player contracts are signed directly with the league. While my previous contract had been with Leverkusen and I was only on loan to MLS, now that MLS fully owns my rights, we can negotiate directly to make my homecoming long term and mutually beneficial. For all the trouble they've gone through to bring me back, Rich thinks he can get me two commas in my annual contract to ensure that I would stay there. Yes, please. We agree on a four-year contract at $1 million annually. Leverkusen's getting almost as much money to let me go to America as I'm getting to stay here, but I don't mind. With this contract, I will become the highest-paid player in MLS. Even better, I will get the security of knowing I will get to play at home in Los Angeles in front of family, friends, and Bianca for the next four years.

Exactly one hour before the World Cup qualifier, the deal is done and my time in Germany has officially come to an end. No one else knows it yet. I take the field in front of 31,000 screaming U.S. fans with wild MLS rumors swirling around. I'm feeling great, and early in the game I set up Eddie Johnson, who hammers home what would stand as the game winner just 11 minutes into the first half. For one night, Carlos Ruiz and I share a field in Birmingham, our careers touching and crossing as my U.S. team beats his Guatemalan team 2-0.

Before the game even begins, Carlos is no longer a member of my new team, and I am no longer a member of my old one; soon everyone else will know it. Tomorrow morning, I will fly to Los Angeles for a one-of-a-kind, surprise press conference to announce I'm donning the #10 jersey for the Los Angeles Galaxy.

86′

THERE IS nothing like a press conference in Los Angeles. And this one, with me standing on the Galaxy practice field, was like nothing I'd ever experienced in my career. The media fully enveloped me, microphones and tape recorders in my face from all sides as I read my carefully prepared statement and answered questions as thoughtfully, yet candidly, as I could.

I stayed there and answered all the questions—calmly, respectfully, professionally. And when the questions were all exhausted... I was too.

I thanked the press and prepared to train for a Galaxy match. The actual wounds would take a lot longer to heal than this first press conference.

Rich, Bruce, and I had ultimately decided to go with 90 percent take the high road, 10 percent hold strong. If pure soccer considerations were the only factor, I didn't understand Jurgen's decision. If being a good teammate was the only factor, I didn't understand the decision. If pure statistical considerations and logical analysis of play, conditioning, and ability to contribute was the only factor, I didn't understand the decision. Any way you cut it, getting cut by Jurgen felt like it was about something deeper than just soccer.

It had been an intensely depressing 48 hours. I was doing my best to quiet and compartmentalize my emotions, but those emotions were fighting back. And in the days and weeks to come, it would be harder to not give in to feelings of anger and bitterness over the opportunity that had been taken away from me. I wanted them to miss me. I wanted Jurgen to know he'd made a mistake. The ego is a funny thing. You bet I wanted the guy who'd made the decision to hurt too.

Rich's main response to how I was feeling was wise advice: "Leave social media alone. Don't respond to anyone—especially on Twitter. Stew all you want, but don't be the narrative. You let Jurgen answer for his failings."

For the most part, I obliged. Kept it calm in public. Cracked some jokes about it, locked the anger in the vault. But I had the awareness now to be brutally honest with myself about my highs and lows. I should have made the team on merit. I wasn't an aging superstar who couldn't cut it, but the end was getting nearer. And yes, there's part of me that thinks that should have counted for something too.

It wasn't about playing time. I would have been fine being part of the supporting cast. If Jurgen just wanted to use me as a sub, I would have had the opportunity to take it all in and enjoy it. I could have told the young guys what I saw out there and helped them handle it when things got tough. I could have brought speed and fresh legs off the bench and a brain with a full career's worth of knowledge. And with all my experience at World Cups, I know I could have helped this team.

It would have been my last chance on the world's stage. I wish I'd gotten to have that moment.

Unfortunately, it's an opportunity I didn't get.

47'

IT WAS another gorgeous Manhattan Beach morning. That this much vitamin D could be attained naturally in December was boggling the mind of my visitor. Sunil Gulati, the president of U.S. Soccer, and I were seated together outside having brunch at one of my favorite local restaurants, and I was in a relaxed and reflective mood.

How could I not be?

My first season in Los Angeles was in the books, and though it had been up-and-down at times, it had ended as well as it possibly could have: with me winning my third MLS Cup (L.A.'s second) a month prior, besting the New England Revolution in overtime in a tight 1-0 game. My old teammate, MLS veteran Jeff Agoos, had five MLS Championships under his belt. At only 23 years of age, reaching Goose's status—or even surpassing it—now sounded totally achievable.

At brunch, Sunil was talking about how far U.S. Soccer had come. "When I started out 20 years ago, I was running a U-16 national camp for U.S. Soccer. It was the first year that FIFA was running the Under-16 World Championship and it was to be hosted in China with 16 nations, us being one of them. You would have been three... You're good but not that good to make that team. There were about 60 kids, and it was a mess. No one had brought balls, so I had to go to Kmart to make that happen. In the middle of our practice at the Air Force Academy, the sprinklers went off and doused all the players. Just a disaster."

"How'd we do in China?"

"We beat Bolivia, then lost to the host nation and Guinea."

"America lost to Guinea?"

"In front of 80,000 people in Beijing. U.S. Soccer has come a long way."

I'd come a long way too, I thought to myself. I could never have expected all that would happen when I joined the U.S. U-16 team: the end of high school, the training in Florida, the international play for America, the professional career. It'd been eight straight years of soccer without a break, and... I was kind of missing that. I was always on my way from L.A. to *someplace*, be it a game for the Galaxy or the U.S. team, an obligation or endorsement, or just to see Bianca somewhere on a set.

"Sunil... I'm thinking about staying in MLS for my entire career."

Sunil hadn't even had time to order his tea. I continued.

"I had an amazing 2002 World Cup. And I really don't feel like I have anything left to prove."

This did not sit well with the president of U.S. Soccer. After officially qualifying atop CONCACAF in September thanks to another *Dos a Cero* victory against Mexico in Columbus, we were now a stone's throw away from the 2006 World Cup, which was to be hosted in my favorite country in the world: Germany.

"You don't have anything, in your mind, to prove against the very best players in the world, Landon? I find that hard to believe."

Sunil couldn't believe I was content playing in the States.

"Landon, don't you want to get better? You really have no interest in going back over to Europe to compete against the very best?"

I'd learned that the grass isn't always greener. The grass here is plenty green. I was making fantastic money playing a game I love. That was already enough for me. I didn't feel the need to go anywhere else to prove anything to anybody. I knew in my heart that I had a good thing going; I was living the life I wanted and I was near my family and the beach.

"Sunil, my mother and sister live up the road from me. I've got Bianca and the dogs living with me. I get to have dinner on the weekends with Rich, Randee, and my goddaughter Eden. I'm committed to the responsibility of growing U.S. Soccer from American soil. And I wake up every day to sunshine and get paid a million dollars to do so while living by the beach. Why would I leave this place to go play in Europe?"

Sunil just shook his head while he buttered his scone.

"Landon, I cannot decide if I want to get up out of my seat and slap you or hug you."

Everyone meant well. And everyone thought they knew best. I heard it time and again: That I needed to challenge myself and that Americans must improve—and prove—themselves overseas.

Test yourself. Get better. Play against the absolute best.

I started out on a quest to be the best. But once I knew who I was—once I *knew* I was as good as I thought I was—it became a quest to simply find peace. That's what frustrated people about me. If they were me, they thought they would make different decisions. They thought that staying in MLS when I could play abroad meant I wasn't testing myself against the best, and that not testing myself against the best meant I didn't want to *be* the best. What if you could do something that you love, and do it somewhere you love, and be with people you love, and get paid more money in a year than you thought you'd see in a lifetime? Would you leave that just because other people thought that would make them happier if *they* had that choice? Did I seem happy—to anyone—in Germany?

I just wanted to be at peace. When I'm at peace, I can play with anybody in the world.

After brunch, I met Bianca to do whatever she wanted to... which was kind of status quo for our relationship. On the agenda *du jour*, in true California style, is a spiritual Zen session that Bianca has booked us for. Bianca has found that, to manage the mental and physical stresses that come with her profession, the only thing that seems to help is meditation. So off we go to a mindfulness meditation workshop. As we enter this studio, we're greeted by a gentle smile from a grounded, middle-aged Iranian woman. There's something calming about her—a quiet strength and a maternal presence that immediately puts me at ease.

The woman guides us through a 90-minute session of self. I know: *How California of us.* However skeptical I felt going in—not that I would say anything about that to Bianca—I *was* curious. What do I know about meditation? OK, I'll try it. And what do you know? I come out of the session feeling lighter and refreshed. It's like a massage for the mind, and I can see how this would help Bianca with the things that she is dealing with.

I believe people and things find you when you need them. When Juliet came into our lives, leading this meditation session, I didn't know her as a therapist, and I didn't know how important she'd become in my own journey with depression and self-exploration. It would be two more years, in fact, until I'd even start seeing her one-on-one, although Bianca started seeing her shortly after that meditation class. There was no stigma around therapy in Bianca's family. I remember how much freer and more balanced she would seem when she'd come home from these sessions, and it made me curious about what therapy could do for me.

I only wish I'd taken the hint from life then instead of waiting those two years. It would have made the stuff I was about to go through in 2006 a whole lot easier to deal with.

49'

___

FEBRUARY 22, 2006: The fax comes through at the Galaxy training grounds with great news: Todd Dunivant, my on-the-road room-mate, and I have both been called in to play in the next USMNT game in Europe. I'm thrilled for Todd—he's currently playing out of his mind, and it's almost as exciting to me as it is to him to see that he has fully made the leap into the USMNT mix and earned Bruce Arena's trust. This will be his third cap. An hour after the fax lands, Todd tears his quad in practice. He is out for at least three months, and it ends not just his season, but also his chance to play at the 2006 World Cup this summer in Germany.

It's a stark reminder of how quickly something completely out of your control can change your life. Todd deserved to make the national team—he earned that opportunity. We rely on our bodies to make this living. We can do everything right to put ourselves in a position to succeed—train hard, eat right, take care of ourselves— but sometimes it's not enough, and not for anything you did wrong. Sometimes luck really is just luck. Todd will make it back from his injury to play another nine years in the league, but will never get tapped again to play for America.

MARCH 9: Rich calls to tell me the terrible news: Doug Hamilton, the president and general manager of the Galaxy, has suddenly and unexpectedly passed away. He was on a flight from Costa Rica to Los Angeles and suffered a terminal heart attack in the air. I'm in shock. I'm trying to imagine the Galaxy without Doug, and I'm having a hard time doing it. He is the architect behind everything we've been able to build there, and he worked closely with Rich to get me to Los Angeles from Leverkusen. He brought in basically everyone I've played with here, including Todd Dunivant. I'm gutted and I'm going to miss him.

MAY 3: Bruce announces his roster for the World Cup in Germany. There are few surprises—we are a young but veteran team filled with players with experience from the 2002 cup: Beas, Claudio, Gregg Berhalter, John O'Brien, Wolfie, McBride, Pablo, Eddie Pope, and Kasey back in goal. Clint Dempsey and Bobby Convey bring new blood up front, and Gooch is in the mix on defense now. We easily qualified for the World Cup this cycle—and are currently ranked fourth in the world.

We could not be more confident heading into Germany. And I am personally looking forward to it. I've still got an axe to grind about my time there; I can't wait to show them what they insisted on keeping on the bench.

The media run-up to this World Cup is out of control, somehow even more chaotic than last time. You can tell that soccer is gathering steam in America. There are so many more reporters, so many more appearances, and so many more channels covering our sport. With my individual success at the last World Cup and in MLS, I'm being rolled out across all forms of media, in America and beyond, as the face of U.S. Soccer, including another late-night rendezvous with David Letterman. I'm basically fluent in English, Spanish, and German, so I'm talking to just about *everybody*.

In between talking about the World Cup, we're also preparing for our brutally tough group, which includes Italy, Ghana, and the Czech Republic. Not a whole lot of people abroad are picking us to even get out of our group—we may be ranked fourth, but the Czech Republic is second in those same rankings, Italy's still Italy, and Ghana has been a perpetual nightmare for us. It's going to be a battle, and we've got a lot of doubters to prove wrong. Fortunately, we've got a team strong enough to do it.

JUNE 12: We feel loose going into our opening match against the Czech Republic at Veltins-Arena in Gelsenkirchen. It becomes rapidly clear that loose is too loose. Five minutes in, the Czech Republic plays a ball over the defense from midfield and down the right side. There's barely a U.S. defender in sight, and it's like we're moving in slow motion as Zdenek Grygera gathers the ball and fires it square across the middle to Jan Koller, who beats our defenders cleanly to head the ball in from six yards out. We look apathetic and sleepy, and it only gets worse. We're at least marking better in the 35th minute when a headed clearance from our box lands around 35 yards out at the feet of Tomas Rosicky, who settles it calmly, plays a soft touch to his right, then fires a shot past a diving Keller into the right side of the goal. He is effectively unopposed for the distance between him and any other U.S. player—only Reyna gets close to him just before he shoots, but we simply didn't see it coming.

I might as well have been invisible. I'm not the only one—as a team, we muster exactly one shot on goal—but that doesn't make it better. We've been awful. Just in case we didn't get the message, Rosicky sends us one last special delivery in the 75th minute, taking a pass about 10 yards past midfield and leaving four defenders in his wake in what looks like an escorted tour of our goal box as he scores his second—and the Czech Republic's third—goal of the match. Rosicky personally scores more goals than we put shots on net. It's a shellacking.

Bruce can be serious, but he likes to keep things light and easy, and he prefers to keep his harshest criticism in-house—it's something I really respect about him. He'd rather tell a player something in a place where they can deal with it in private than hit them with it publicly. But after the game he calls us out. He says I showed "no aggressiveness," that we got "nothing" out of Beasley. That we didn't have the courage to attack. The worst part is ... he's right. We looked like we were in shock out there.

JUNE 17: Whatever overconfidence we brought into our game with the Czech Republic is long gone—they cleared that right out, along with most of our chances of moving past the group stage. We all feel—for whatever reason—we weren't ready to compete five days ago. That won't be an issue here. We need points if we're going to claw our way back into this. Unfortunately, we also must play Italy, who just did to Ghana what the Czech Republic did to us, albeit in a harder-fought 2-0 win. Bruce has made some changes at the front and back—Beasley and Eddie Lewis are out, Dempsey and Carlos Bocanegra are in. We take the field at Fritz-Walter-Stadion in Kaiserslautern knowing we need to attack.

It is an ugly, dirty brawl. Bruce will not be able to complain about lack of aggressiveness this time. Italy follows their formula; they drop off, defend, and counter. Bobby has an OK look in the 15th minute, but it's a tough angle and he sends it wide. Clint turns and fires one about two minutes later, but it misses left. There's no score, but we're clearly alive, and pushing the action the first 20 minutes. But it gets away from us in the 21st, when Andrea Pirlo's free kick perfectly leads a diving Alberto Gilardino, who heads it home from eight yards out.

To our credit, just five minutes pass before a cross in the 26th minute finds an open McBride ready to put it in and tie the match ... but hits off Cristian Zaccardo, Italy's right back, before McBride can touch it, and rebounds in for an own goal. We don't care how we got it; we're back in the match.

McBride doesn't get the goal, but not long after that he does get something else—a brutal cheap shot elbow to the face from Daniele

De Rossi. Blood streaming from a gash in his face, McBride can walk off to get cleaned up, but it will require multiple stitches. De Rossi is sent off with a deserved red card. At 11 on 10, we can see a little daylight and maybe a way through. As we get close to half, Pablo Mastroeni fires a shot from almost 40 yards out that's dipping, but not enough—it just clears the crossbar and out, but we're feeling some momentum. Minutes later, Pablo tackles Andrea Pirlo, earning a red card of his own. And two minutes into the second half, Eddie Pope gets his second yellow of the match on a tackle where he first wins the ball . . . and now we're fighting nine against 10 for 45 minutes against the Azzurri.

Bruce subs Beas in for Clint to give us fresh legs in the 62nd minute, and Beas immediately makes things happen, taking the ball at the top left side of the box in the 66th minute and sending it into the net . . . only to have what would have been the game winner called off for another player being offside. After that, being down a man catches up to us and it's all Italy, but we hold on, leaving Kaiserslautern with a 1-1 draw—and a much-needed point—against the eventual winner of the 2006 World Cup. Even better, we leave with a chance, as Ghana has upset the Czech Republic. A win against Ghana and an Italy win over the Czechs and we are, miraculously, moving on.

JUNE 22: With everything still on the table, we have a chance to turn our first game sleepwalk into a dream finish. But we don't. It falls apart, in a death-by-a-thousand-cuts game that had been there for the taking. Ghana starts the scoring in the 22nd minute, when Haminu Draman strips the ball from Claudio Reyna and beats Keller with a quality finish. I have a nice chance in the 34th minute, but my touch is not there. I take it on one bounce and fire, and it sails harmlessly off target.

In the 43rd minute, Beas breaks through the defense on the left side and plays a beautiful ball across the middle behind four Ghana defenders. A streaking Clint runs onto it and, with absolute killer instinct like only Clint can do, hits it first time into the back of the Ghanaian net. It happens so fast their keeper doesn't even move. We are tied 1–1. The whispers on the sidelines have Italy up 1–0 on the Czech Republic. The stars have aligned—one more goal, and if all else holds, we are going through. For a glorious moment, there's a chance.

Two minutes later the goal comes... and it's not ours. The half is approaching. We're a minute into extra time. A ball is played into our box, and Gooch goes up to head it. But Razak Pimpong—all of 5′8″—falls trying to front our 6′4″ defenseman, and the referee calls it a foul on Gooch. Minutes away from entering the half all tied up at one, Ghana is gifted a penalty kick, and they turn it into a goal. With both halftime and the second round firmly in sight, we go from needing only one goal to now needing two.

In the second half, we have our chances, but you have to get one to get two, and the one never comes. And what does Ghana do when they have a lead? They foul. They stall. They attack when the chance presents itself, but mostly they sit back. McBride gets us closest to even with a shot off the post at 66 minutes, but that is the best that we get. When the whistle blows and it's final, I almost can't believe that that's it. Italy does their part with a 2–0 victory over the Czech Republic. We don't do ours, and our World Cup comes to an end.

We scored one paltry goal of our own and picked up another on an own goal. We had phantom calls, missed calls, injuries, bad play, and a wiped-out goal. Somehow, we still had a way to go through and we failed to make it happen.

The game against Ghana remains my least favorite of the 12 World Cup games I've played. I have a vivid memory of receiving the ball in the 89th minute of the match. We're down a goal and need something—anything—and it comes to me on the right side of the pitch, near the top corner of the box. When I'm aggressive, when I'm playing well and feeling like *me*, these are the moments I relish. But instead of taking on the defender, I passively pass the ball back, and we get nothing out of it. If I had taken it to the goal, if I had dribbled, or turned and shot, maybe nothing would have happened. But I look at it now, and I feel like I wasn't playing freely, I was playing not to mess up. You can't shy away from the challenge and the risk. You can't play not to make a mistake.

In a World Cup, you get three games to make it through. Any person—any team—can have three bad games. The best team doesn't always win. Sometimes your bad streak just hits at the exact wrong time. But we came in confident. We came in good. And we came home more than empty-handed. In my first World Cup, I scored two goals and helped get us further than a U.S. team had gone in more than 70 years. In my second one, I scored zero goals, had zero assists, and barely made the U.S. highlights reel... if you can even find one.

Even after all this time, it never goes well for me in Germany.

JULY 14: Eight years after taking over the USMNT coaching duties, and barely three weeks after we flame out in the first round of the World Cup, Bruce Arena is removed from his position. He led the University of Virginia to five national championships. He led D.C. United to two MLS titles. He led the most successful USMNT World Cup push in almost a century. It's not enough. Our miserable play in Germany has doomed him. It doesn't matter that we tied the eventual World Cup winner Italy. It only matters that he raised expectations for us so high and we all then failed to achieve them.

With this news, I feel everything. Guilt. Remorse. Responsibility. Bruce and I have been together for five years now. He put his trust in me when I was a kid, and with four years more experience under my belt and a great team around me, I was... invisible. We came in loose and with such swagger. We left with tails between our legs, leaving Bruce without a job.

How could this happen? I thought I would stroll into the World Cup and be one of the world's best players. How could I not? I was lights out four years ago. It seemed like the next step. Instead, I let Bruce down, and it led to his firing. I let the country and our fans down. I let MLS down. I let myself down. I feel personally responsible for our poor performance.

For the first time ever, I receive heavy criticism in the American media. Yes, there was heat when I went to L.A. instead of back to San Jose, but this time it's different. This is national media and the national team. This is about the expectations of America. Before 2006, the focus has always been to build up soccer, to work together to lift the game and do it together. But now? I lay these losses on myself, and to some extent, they do too. The media has always appreciated me for my honesty, but now... my honesty takes a toll. So does theirs. I failed to meet our expectations. And it cost us. It cost Bruce. It doesn't matter that there's an entire team beside me. When your whole life you've been on your own, the burden falls on you. It certainly feels that way.

OCTOBER 14: My second season with Los Angeles is over, and we haven't sniffed the playoffs. In MLS, this is an almost comically difficult underachievement. Somehow, it's even worse than it sounds: After winning it all last year, this year we have finished with the worst record in the Western Conference. The L.A. Galaxy played so badly that on June 6, while I was away preparing for a World Cup, they relieved head coach Steve Sampson of *his* duties there, turning the reins over to my old Earthquakes boss Frank Yallop. Alexi Lalas has been brought in to fill the shoes of our departed friend Doug Hamilton. They're getting the Earthquakes band back together, and on some level that should feel good, but... it doesn't. Not after this. That's two coaches gone in a year on my watch. Last year we were champions. This year, we don't even qualify for a shot at repeating.

Two coaches fired. World Cup flame-out.

MLS fail. Negative media.

A real champion would test himself overseas.

You've got to play the best to be the best, Landon.

Don't you want to be the best?

Who doesn't want to be the best?

I did this. I failed them. And I feel awful.

That old gray Leverkusen cloud has settled back around me.

I go back to my California home and try to block out the noise, but when half of it's coming from your own head, you hear it. I should have gone to UCLA. I should have stayed in Germany. I should have retired from the national team. I should have been more aggressive on the field. I should have done something.

I'm still knee-deep in sadness when I get a call from Tris. She's sobbing when I pick up the phone. I ask if she's OK. Of course she's not.

"Where are you?"

"City of Hope in Nashville."

"Why are you there?"

"Dad has cancer."

50'

IT RARELY SNOWS in Santa Barbara. While the nearby San Rafael Mountains might be no stranger to sporadic blankets of snowfall, there was simply no way our guests could have expected they'd embark on a festive Winter Wonderland.

This was no miracle. We had purchased the best snow money could fly in.

Bianca and I tied the knot on New Year's Eve at the ritzy Bacara resort on the tranquil Gaviota Coast. To Bianca's credit, it was no easy feat having to plan a wedding for a guy who lives out of a suitcase. I suggested getting married in the winter—my off-season—and she lit up.

"I love that. How about New Year's Eve?"

"Wouldn't that be really expensive?"

"Who doesn't like a party on New Year's Eve?"

Winter's not wintery in Southern California, though, so if for some reason you were to decide you really wanted to capture that North Pole feeling, you would end up with something like, say, an extremely expensive snow delivery service. Among other things, Bianca went to town planning our over-the-top wedding soiree. If you happened to pop in over the course of those nine months, you'd have thought money grew on trees. Some people, like Bianca, gain energy from planning colossal social events. Others, like 5'8" soccer players, are far more at peace being thrown in the trunk for the ride . . . or preferably, not being on the ride at all.

That last part didn't seem to be an option, so along for the ride I went.

It's probably not a great sign when you're having a hard time getting excited about planning your own wedding, but it felt like the big celebration was more her thing anyway, and there were a lot of other things presently competing for space in my head. I was still reeling from my 2006 World Cup performance and the brutal media fallout that came with it. We had returned to America with nothing but questions and takedowns about our failures, both as individuals and as a team. My teammates who played overseas at least had a little time to lick their wounds; we in the MLS were thrown right back into the grind of a season in progress. There was no time to process the blowback—I rejoined the Galaxy with our season on the brink and a new coach to adjust to. All while the manager of my home life was a runaway train planning our wedding.

None of this was Bianca's fault. I didn't have the backbone to say no. Bianca wants a karaoke machine for the late-night afterparty? We're having a karaoke machine. Bianca wants a surprise midnight In-N-Out food truck? Just a little something extra to top off the evening for our tuxedoed and ball-gowned guests, already filled to the brim with filet mignon, seared halibut, and enough passed food to feed a small village? We're having a food truck. And if Bianca thinks we should get our eyebrows plucked together a few days before the wedding, looks like I'm doing that too.

And while this all seemed a bit extravagant to me, we could afford it. Bianca was doing well in Hollywood. I was making quite a lot of money compliments of Nike, Gatorade, and Major League Soccer. When it's your wedding and it's going to make your soon-to-be wife happy, it's easy to go along.

And if it seemed extravagant to me, I could only imagine how it must have seemed to most of my teammates: MLS's coffers weren't exactly overflowing. And to my Redlands crew, this had to seem like an insane amount of money to spend on anything. Two very different classes would come together on our special night. While the Hollywood types and soccer elites were able to afford the lofty cost of the resort, I know a good chunk of my closest would be sneaking away to stay someplace off property with a more agreeable price point. I just hoped they stayed long enough to grab an In-N-Out burger on the way out.

Regardless, for the two of us and 150 of our closest friends, it was a heck of a way to cross into 2007. Bianca had much to celebrate this evening: a new husband, every wedding indulgence her heart desired, and a recurring role on *Rules of Engagement*. To top it off, she had successfully followed her own #1 Rule of Engagement: Get hitched before turning 30. I was thrilled that I was able to provide my very happy wife *her* perfect wedding. And while I'm usually more of a keep-to-myself type, even I loved seeing so many people I cared about enjoy a top-shelf evening together in one oddly snow-filled ballroom in Santa Barbara.

I could look in any direction and see someone who meant something to me: Rich and Randee, Bruce Arena, Sunil, Todd Dunivant, Coach Ellinger, Michael Kammarman, and a bunch of my teammates from my soccer world. And, of course, my whole Redlands squad: Mom, Paul, Tris, Joshie, Adam, and Coach Hafley.

Not on the guest list? My dad, Tim Donovan.

It had been five years since Dad and I had had any communication with each other. There had been no change to this status quo after Tris's recent phone call, and Tris was not particularly pleased about that. To her way of thinking, he was still our dad despite everything he'd put us through. He had nasal cancer. Tris was going to be there for him; she couldn't believe that I was not. She'd told me I needed to go see him. I had no plans to do so.

I suppose all children are some sort of blend of their parents' traits. Tris was like an 80/20 blend of Mom to Dad. The bulk of her personality comes from Mom's side: She has a wonderful strength and a special kindness to her that I've seen in Mom. But in her relationship with me, I can see that 20 percent of Dad. Tris—like Dad—is not afraid to rip me a new one if she thinks I deserve it. My refusal to interact with Dad was one of those moments.

"No matter what type of falling out you guys had, or how you feel, the worst thing you can do is nothing at all. If something happens to Dad and you don't have closure with him, you're going to always regret it."

I heard what Tris was saying, but I didn't want to listen. How many times had I given Dad chances only to be let down by him? How many times could I invite Dad back into my life only to have him hurt me? And how could Tris forgive him after all that he had done to hurt her? Didn't she remember Dad's needless custody battle? Being dragged through years of excuses, stress, and useless legal wrangling? How do you forgive a man for that?

"Landon, that was 15 years ago. You have to move on."

Move on? I wasn't moved by this idea. But if Tris wanted me to try... fine. I agreed I would reach out to Dad when I thought it was the right time. I just wasn't sure when that would be. It certainly wasn't going to be during my wedding.

51′

MANHATTAN BEACH is nice, but the beaches of Maui have a way of soothing even the most overstressed people in a way Southern California just can't.

Bianca and I had greeted the second day of our week-long resort stay with a workout and a yoga session. We were heading up to the suite level at the Grand Wailea hotel when we were joined on the elevator by a sunburnt American who was clearly a soccer fan, as he rapidly went from overjoyed to overwhelmed when he realized who he would be riding up with.

"Oh... my... god. You're... Landon... Donovan. You're! Landon! Donovan!"

He was, in fact, correct: I am Landon Donovan. That was apparently a bit too much for this man, who was in a state of tears. Just by standing in an elevator, without murmuring a word, I had somehow taken this other human being to an emotional place where he seemed to lose all ability to function.

This was starting to happen to me more and more, and I can't say I was loving it. The downside of breaking into the American consciousness was that my privacy was becoming quite public. Even at the edge of America in Mahalo country, I was now being ogled and hit up in Hawaii for photographs, autographs, and conversation. I appreciate that fans want interaction or connection, and I recognize that I'm lucky to get paid to play a game and have people recognize me for it. It's just that when you start playing a game like soccer, you never think you might be trading off your ability to be out doing things undisturbed. The irony is that Bianca would have loved to have more of this type of interaction. If a glowing fan had spotted her and short-circuited right before her eyes, she'd have taken that as a high compliment.

There's something that fascinates people about celebrities or people with fame, wealth, or power. But I think people are mostly enamored by those who seem to have mastered something. You don't have to know much about playing the violin to be captivated by someone who can really play the violin. Watching a potter make a masterpiece out of a lump of clay is like watching magic happen. And witnessing a professional athlete—particularly one who excels even by professional standards—allows people to dream of having that mastery in their own lives. I knew how much work and sacrifice had gone into my success, though, so it didn't really seem all that special to me.

For me, soccer had been my obsession and full focus since as far back as I can remember. Even among other soccer players, I had a one-track mind about it. When my Residency teammates in Florida would head to Walmart on a Sunday night, I'd head outside to practice. When most families were starting their Friday movie night, I was starting to work on my finishing. I was maniacal about my methods.

And while I happen to be crafty when it comes to scoring goals, I don't think that means I should be looked at as some divine figure or put on a pedestal. I just happen to be good at something—soccer. Other people are masters at other things. Imagine if we were more interested in getting close to the best teacher in the world than to the guy who's really good at sports? That seems like it might be societally healthier to me.

The truth is I worked my ass off to have a chance to succeed. It's the part of the make-your-own-luck equation that I can control.

Before this vacation in Hawaii, Bianca and I took a trip to Bora Bora—we always seemed to escape sun for more sun. She was reading a book called *Fast Food Nation,* and when she was done, she told me I *had* to read it. I did, and it completely changed the way I looked at food and what I put in my body. I'm fortunate that I've always had a healthy relationship with food, because we didn't have much money growing up and never saw food as something we could afford to overindulge on. And playing soccer from such an early age, I always took care of my body. *Fast Food Nation,* though, kicked my healthy eating habits into hyperdrive. Being very careful about the food I ate became part of my regimen.

You wonder why all these soccer players around me were getting hurt? Some of it is surely bad luck. That can happen to anyone—you simply can't control that. But sometimes, it's a body breaking down because it hasn't been taken care of off the field. What you do off the field is just as important as what you do on it. Don't eat right, don't sleep right, don't take care of yourself... maybe you can do that for a while, but at some point, it's going to catch up to you. I wanted to do everything in my power to maximize my opportunity, right down to the fuel I put in my body. *How you do anything is how you do everything.*

I owe a lot of that to Bianca. She was always working on herself—mind, body, and spirit. Pilates. Yoga. Acupuncture. Meditation. And, of course, therapy. She brought all that into our relationship. Her search for self-improvement became my secret weapon for maximizing what I could do on the field and, ultimately, for bettering myself off it.

My Redlands friends and family would always say to Bianca that I was so different after I was with her. That's true. I was always curious by nature, but Bianca was far more exploratory, and by proxy I became that way too. Bianca set the path—she was the caretaker—and I came along for the ride. Our trip to Maui was no different. Bianca would scour the resort brochure planning what we would do next. I would work on a crossword puzzle and get rest and rejuvenation until the next thing she'd lined up for us.

I recognize the irony of this now. When things were going well on the field, it was because I made something happen. But I went with the flow off the field, avoided confrontation, followed someone else's lead. I didn't know those things were even in conflict with each other inside me. It would catch up to me eventually, but I thought I was doing just fine.

All that "fine" would fade away when a message from Frank Yallop found its way to my phone on my vacation.

Frank, who was now the coach of the L.A. Galaxy, had sent over a text that I was sure was a joke. But the joke would be on me when a certain British superstar and his spicy wife came to Los Angeles and for my Galaxy captain's armband.

53'

THERE WAS a sense across U.S. Soccer even before 2006 that the national team program had gotten too "loose" under Bruce's stewardship. After the 2006 World Cup flame-out, the thing that players adored most about Bruce—his willingness to give us the flexibility to be ourselves—was now viewed as problematic at the very top of America's soccer governing body. Our failure to advance was all they needed to justify a change to someone who was less a "player's coach" and more a disciplinarian. So it was no surprise that when they decided to tighten the strings on the national team, someone like the tougher-than-nails Bob Bradley would be brought in to try and reset the bar.

This wasn't Bob's first time working with us. At Bruce's request, Bob had assisted in many national team training sessions during the last World Cup cycle, and he'd been an assistant on Bruce's coaching staffs before that. When Bob was named the interim coach in December 2006, he was already intimately familiar with the way Bruce worked, which meant he was intimately familiar with the way we worked.

Bob was a born-and-bred "Jersey" guy. He was tough. Disciplined. Prepared. Bob was a tone setter—a little bit Rutgers, a little bit Princeton, a lunch pail guy with a market price education. You didn't necessarily feel the Princeton in his personality, but it was always there under the more rugged surface of his training methods.

I wasn't sure how I felt about the coaching change. My loyalty was to Bruce. He'd brought me to the national team and given me the freedom to be myself. Bruce was a big team guy who had a way of inspiring and motivating us. He spoke fluent subtext, using humor and sarcasm to get the most out of his players. Bob was... not that. Where Bruce used subtle humor, Bob fired straight-shooting heaters. He was deliberate, focused, and committed to having us do things a certain way—his way. He didn't mince words. He probably felt no one had the time for that anyway.

Bob's USMNT office was located at the Home Depot Center, which is also where the Galaxy train. I was working out in the Galaxy gym one day when Bob came in and told me he wanted to see me when I was done. I finished my workout and walked over to Bob's office. Four months into the 2007 MLS season, we had only three wins under our belt; our Galaxy squad was following up last year's disappointment with a truly blackhole type of season, despite last year's late-season coaching switch to Frank. But we had just pulled off a surprising North American SuperLiga tournament upset against Mexico's Pachuca 2-1, and in classic "me" fashion, I let the press know how I really felt about our lucky win. Well, Bob had watched the game and had a few choice words to get off his chest:

"Landon, man. I watched your postgame interview. You know... you want to be a leader? Let me explain something to you. Your team is going through a rough season and Frank's taking a ton of shit. When you guys win that game, even if it's lucky, you don't need to bare your soul to whoever asks that question. You love Frank, right? Perhaps try, 'You know... the season hasn't gone the right way, but Frank continues to push everybody in the right direction.' You've got to see the bigger picture of the group, Landon. If Tiger Woods was playing shitty and the press asked him a question he wouldn't say, 'I'm playing shitty.' He wouldn't want his competition knowing that."

Everything was a teaching opportunity with Bob, and the ruthless strategist got us on the same page shockingly quickly. Just two months after the "interim" was lifted from his coaching title, we were once again lifting the Gold Cup, beating Mexico 2-1 for our fourth CONCACAF trophy. I tied the game on a penalty kick that also tied me with Eric Wynalda atop the list of all-time U.S. goal scorers, and 11 minutes later, Benny Feilhaber put us ahead for good with an absolute rocket. The ball never touched the ground from the moment it was put in play: A corner cleared to the top of the box fell to Benny's foot and he smashed it into the left side-netting. Just as beautiful was the feeling of putting 2006 in the rearview mirror with Bob Bradley firmly in the driver's seat of the USMNT.

That trophy heralded the beginning of a new team under Bob, and there were a few of us that he expected to step up as the new core of the team. They included Carlos Bocanegra, Steve Cherundolo, and my old Residency teammates DaMarcus Beasley and Oguchi Onyewu. Then there was me, Clint Dempsey, and Tim Howard holding down the fort behind us. Bob liked what he saw from this unit, and he was clear from day one that he intended to build around us for the 2010 World Cup.

In September, just before a friendly against Brazil, Bob pulled the handful of us aside and shared as much:

"When you're in a cycle to get to a World Cup, every time you come in, you've got to build on the work. You can't just get to the end and suddenly find an identity. You must develop that identity, and you must develop that leadership. *You* guys are that nucleus. You're the ones I'm counting on."

Naturally, Bob couldn't promise every one of us that we were going to make the cut. But he wanted all of us to know that we were the players he was going to expect the most from, and that he was going to hold us responsible for providing leadership to everybody else.

This was Bob's way of reestablishing the pride that comes with being part of America's team. It was his way of demonstrating that when you play for the United States, it's bigger than any one player. His plan was simple enough to put into words but required everyone's buy-in to make it real: Work hard for each other and make it hard on the other team. It was a clear direction with clear expectations. Whatever lingering feelings I might have had about Bruce being gone, there were no questions about what Bob expected from all of us. I was going to have to adjust, but at least I knew what was to come.

Unfortunately, the same was not true almost anywhere else.

The shift from Bruce's loose, sly humor to Bob's no-nonsense approach was tough but manageable, but it felt like every other part of my life was changing fast. Rich and Randee were less present than they had been in years, partially because my own marriage meant I was spending less time at their house, but mostly because they were consumed with a major change of their own: twin boys. Eli and Sammy had been added to Team Motzkin a few years earlier, and they understandably had their hands full.

While the twins were the most notable addition to the lives of my favorite power couple, one half of an entirely different kind of power couple—and all that came with them—had been added to my own life: David Beckham. The rumors of David's interest in playing in MLS had already been flying in 2006, and the signing became official in early 2007. But none of us had any idea how his celebrity would impact our league or our lives until David showed up.

David's signing was a tsunami, and, at least at first, the rest of us were but small, unprepared craft riding those surging waters.

David's introduction was a massive affair. League higher-ups. An overwhelming number of fans. A circus of reporters. If the sudden worldwide interest in our little league and the European glitz and glamour of his introduction weren't enough to tell you that something far beyond the standard MLS fare was happening, they threw in a full overhaul of the Galaxy's colors, crest, and kit, as if to underline that things here were about to be very, very different.

Walking into a brand-new locker room and meeting new team-mates is awkward for anyone. For David, I imagine it was strange beyond even that. David was a global star with a level of celebrity far beyond anything any of us had ever experienced. I had some notion of Hollywood celebrity through Bianca and her work, but this was magnitudes greater. David was someone who'd played for Manchester United and Real Madrid and been captain of the English national team—a place where they *really* care about soccer. His wife's every move was tracked like she's royalty. Some of the players on our team barely made enough to afford a quality suit—the Beckhams ran clothing lines. He was pulling down literally millions more than anyone on our team, and yet he still had to walk into a locker room and meet the people he'd be playing alongside. It was a disparity unlike any I'd seen in any previous MLS locker room.

When he walked into the locker room that first day, the strange uncomfortable feeling of us mere mortals meeting this global soccer star barely lasted a few seconds before Alan Gordon—a man making roughly $5,950,000 less than David—waltzed over, his long hair hanging down, put out his hand, and introduced himself to our stylish, new, close-cropped addition.

"I'm Alan. And what's your name?"

Momentary confusion flashed across David's face.

"I'm David."

"Uh, yeah, man. I'm just fucking with you."

It was classic Gordo, who was fun, funny, and easy to love, and we all—David included—burst out laughing, as the apprehension that had been floating around the locker room dissolved.

I introduced myself to David too, and it was clear he was genuinely excited to be here. I was just as excited—to have him as a teammate and to see what his arrival meant for MLS. I was all in on the league, and having someone of his caliber step in felt like a major leap forward. He didn't need us—he was fresh off a La Liga title with Real Madrid—but he still chose to come. That said a lot. And after a season where we'd missed the playoffs, I couldn't wait to see what having a world-class player like David would do for us on the field.

Frank had David's locker set up next to mine. It made sense—I was probably the best-known player in the league prior to David's arrival, and the face of the Galaxy up until then. Upon arrival, David immediately took over both honors. For us to make the transition work, we were going to have to be partners. And as captain, it was up to me to do the most bending.

It didn't take long, though, before I encountered the first real bit of fallout from Beckham's continental hop. Later that day, I was pulled aside by Alexi Lalas, our shoot-from-the-hip general manager, with a "suggestion": "Hey, Landon. I just had a thought... to make David feel more comfortable, maybe he could be the captain?"

Was this a question, a suggestion, or an order?

A day later, Frank called me into *his* office and brought up the same "suggestion."

Is this in his contract? That he is going to be the captain?

I called Rich to find out what was going on with this request. Was this coming from David? "Rich, if I was going to a new team, there is no way I would ever—ever—ask to be the captain. And if their captain came up to me and suggested that I'd say, 'No way.'"

Rich had heard the push was coming directly from Beckham's camp, so it seemed this was something that he—or someone close to him—wanted. I didn't get it; it seemed such a strange thing to want when we hadn't even played a minute together yet. But if that was what it took to make him feel part of the team... I needed to consider it. He'd been captain of the English national team. Maybe he just couldn't see how he'd be anything else here. Either way, I didn't want us to get off on the wrong foot, and I could see how turning over the captaincy might be the most captainly thing I could do, to demonstrate that the team's needs came first. I told Frank and

Alexi I needed to think it through, but that the door was open. And a few weeks later, I acquiesced.

There were other issues. David barely played that first season—he'd had a nasty ankle injury long before arriving that needed tending to all season long. But without him on the field, we were suffering. Alexi seemed to be bringing in player after player looking to find the right mix to put around us, and we had little consistency from game to game. The massive media onslaught that came with David's acquisition put our terrible play even more under the spotlight. Everywhere we went, it was like a rock concert with the number of fans wanting to see David—and because of the injury, most of the time he wasn't there... And with our revolving door of players, we barely were either. We went 9–14–7, even worse than the previous season, but with far higher expectations and the eyes of the world—not just America—truly upon us.

At the end of the season, with rumors swirling that he would be relieved of his duties, Frank instead resigned.

A few good things came out of that year. One of Alexi's mid-season moves had brought in Chris Klein, an incredibly likable veteran player—and a former U.S. team roommate of mine—who had a strong season and had been a great addition to our mix. So much so that a week before the season ended, when the L.A. Galaxy Most Valuable Player for the season was named—as voted on by the local media—it was awarded to Chris.

When a season is already this weird, you can count on it getting even weirder, and it almost immediately did. When the news of the award was released, a reporter from the *L.A. Times* came up to me with some really unusual information: "Hey Landon... I don't know if I'm overstepping here, but we all did a straw poll between us and basically every one of us chose you as the player of the year."

This was perplexing. And infuriating. I didn't mind that Chris had won the award, but I did lead the team in scoring on the season, and I could see how they might have voted for me. Beyond that, winning the award triggered a $25,000 payout under my contract. That and the strange thing I'd been told spurred me to call Alexi to find out what had happened. I told him what the writers had told me—that I had been their near-unanimous selection.

"Alexi. I wouldn't care about this except that winning the award triggers a $25,000 payout per my contract."

Quite dryly, Alexi pointed out that Chris Klein had won.

I asked him how, though?

The media brought him their vote, he explained, and he thought Chris Klein was more worthy, so he gave it to him.

What the fuck?

"Alexi, this award isn't 'the general manager's Most Valuable Player'; it's 'the media's Most Valuable Player.'"

Still, Alexi stood firm; it was his call.

I hung up. I truly couldn't believe what Alexi had just said to me. I called Rich angry and befuddled, and at the end of the conversation we connected with Tim Leiweke, the president and CEO of AEG. Tim was a busy man, as AEG owned the Galaxy, Lakers, and Kings. We explained that we weren't trying to rat anyone out, but this was now a contract conundrum—if they were taking money out of my pocket that I rightfully earned and was voted on, that was an issue. I wasn't interested in them announcing anything different— Chris Klein was welcome to remain MVP—but I expected to be paid what I'd rightfully been awarded by the media vote.

In the end, they ended up paying both of our bonuses, but I couldn't believe this incident could happen in a professionally run organization. For Alexi to do that on top of effectively stripping me of the captain's band didn't exactly make me feel appreciated. I'd chosen to come to Los Angeles. I'd committed to being here and already helped us win a title. Now? The Galaxy was making me feel like my commitment to them didn't matter.

It all weighed on me. Beckham signing. Frank "resigning." Bruce getting fired. Bob getting hired. The media criticism for our 2006 failure, and the media crush that landed me in the shadow of Beckham's first year. The lack of respect and honesty from the Galaxy management and our failures on the field two years running shattered a little part of my ego. I was giving my all on the field and sacrificing off it, and it sure didn't feel like that was coming back my way.

Ironically, the media was covering our absurdly forgettable season more than any I'd been part of. I'd been to World Cups with less press than we had during Beckham's first season. The media were out in droves covering David's every move on—and, that year at least, mostly off—the field. Our world was turned upside down from the moment he arrived. David proved that first year that he really could fill the stands from Toronto to Dallas. We'd never had higher attendance across the league.

This was the double-edged sword of David's celebrity. He undeniably raised the profile of the league and made soccer bigger in America—a thing I absolutely wanted. He raised the profile of the Galaxy—a thing I wanted just as much as he did. But David's arrival simultaneously thrust me somehow both even more and less into the spotlight. More eyes than ever were on everything we did, meaning even less privacy. Unfortunately for us, that meant we've never had more people watch us play embarrassingly bad soccer and get our asses kicked across 13 MLS stadiums.

54'

THE SEASON OVER, and me stewing, Bianca decides one night that we should go to see a movie around the corner from our Manhattan Beach home.

On the agenda for the evening is a film people are raving about called *Into the Wild*.

As the lights fade, so do the loud, sharp edges of my thoughts, and I am pulled into the story of Christopher McCandless liberating himself from the world as he knows it. He abandons his fears, his family, his money, and his possessions. As I watch his growing independence, my arms fold upon themselves with a tension I cannot release. In McCandless's solitary journey, I recognize something that I desperately wish for myself. I feel something shifting inside me that I cannot stop.

This man is living how I wish to be living.

My thoughts are flying along with the movie. Seeing him release his societal bonds, I suddenly feel the full weight of burdens that I have been carrying.

Chris changes his name.

I wish I could change my name.

Chris disappears from life as he knew it.

I wish I could disappear from life as I know it.

Chris frees himself by giving it all up.

I wish I could free myself and give it all up.

Chris was 24 when he undertook his quest to escape it all. I am 25 and stuck fully in the shackles of professional soccer. I want to get away and forget it all for a bit. The final moments of the movie present themselves—Chris's slow realization of what he has in fact given up in isolation—and we see Chris shaking as he scribbles in his journal:

HAPPINESS ONLY REAL WHEN SHARED.

The screen cuts to a real-life image of Chris, from the undeveloped film found in his camera after his death. It's a self-portrait of Chris up against the bus in which he lived in the Alaskan wilderness, a huge grin on his face. I study him intently and see no signs of pain or sadness.

Out there, Chris looks... Free. Alive. Happy.

I couldn't feel more claustrophobic.

Am I free? Alive? Happy?

Is my life even... my life?

The credits roll, and tears roll down my face.

We sit in the darkness as the credits scroll, Bianca confused as to why we're not moving from the stadium seats. I remain speechless on the outside, while inside I crumble.

I think of our 2006 failure in Germany: no joy, no limelight, no love. Just disappointment and loneliness. And the feelings that had followed:

I let the country down.

I let Bruce down.

I let MLS down.

I think back to the kid who loved Residency. Who won the Golden Boot at the U-17 World Championship. Who played endless games of anything he could on those endless hot summer days.

I'm not that kid anymore.

As an adult I'm still playing, but the pain has caught up. In all the time I've played this sport that I have both loved and hated—often simultaneously—there is only one soccer player I haven't been able to outrun. *Me.*

That hits me hard. I know I'm onto something, but there's a cold, gray, cloudy heaviness that leaves me in an uncertain fog.

Soccer used to be freeing. It used to be play. It was where I could go to outrun my other troubles. I could not perfect a father, but I could perfect a pass, or a shot, or a move. Soccer let me be me.

Now... I can no longer escape my troubles in soccer—soccer keeps bringing me more of them. Soccer is a job.

Something in me is dragging me to a thought I have been deflecting for years. My feet have always kept my mind off my mind. Not tonight. Tonight, I need to know what it is. I am *conflicted*... no, that isn't it. I am... *confused?*... no, but close. I have fallen out of love with soccer. I want to break up with the game. I want to break free from the pressure of it. Homing in, but not quite there.

It's becoming clearer now. I completely define myself by how I perform as a soccer player. My *marriage* is to soccer. My friendship is with soccer. What am I without soccer?

I don't know. Sitting in the darkness, I have no good answer.

I've always gained energy being alone. But right now, with my wife sitting by my side, I feel as if no one is by my side. This is as alone as I have ever felt. I am deep inside myself, and there is no energy, just an emptiness I cannot explain.

My entire being is soccer.

The endless gray of Leverkusen.

I should be more than that.

Another lonely day.

I am... *depressed.*

That's it.

That's the word.

Depression doesn't care if you're rich and famous and popular. Depression is selfish. It never asks for permission to show up, and it comes and goes as it pleases. It doesn't care about your gender, your class, or your age. It will tell you your successes are failures; it will turn you against yourself and will refuse to let you off the hook.

I have always wanted to talk to someone about my problems but have always made excuses.

I've never felt more alone.

I'm ready to talk.

HAPPINESS ONLY REAL WHEN SHARED.

I need help, and it's time to seek it.

56'

I'M HUNCHED DOWN in white, 12 yards out and crouched in a kneeling position. The Swedish keeper is trying to project himself as being bigger than he is. I'm unaffected. I work my way through my penalty kick ritual.

It's January 19, 2008, and we are in front of 14,000 fans for a friendly against Sweden at the Home Depot Center. I have an opportunity to extend USA's 1-0 lead thanks to my teammate Jozy Altidore, who earned a foul in the box just two minutes into the second half. Less important to the game, but present in my mind nonetheless, is the fact that if I make this penalty kick, I will become America's all-time leading goal scorer.

But these thoughts are far away from my routine as I approach the ball, then deliver a decisive shot mid-height to my right . . .

I never set out to earn the honor of being the American men's all-time leading goal scorer, but it matters to me. It means consistency week after week, year after year. To have been in so many games for my country already at age 25—to have had that many chances and the ability to score that many goals *for America*—my 35th goal, extending our lead to 2-0 on this day? I was proud of that.

Some awards mean more. A player of the year award voted on by the media and subjectively changed by a general manager? Not terribly fulfilling. Breaking a record with no subjectivity to it? That's on an entirely different level. I was able to pass my now-just-retired Galaxy teammate Cobi Jones as the USMNT's all-time assists leader a mere two years ago. With this goal, I was now the all-time scoring *and* assists leader for the national team.

Cobi and I weren't just linked in the record books. We were also getting ready to go through an entirely new experience together: getting our first taste of Ruud Gullit, L.A. Galaxy's new head coach. Cobi was turning in his cleats for a clipboard as a first-time assistant coach. Ruud had first been introduced to us just after last season's debacle. We had a special trip to Australia planned by the Galaxy's main sponsor, Herbalife.

Ruud decided he would immediately set the tone as our new coach by calling us together after the 16-hour flight for an *I'm-the-fucking-boss* two-hour training session.

He makes his point—he's the Head Dutchmen in Charge. We are now exhausted. Between the flight and the practice, our bodies and backs are in pieces, our necks sore, and our moods... not good. I walk into the treatment room and there's our seasoned trainer Ivan Pierra working his butt off... but not on any teammate. As I look closer, I can see it's Ruud on the training table. *Are you fucking kidding me?*

So that's my first impression of our fearless new Dutch leader: He's someone willing to put us through misery and then jump the line to take care of himself first. We're not off to a great start.

When Ruud was hired back in November, I was disheartened that Frank was leaving, but at least intrigued to play for an attack-minded player like Ruud, who had achieved great things with the Dutch national team. How could that be a bad thing? Two quick experiences into our get-to-know-you trip to Australia, and I was getting to know: Ruud was clueless as a coach. The season hadn't even started, and I could already sense we were in for another dud of a year. Just what I needed with all the other shit going on in my life.

I had already decided to address some of my other issues when we returned to America. Bianca always seemed so fresh and free when she came back from seeing her therapist. My *Into the Wild* epiphany had pushed me to give therapy a shot. Bianca was legitimately surprised; she thought there was no way my ego would let me dip a toe into that arena. When I returned to the States, I set up an appointment with Juliet, who I had met a few years earlier at that meditation session.

It seems strange that the people who have the most are sometimes the most likely to be depressed, but it was also now clear that everything I had gained and achieved wasn't making me happy. And while there should be no shame in seeking help for depression, I was new to this, and I did feel shame. Surrendering to the notion that I needed help weighed me down even more. I hated feeling that I couldn't figure "me" out for myself.

I pulled up to Juliet's office early one afternoon for our first session. Leave it to the universe to park her office right next to a sports complex where multiple youth soccer games are in progress. Ah yes... my old happy place. I parked and walked up 20 stairs and into Juliet's workspace.

It had been a few years since I had been here, but I remembered the calming, almost predictably Zen music that was still helping set the aura of her office. In front of me was a compact glass table with two wicker baskets, one containing pamphlets for the classes Juliet taught, the other with the word "Dana" scribbled on it in a sharpie. I read it at first as "Donna," my mom's name, then remembered that Juliet's meditation class was free unless you chose to leave a Dana... a donation.

I noticed a two-seater couch lined up across from what I imagined was Juliet's chair. This would become the hub of our work for the next two years. The adjacent room I recognized. That open area was her spacious meditation Zen den where Bianca and I had worked on breathing techniques 18 months back, filled with big, plush cushions surrounded by seated Buddha statues.

Juliet sat down across from me holding a mug of tea, and even though I knew she was there to help dissect me, I couldn't help but try to dissect her. She smiles—a calm, spiritual sage with a Middle Eastern accent—settles into her chair, and we begin.

"You should know I'm not a 50-minute type of therapist."

I'm not sure what that means. I don't really know what therapy is—I've pictured it as some deep, cold, overly cerebral questioning, like a cross-examination. Juliet seems warm and welcoming despite my obvious discomfort. She asks me to share a bit as to why I am here, so I start to spill my guts. It feels like a never-ending tell-all. As I share, she listens. Occasionally, something triggers her to grab her yellow pad and write something down. But even then, her eyes rarely leave mine. For an hour, I talk, sharing my story, and I end with what I think the goal of me being here is:

Who the hell am I?

Juliet smiles at this. She puts down her yellow pad and lifts up her teacup.

"See this cup? Imagine this cup is who you truly are."

She looks for an item nearby and picks up a tube of ChapStick.

"This is your mom's voice."

She pushes the ChapStick against her tea, then finds another item—a piece of candy.

"Here's your dad's voice."

She puts it next to the ChapStick. She picks up a remote and presses it up against the other items stuck to the outside of her teacup.

"Your Josh experiences. You get the picture? As we go on in life, this magnet gets bigger and bigger and bigger. And if you're famous, it's even bigger, Landon. And more solidified, because everyone is telling you who you are, what you are, and what you should do."

Juliet rests all the items on the table next to her, then holds up nothing but her tea.

"The true nature of who you are at birth is just the magnet. An empty magnet that has no attachment and nothing around it. And as you go through life, the magnet takes over."

Juliet once again sticks the ChapStick to the cup.

"The voice of Mom saying a certain sentence with a certain inflection sticks."

Then the remote control.

"Then something a coach says."

The piece of candy.

"Then an experience with your sister Tris . . .

"So the courage needed is, one by one, to examine: What do you truly believe? When you hear something that upsets you, to examine: Why does this upset you? Is that really you being upset? Or is it your conditioning? Something related to the attachments you have brought on from all those other people? The goal is to dissect and demagnetize the stuff sticking to your psyche that you now know is not you. So, to your question. Who are you? The goal of our time is to help you separate out everything that is sticking to your magnet. If you want to be free, it will take time, but let's get you free."

She has my attention. I am intrigued by the conversation and the way she thinks. Therapy has come a long way since that therapist Paul and I had made fun of so many years ago.

"Now . . . you do have homework. Some days you will and some days you won't. Today is one of those days. It's quite an extensive questionnaire I'd like you to take. What are some of the themes you want to accomplish? What are some of your struggles? Let's try to limit what you'd like your goals to be."

She hands the survey over and we agree to connect in the next week. She is aware my schedule is all over the place, but she is willing to be available over phone or Skype if I need her when I am on the road.

I understood now what Juliet had meant: She wasn't a 50-minute therapist. We had talked for 90 minutes in a blink, and that was barely introducing the surface we were going to have to scratch. I wasn't sure where all this was going, but I knew for certain that my interest in doing this was far greater now than when I'd walked in. I'd committed myself to doing what I needed to do to be a world-class athlete. Could I put the same energy, focus, and tenacity into becoming a world-class human?

We were going to find out.

57'

DAVID BECKHAM and I should have gotten on better. We have quite a lot in common on paper. We both had tricky relationships with our dads. We both have special connections with our moms. We both had epic memories surrounding the 2002 World Cup, David's being his nail-biting, last-second free-kick goal against Greece to seal a spot in the tournament for England. The 2006 World Cup is a sore subject for each of us. We both experienced a coach we viewed as a father figure. We had each reached the quarterfinals of the grandest soccer tournament on earth, and now we had each also worn the captain's band for the L.A. Galaxy.

Most importantly, we were compatible on the pitch, which is all that really mattered. Our interests off the field couldn't have been further apart. I had no interest in mingling with Hollywood superstars and being featured in the culture pages. David enjoyed living in the bright spotlight of Beverly Hills; I preferred the sunlight of Manhattan Beach. He could have the iconic Hollywood Hills and I my chill beach—we could still play together just fine.

I am in my home near that beach, and for the first time since sophomore year of high school, I am doing homework. Today, I am the center of my own attention. I have committed to therapy because committing to therapy means committing to me.

The exercise in front of me has me looking at all facets of my life and identifying the different versions of me and the groups they interact in. One by one, I methodically take out each Landon from where they are nestled inside one another. I can easily identify On-the-Field Landon, Redlands Landon, and Married Landon. Whether I like it or not, I also now see Famous Landon. And there's the Landon I don't see clearly yet, but who I aspire to be—for now I just write Free Landon.

I go to town deconstructing myself, explaining the pros and cons of each of these personas as I see them, and the guardrails holding each of them in place and helping define them. It's complicated to tell where one Landon ends and another begins, but it gets easier when I realize that Free Landon—the Landon I aspire to be—is a much simpler version of me. *That* Landon seems most like Redlands Landon, but with a dash of *Into the Wild*'s Christopher McCandless in it. *That* Landon seems curious and unfettered to me—an explorer of the world who doesn't need a lot beyond himself and new experiences to immerse himself in.

The exercise also forces me to examine my soccer goals. My mind slips to Ruud Gullit's attempts to remake the Galaxy, decisions I mostly don't agree with and feel frankly slighted by. Ruud has focused his attention on adding a pure goal scorer to the roster—he said he didn't feel we had one. He's made our back line even worse by parting ways with our keeper, Joe Cannon, so he can spend the last penny we have under the MLS cap (which he doesn't understand, coming from Europe) to reacquire Carlos Ruiz. Two eras of Galaxy goal scorers united on the same field— it sounds nice in theory, but who is going to stop the other team from scoring?

Carlos's acquisition does help me lock in on a soccer goal, though. If there's one good thing about having David here, it's that I can put all my energy into my game. There were days where my focus had waned. So I take this moment for what it is: a challenge. OK, Ruud doesn't think I'm enough of a goal scorer? Let's prove him wrong. On-the-Field Landon sets two goals:

1   I want to lead Major League Soccer in scoring.
2   I want to win the Most Valuable Player award.

That would be something.

I've never done either of these things. Most people forget that my obligations with the national team mean I invariably miss playing in roughly a third of the Galaxy's games in an MLS season. It's damn near impossible to lead the league in goals when you're out of the country for eight games, or just back from CONCACAF qualifiers in Costa Rica and needing to recover from the heat, humidity, and travel. Can you lead a league in scoring playing only two-thirds of the matches? Can a 66 percent player really be *the* MVP? I've never thought so, but I will no longer allow that to be an excuse.

Excuses have never been my thing. From a young age, it was engrained in me that excuses don't help you get better.

When I really think about it, I probably got that *not* from my Mom but from my...

I think back to the promise I made Tris. I pull out my phone.

For the first time in years, I fire off a text to my dad.

58'

BIANCA WASN'T the only one who was happy I was giving therapy a chance—Rich was too. There was no shame or stigma to therapy for Rich; he came from a family of therapists. To Rich, going to a therapist didn't mean you were broken; it was just taking your mind to the gym for mental reps.

I've never been one for small talk. One of the joys of Juliet's sessions is that we jumped right into it from the get-go. I wanted to solve all the problems, and I wanted to do it right away. But it turns out that being a world-class athlete does not make one immediately capable of handling world-class therapy. I had fantastic instinct and awareness on the field; off the field, the right moves were cloudy and flickering. I was willing to put in the work, but it quickly became clear that this was going to take a lot of effort.

I didn't want to take time to rehash subjects, but your experiences are like an onion, and you must face each layer of the onion as it comes. Each new layer reveals something new that must be examined, addressed, assessed, discussed, and accepted. And—if you're lucky—reconciled.

It is our second session, and I am back on her couch. Juliet scribbles intently in her yellow pad, then flips the pad around to reveal five categories, each within its own little square:

- Little Boy Landon
- Landon "the Man"
- Famous Landon
- Landon the Leader
- Landon the Soccer Player

"I want to get through your goals and then we are coming back to this first square." She points to "Little Boy Landon," and I nod in understanding.

I have listed out my goals—the things I want to work on—and ranked them in the order that seems most important to me:

1 My father and our relationship.
2 Becoming more consistent as a soccer player.
3 How to process anger.
4 Dealing with fame and money.
5 My relationship with Bianca.

I fully expect to hear an "interesting" or "I see." I get nothing but a small, focused nod and smile as I go through them. Like a poker pro, Juliet gives me little to get a read on.

"Thank you for sharing these. We will continue to come back to them."

She asks me to turn in my homework, so I hand it over, and into the first square we leap: Little Boy Landon. It's like diving into a pool of memory, and I am splashing all over as I try to explain my childhood. How we grew up what I call "American poor"—not on the street, but just eking out a living. How we ate whatever Mom could afford to get us: Spam, cereal, Cup of Noodles, hot dogs, canned fruit. I talk about life with Joshie, my relationship with Tris, the long afternoons playing outside with no one around, and the lack of supervision that defined our childhood. I share details about my parents, their phone calls and arguments. As Juliet probes further into these relationships, the onion layers peel away, and we go deeper and deeper.

I'm remembering something and she stops me.

"Stop storytelling, Landon. I don't need the story. I need to know what you're feeling. Then we can address why you're feeling a certain way."

It's a jolt, but I appreciate her directness as this session winds down.

The following week, near the end of a session, I'm telling Juliet about McDonald's, and how my dad was supposed to pick Tris and me up on Friday nights but almost never showed. I'm upset about it. I'm upset about him.

"My dad is a horrible guy. He just flaked on us."

"Does that make him horrible? Just because he didn't show up? That might not make him horrible."

"But he was supposed to pick us up, and he didn't show up. He's an asshole."

"Maybe him not showing up was less about you and more about how he felt about your mother."

This is not what I expected to hear. I thought Juliet would confirm what I'm saying, but she's challenging me on my assumptions, making me think about why I see the world the way I do. It gives me pause, but I like being challenged. I can tell she's not doing it just to negate what I'm saying—she is setting a tone and trying to get me to stretch and think about Dad differently.

"Your dad may not have that level of awareness, Landon. He is making it about himself. But you, Landon, do have that level of awareness."

"What are you suggesting?"

"Perhaps it's time you go see your dad."

Had she talked to Tris? I really didn't expect her to say that. I shared that I had recently opened a dialogue again with Dad by text, but I wasn't sure that I was ready to see him in person, even with his cancer. She slowly stirred her tea with a spoon, then ever so delicately unveiled why she perceived this to be the necessary remedy to my dad problem.

"Landon, you are going to have to address this if you want peace. It's the very first goal you listed. You are toeing a line that could lead to Little Boy Landon regretting it if you don't mend this relationship. You have the power to fix what needs fixing. But you will need to talk to him to do it, and you might need to examine more deeply what happened in your dad's life."

This was a lot to process. I was exhausted. And although I may not have wanted to admit it, Juliet was making sense.

The only way forward is through the thing that's in your way.

And I couldn't shut off a cadence my mind had suddenly chosen to repeat to me:

How you do anything is how you do everything.

60'

DAD DIDN'T look different, but something about him seemed new. I hadn't given him much of a heads-up that I was coming to Nashville, nor did I share straight out of the gate that I was putting new tools to use from therapy. Mostly, I just started talking sports with him.

Sports was always our icebreaker. The beer didn't hurt. I'm not a big drinker—I'm not even a middle drinker—but beers, sports, firepits, and backyard hangouts felt like something dads and sons were supposed to do. So here we are bantering about Dad's favorite topic: hockey. It's March, and the L.A. Kings and the Edmonton Oilers are both at the tail end of a terrible season. Fitting that both of our teams find themselves in the cellars of their divisions with nowhere to go but up.

Eventually, we move on to Dad's second favorite topic: my soccer career.

I let it go on for a little while.

We discuss the hiring of Bob Bradley, and the surprise limbo Bruce finds himself in—he had been tapped to coach the New York Red Bulls after he was let go from U.S. Soccer but was suddenly back out of work. Then on to one of Dad's favorites, Tim Howard. They shared a love of music and records. I was fairly certain Tim was now "the guy in goal" for this World Cup cycle—that brought some joy to both of us. Tim is a consummate pro, and he's fought through his own set of uncomfortable circumstances with his dad and his own parents' divorce. The topic flips to the Galaxy, and I confess my tepid relationship with Beckham, my low hope for us entering the season, and my ambitious personal goals for 2008.

Night falls, and the soccer conversation does as well. We can't seem to advance beyond it. It's a safe place but also a sticking point. With more liquid courage now gliding through my veins, I make a late run at nudging us from small talk to big talk.

"Dad, I have a request."

The fire in his backyard burns, and I have Dad's undivided attention. He's looking at me and waiting to hear what I have to say.

"For a little bit, I'd like us not to talk about soccer. If you don't mind, I'd like to use this as a fresh start, one where you try to relate with me as your son first, rather than as a soccer player. I want to be more than just that in the relationship. Can we try that?"

While he's processing this, I figure there's no better time to share where this idea has come from. Dad nods as I tell him I've been in therapy for a few months now. I want him to know why I'm doing it and that I feel it's working for me. And I share that the work in therapy has helped me find what I need to hopefully turn our relations back into a relationship.

Dad stares into the fire and gives me a short but sufficient response.

"You got it, son. Let's try it."

I wanted more, but I didn't know if he could go deeper than that. It's possible he couldn't. I had been working on my awareness and tried to really pay attention to my dad, and then I tried to put myself in Dad's shoes and see if we could go further.

Cancer can be a truth serum. It can force someone into having the sort of man-in-the-mirror conversation they've avoided their whole life. And usually, it's like their entire family gets part of the cancer too. Everyone around them is affected. I was affected by Dad's cancer. I just wasn't involved.

"Dad, I'm sorry I never reached out when you had cancer. I'm sorry I never called or visited. I can't imagine how hard that must have been."

I meant it.

"Landon, there's a lot we can't change about our pasts. I feel bad about a lot of things that went down when you and your sister were young."

Sitting and looking at the fire, it felt like one more line should have followed. I yearned for more, but this was a start.

The next day we were back to small talk, but that was OK by me. He didn't ask me about soccer. I learned his nasal cancer was in remission; dealing with it seemed to have made Dad a bit more mortal. Whatever he had been running from, the cancer had slowed him down.

At the end of the weekend, I felt like we had at least started to communicate—that whatever was between us had been better stated, or at least reestablished. Dad drove me to the airport, and maybe I shouldn't have pushed my luck but I couldn't help myself.

"Dad?"

"Yes?"

"You know... you've never once apologized for how you treated us. You never once said you were sorry. Do you know how far it would go if you did that? All I've ever wanted is for you to apologize."

Dad pulled off to the side of the road. He put the car in park and looked me dead in the eye.

"I'm sorry, Landon. I can't change what happened. That's the road I took, and it took me far from California. I know my leaving had effects on you and Tris. I regret that. But like I said, all I can do is try to be better."

I don't know if it was the cancer, the fact we hadn't seen each other for so long, or just an older version of Dad who now had time to reminisce by a firepit about his past, but I knew he meant it. It wasn't perfect, but it was something, and that felt like the closure I needed to move on.

61′

WE'RE OVERWHELMED 4-0 by the Colorado Rapids at Dick's Sporting Goods Park in our March opener but earn a 2-0 win at home against my old friends at San Jose in the second game of the MLS season. I'm involved in both goals, grabbing an assist on Beckham's ninth-minute tally, with him returning the favor on my goal in the 37th. Our third game sees us helping Toronto FC to their first win of the year on our home turf in a match they never trail. I tally both goals in the 2-3 loss. I score a pair in a 2-2 draw against previously winless Houston in our fourth game, and in our fifth, we shred Chivas 5-2, with me scoring a hat trick and an assist.

By the end of April, we've broken about as even as one can, with 2 wins, 2 losses, and 1 draw, but I've tallied eight goals and two assists in five games and am named MLS's Player of the Month.

We mirror our April record come May, once again going 2-2-1. David Beckham is healthy, and, on the field, our games come together beautifully. But our defense is horrendous, and Ruud... aside from moving us around and dictating starters, subs, and formations, I don't know what Ruud does. I haven't had this little hands-on coaching since I was a kid. There are days when Ruud's left the facility before I finish with my extra work on the field. I don't know what Ruud's doing with 21 hours of his day, but he sure isn't doing it here.

We're scoring a lot of goals and giving up almost as many. Two months in, we're treading water. With Ruud at the rudder, it just feels like choppy waters ahead. But from May 18 to June 14, we rattle off four wins in five games, and score at least three goals in each win, even with me missing two of those weeks with the national team. Edson Buddle is a revelation in Carlos Ruiz's absence—he's playing great and making David's life and mine easier on the field when we're out there together.

Then summer hits, and the shitstorm arrives. We're no longer treading water. We're under it. From mid-June to late September, we don't win a single game—a disastrous and unheard of 12-game winless streak. The Galaxy had become a black hole.

63′

I'VE SEEN Juliet enough times that it's become second nature for me to grab my own tea. Months into our work, I can feel how Juliet's couch works its magic. I've run these drills enough now that I can see what skills they work. The game is coming into focus. We're not just here for her to sift through my life story—we actually need to *dig*. It's a turning point.

We bury things we don't want to remember. And when those memories finally bubble to the surface, we often tell ourselves something other than the truth. It is the blessing and the curse of our minds and of Juliet's couch. She summons memories from the past. Sometimes it's just a memory. Sometimes it's a lot more.

Today's topic?

Germany.

It's my second stint with Leverkusen. I have returned to fulfill my contract. I have been promised a real opportunity. It's my seventh appearance in nine games for them. I have mostly come on as a late-game substitute and have never been granted the luxury of getting into any type of rhythm. But today, Coach Klaus Augenthaler has started me out of necessity. It's a UEFA Champions League game against Liverpool, and Robson Ponte's booking from the first leg means I'll get my shot to start.

I haven't done much coming on as a sub. I feel like I'm still getting my legs under me here and it's hard to get in the flow. But this is different—a chance to play a full 90. I'm excited but tense. I have been waiting for this moment for 22 years. And in the first 22 minutes of the match, an opportunity comes my way... but I miss a sitter. It would have put Leverkusen ahead. It's a play I've made time and again in MLS, but I rush it and don't hit it cleanly. It sets me off the rest of the half and I play poorly.

It's not my finest hour. And it's only an hour, because Coach Klaus pulls me off the pitch moments after halftime. It's a downright poor performance that I wish I could get back.

I *did* get a shot. The shot was short, but it was a shot on the field. And a shot to my ego.

Juliet sits up in her chair. She gives me that slight, knowing little smile, and I know we're digging deeper into this.

"Do you think that coach believed in you?"

"Not after that performance."

"But do you think he believed in you before it?"

Before I can reply, she stops me.

"Think about it, Landon. We're in no rush."

Juliet does this a lot—tells me not to reply just yet, to stop and think about it first. I am learning to not just immediately spout out what I'm feeling. I sip my tea; it gives me space to not answer Juliet's question so quickly. It's not just a fair question but the right one, and I've thought about it before. I remember being demoralized at halftime of that Liverpool game.

That asshole subbed me off in the 53rd minute, just eight minutes after halftime.

"No. No way."

Juliet nods as if she already knew the answer.

"You seem to have a track record of not wanting to perform for men who reject you. Have you noticed that?"

"What, like my dad?"

"Your dad, yes. This German coach. Your current coach. And you seem to have a track record of performing for men who believe in you, yes?"

"Coach Ellinger. Bruce. Frank."

Juliet adds a name to the mix:

"And Rich."

"Rich?"

"Yes, Rich. I recall the first time you played in front of Rich in high school you told me you had played poorly and he still wanted to get to know you and signed you."

I have never thought about that before, but it's true.

"There's nothing wrong with any of this, Landon. It's about understanding why you respond well to certain people and why you might not respond well to others."

I nod, following the logic. It is, as always, a lot to take in.

"Have you ever studied Rumi?"

I haven't.

"Rumi was a mystic Persian poet whose words still stand today because they speak the truth. Rumi believed that everything, even suffering, brings us closer to something greater. 'Be like a tree and let the dead leaves drop.' Landon, your soul is learning how to let go."

"I'd like to let go of Germany."

I say it in a joking fashion but Juliet remains Juliet.

"The sooner you let go of what no longer serves you, the sooner you'll be free. As the saying goes, 'This too shall pass.'"

While I'm a fast learner, *This too shall pass* is easier for Juliet to suggest than for me to actually live out. But the sentiment is landing.

I peek down at my watch and realize our session today needs to be over. I have to head home for a social gathering at our house that Bianca has put together, one which I don't particularly want to partake in.

In my car, the fog in my mind seems to clear. I think back to my memories of Germany and remember the feeling I had there when I knew it wouldn't work. It feels eerily similar to how I feel now, walking into a big dinner party at my chaotic house.

I don't have this in me tonight. This too shall pass?

Our neighbors all seem to be socializing in my kitchen this evening, but I am feeling antisocial. Instead of talking to them, I sneak upstairs to my office and close the door. Bianca needs nights like tonight—bouncing off all these people is where she gains her energy. It drains mine. Not like I have any energy left to be sucked from me. It's exhausting enough being a professional athlete. Layer on a session with Juliet and my brain is at capacity. I'm not trying to be rude to anyone, I just have enough conversations going on in my own head tonight that need to be worked out.

With the house full of people, I sit at my desk and it's like I am sitting on Juliet's couch in my brain. She was right. I would run through a brick wall for a coach who believed in me. And I'd run the other way from a coach who didn't.

Luckily for me, a coach I didn't have an iota of faith in would soon be out—and a coach I'd scorch earth for was coming to Los Angeles.

66′

FOUR OF my roommates were loud, messy, non-paying tenants. Their rent covered in unconditional doggy love. But if you entered our modern, two-floor California coast home on this evening, you could have smelled the beach on the breeze floating through our patio doors.

The Beijing Summer Olympics were background music on the TV to the six of us. I glanced up at three American men—Kerron Clement, Bershawn Jackson, and Angelo Taylor—hurdling their way to an all-American 1-2-3 on the podium. It seemed like eons since I had played in the Summer Olympics. I was a different Landon back then.

Bianca and I were buried deep in our laptops on opposite sides of an invisible border on the living room sofa with our dogs. Our youngest—Santi, a vizsla mix—was currently invading my space while I was scanning the breaking news that was now old news to me.

Tim Leiweke, AEG's CEO, had sought me out a week back and confided that the dysfunctional Year of Ruud was coming to an end. I liked Tim for a lot of reasons, and not just because he was sharing this snippet. Tim was another attendee of the School of Hard Knocks who had never gone to college but was doing just fine for himself—if you consider running a multi-billion-dollar company "just fine." Tim had sought me out to tell me they were looking at bringing in Bruce Arena and asked me what I thought.

I didn't hesitate.

"Do it as fast as you can."

Tim had seen enough. It felt like he had been engaging with Bruce for a few weeks and knew bringing him in would excite me. I trusted Bruce. He was the most successful coach in American history. Nothing would bring me more joy than to play for Bruce again. He was a coach who already knew who I was—not just as a player, but as a person. And yes, we were both competitive and driven to succeed.

Bruce was also aware of the nuanced details of the salary cap and roster rules in MLS, all the blind spots that kept tripping up the foreign coaches MLS teams brought in. He was a proven portrait of stability. Bruce could equal in a day the number of hours Ruud would be at our facility in a week. If it wasn't for his wife, Bruce might just live at the facility. That level of professionalism and preparation translated to his teams.

My eldest, Thor—a shepherd / Labrador retriever blend—was now residing at my feet, as I reached the *new* news—an intriguing piece of information that Tim had not shared with me: Alexi Lalas, the man responsible for hiring two coaches in two years who were each shown the door, was now being shown the door himself. Given the MVP issue I'd had with him, I was no great fan of Alexi's run as our GM, but this seemed to have less to do with Alexi's failures and everything to do with Bruce wanting to clean up the politics that often exist in management.

Bruce is no dummy. He wouldn't be taking this job if he had barriers in the way to acquiring the guys he needed. And whatever my issues were with Alexi's time as GM, none of us blamed him for Ruud. We all knew by now that Alexi had little to do with Ruud's hiring. Tim had apparently been strong-armed by Terry Byrne, a key member of David Beckham's management brass. With Ruud and Alexi out and Bruce coming in, there was genuine hope of the Galaxy running like a successful franchise again.

While quite a lot of things were already being turned upside down in my soccer world, there was one more still-unbelievable inversion: I had been invited by Bayern Munich coach Jurgen Klinsmann, who had a home in California, to train with his team this November. And he'd said that if the sessions went well, he'd offer me an opportunity to join the Bundesliga powerhouse on a three-month loan come January. It was late August, and the Galaxy were pretty much out of playoff contention again, but I'd scored 17 goals in 18 games and was on pace to achieve my preseason goals. I was intrigued to have another chance to show myself back in Germany.

Bianca was far less intrigued. Maybe she was so used to our jobs dictating where we'd roam in the world that it was no big deal to her. Perhaps she just couldn't believe I would consider going back to Germany after all the bitterness from my first two stints, even if it was just for three months. But I'd been doing a lot of thinking about my first two opportunities there. They hadn't gone well. I'd been young and inexperienced, then older and hot-headed. I was a neophyte to their climate and the rigidness of their structure. I couldn't change the Germanness of Germany, but I could approach it as a different me. Perhaps the third time would be the charm.

From the other side of the couch, with our other two tenants—Loki, our four-year-old black Lab/ridgeback mix and Luna, our purebred Boston terrier—Bianca caught my attention.

"These dogs... I love them, but they take up so much space. We need more room..."

Here we go again, I thought. Bianca had literally just finished furnishing and decorating this place.

"More outdoor spots for socializing... for when people come over."

Bianca's vices were houses and hounds. I peeked at her screen and my suspicions were confirmed: Bianca was scrolling through real estate sites, which meant it was only a matter of time until we'd be talking about moving again. In our short time together, we'd already been through as many homes as we had dogs.

We'd started with the little community home I'd bought in Willow Glen in San Jose. Then a beautiful, brand-new four-bedroom, five-bath with 2,500 square feet in Manhattan Beach. After that, our current stylized-to-Bianca's-liking Mediterranean-style beach nest on Pine Street. Bianca was now dreaming up a creative idea that included an existing house and an adjacent open lot a whole two blocks over and across the Manhattan Beach wood chip walking path.

"It would be cool if we had a movie theater. And a grotto. Wouldn't that be fun?"

All this moving was starting to make me wonder why we couldn't just sit still with one another. Therapy was giving me the tools to recognize my reality, step outside of my body, and reflect back with real awareness on where I stood. The more time I spent with Juliet, the more I saw the power of having an accepting sounding board—someone who helped me see myself more clearly.

When my body hurt, I would go to a massage therapist. When I had an injury, I would go to a physical therapist. But when I had mental challenges, my ego would never let me go to a psychotherapist. America stigmatizes therapy in a way we stigmatize no other medical practice. It had kept me from trying it for so many years and created a whole other hurdle to overcome before I could even begin the work. No one questions going to a gym to get stronger or going for a run to build endurance. If we just treated therapy like we do every other thing we use to help improve ourselves, we would all be better off for it.

With Bianca and me both seeing therapists, you would think the question of whether we were right for each other would have already bubbled to the surface, but somehow it hadn't. We were each still working on ourselves, bringing our childhood baggage and career issues into our sessions to be examined. Our relationship with each other, how we interacted, had not yet been placed under the microscope. In our relationship, we were still allowing distractions to take precedence over actions. For Bianca, that meant distracting herself with moving and remodeling, an expensive diversion. My distraction, outside of Dad, was focusing on more consistent play and righting the wrong of the 2006 World Cup, which now included an opportunity to again prove myself in Europe.

Was there some other reason we were always on the go instead of confronting what was on our minds or in our hearts? We'd come to that in time. And when we did, none of our distractions—soccer, the dogs, moving—would get in the way.

67'

WINTER IN BAVARIA.

I was sitting solo at a quaint sushi bar surrounded by people speaking a familiar foreign language. It had been a decade since my first sojourn in Germany. This stay would probably be my last. I was learning that loans were double-edged swords with respect to my mind and body. I got better, but I also got incredibly tired. Training with some of the best players in the world like Franck Ribery and Philipp Lahm for a few months will do that to you.

But for all the talent on the field, it was equally toxic off it. Political. Strategic. Cold. Jurgen seemed ganged up on, set up to fail here. While I was looking for more consistent playing time that, once again, was not consistently presented to me, I would not let it rattle me this time. I wasn't looking for a full-time contract. I was not invested in proving what I could do—I was simply invested in getting better, enjoying my time here, and steering clear of the internal bureaucracies I could now see ruling Bundesliga life. This was an opportunistic time-out; my real life was back in America. California's sun was waiting for me.

Back in Los Angeles, Bruce was working fast to build a spine and an identity for his new team. In 60 days, he had already turned the Galaxy roster over, letting 19 of my teammates from last season go. Just four of us would carry over from Ruud's roster: Alan Gordon,

Chris Klein, myself, and David Beckham...assuming David chose to return from his loan to AC Milan, a prospect that looked 50-50 at best. It wasn't lost on any of us that David was playing his best soccer in two years in Italy. Last year's winless streak had left him seeming adrift and uninvested. AC Milan had reinvigorated him. It would be embarrassing for him to give up on his L.A. project now after starting it with such fanfare, but he clearly seemed happier playing in Italy. I was interested to see what would happen with him.

Bruce had signed a slew of disciplined veterans like Gregg Berhalter, Tony Sanneh, and my dear friend Todd Dunivant. He also drafted lanky center back Omar Gonzalez with the third pick in the SuperDraft and traded a second rounder for attack-oriented midfielder Mike Magee. And he had just brought in goalkeeper Donovan Ricketts.

As I sat sipping my German brew on a Saturday night, I thought about how happy I was that Bruce was now in charge of things in Los Angeles. I thought about how proud I was to have kept playing hard even amid the wreckage of last season—hard enough that I had achieved one of my goals by winning the MLS Golden Boot, with 20 goals and nine assists. But most of all, I thought about how excited I was to play at home with the hopes of winning again. Three years without a playoff game was wearing on my soul.

I turn to the waiter at the sushi bar, hold up my beer and say, "Hey, buddy—can I grab one more?" He nods a *ja* at me and goes to grab me another.

"Excuse me."

I turn around.

"Were you speaking English?"

"Yes."

"Cool. I'm American. My friend's Australian."

"Wow, really? Nice. I'm from California."

They invite me back to their table.

I oblige.

68'

I HAVE BOUGHT a million-dollar home *and* an adjacent lot just because my wife wanted to build a killer playhouse equipped with a pool, movie theater, and grotto.

I've heard about it all winter and have finally returned home to see it for the first time with my own eyes. The dogs are ecstatic to see me. Bianca is happy I am home, but she mostly seems excited to show me around our new double house. Bianca showcases everything she's had torn down and designed up. A pool with a waterfall, a swim-up bar, a hot tub, the grotto.

So that's what a grotto is. That does look expensive.

A subterranean movie theater/viewing lounge. An amazing shower just off the master bedroom.

I'm barely taking in what she's sharing. Something doesn't feel right.

How long was I gone? Three months? Three years? The distance between the two of us makes it feel more like the latter. My time in Germany triggered something I had never felt before in my head, and I'm repeating a simple sentence over and over, trying to figure out how to get it out of my head and into the actual world. There's no way I can't tell her what I'm feeling—but the Band-Aid is hard to rip off.

We enter the luxurious backyard of Bianca's newest playlot. She's crafted a beautiful patio just off the master bedroom. It's a calm but cultured space filled with comfortable seating and bright red cushions. As she starts to tell me about the gorgeous, imaginative work she's done here, I can't let her go on anymore—I cut her off.

"Bianca... we need to talk."

70′

——

THE TEXT from Bruce arrived midafternoon.

He wanted to have a one-on-one with me and David before training the next morning. It sounded more cordial than it was. This was an order.

The Beckham Experiment, Grant Wahl's in-depth book chronicling David's decision to join the Galaxy and his first two years here, was officially hitting the shelves, and the media mafia were expected to be in more than their usual tizzy—buzzing around our facility with questions to be answered. Of all the years to follow the Galaxy, Grant had stumbled into two doozies. Shitty results on the field often lead to golden stories—our trash season was Grant Wahl's treasure.

Part of Bruce's problem was that unnecessary comments had already leaked out from both camps. I had questioned both David's commitment to the team and his leadership in the book; Beckham had called me unprofessional for doing so. With David now officially returning to L.A. from his loan to AC Milan, Bruce knew we needed to get on the same page. If this was going to work, it would only be because we had found a way to work together.

Bruce, David, and I would have our uncomfortable conversation tomorrow.

Today I was amid a marathon session with Juliet.

The Beckham Experiment had launched, and the Bianca Experiment had ended—72 hours from now, the news of our separation would hit the presses too. With so much swirling around me privately and publicly, my mind was everywhere but here, and Juliet thought it was best to start our session with some meditation to help us focus in.

Juliet was teaching me how to be aware and present. I'd thrown myself into the work and was getting better at staying present as my mind tried to drift elsewhere. I wanted to be a world-class meditator. Juliet would frequently remind me that this wasn't a competition. While speed is preferred on a soccer field, she'd pull me back to make sure I wasn't racing ahead of myself in her office. She'd remind me that sorting through a life is a delicate process and we would not go through it too fast.

When I have too much going on in my head, it doesn't just weigh me down, it weighs down my game. Perhaps this was part of the problem—soccer always came before Bianca. The arrival of David just complicated my life. The two years of Beckham's Los Angeles experiment felt like something that was happening *to* me rather than *for* me. There was so much to think through and deal with; at times it left me feeling frustrated, overlooked, or paralyzed.

Meditation is the art of accepting what's going on in your mind. It's the act of being present, not "quieting the mind." With Juliet's help, it was becoming a tool in the mental arsenal that I could use to find peace. I lay on Juliet's couch with my eyes closed, breathing through my nose and focusing all my attention on the actual cadence of my breath. Most people start thinking about something else when they lie back like this. Your mind goes to work. The goal is to, without judgment, keep yourself present and focus on your breathing. I needed that if I was going to be able to dig into things with Juliet today. My mind had done enough wandering in the four months since Bianca and I had split up.

Most people would immediately tell you to screw off and start packing. Bianca, to her immense credit, didn't do that. She wanted to understand why I felt the way I did and where it was coming from.

Unfortunately, I had already started to realize that it was less about coming from someplace and more about where I needed to go.

For over a decade now, my schedule had belonged to other people. Between U.S. Soccer, MLS, and life at home, I went wherever I was told. Bianca had fallen easily into her role of caretaker. And like everyone else in my life since money showed up, I let her tell me where to go, what time to be there, and for how long. I had been given a path in soccer at 15, was a professional overseas at 17, and was on my way to marriage at 20.

When most teenagers were studying for the SATs, hanging out with girlfriends, or experimenting in college, I had been shackled to one rigorous path: soccer. At the time I loved it, but now, I knew something was amiss. I had lived a wider life now and felt I needed more. I didn't know who I was anymore, with or without soccer. Or Bianca. I needed to find out.

Shortly after I told Bianca all this, we visited Juliet together. Juliet knew both of us and we knew her office would be a safe arena for a brutally honest conversation. After listening to what we were saying, Juliet had delicately shared with Bianca what she heard me saying:

"He needs to find himself."

Bianca disagreed.

"I don't think this is about him finding himself; I think he wants to be with other people."

Four eyes turned on me. As you have by now gathered, I enjoy confrontation as much as I enjoy playing for German coaches. But we weren't going to progress if I didn't share my truth. So I turned to Bianca, took a deep breath and went for it.

"I have something tugging inside me that's telling me I need to leave. I don't know if it's short term or long term. I just know I need to follow it. That's as far as I know... for now."

No amount of therapy was going to reverse this feeling inside me. We discussed our feelings and where this need was coming from, and Bianca agreed that she was going to allow me space and time to figure things out. The only caveat? If I were to be intimate with another person, that was a non-negotiable deal-breaker for her.

And so, having just returned from Germany and just moved into our grandiose new home, I had also just moved out and maybe even moved on. I had packed my clothes into my car. I didn't have a plan, but I knew I needed to see where all this took me, which happened to be the Beach House hotel in Hermosa Beach, as good a place as any to sort things out until I could see where this pulsing nag in my gut was leading me. I would try to live both in the moment and moment to moment. I'd taken the best room they could give me for a week: $300 a night on the top floor, overlooking the ocean. After checking in on that first night, I went out on the balcony, looked out over the water, and breathed.

I came to from my meditation and recalled that feeling of being on that hotel balcony four months back. It felt liberating. "For the first time in a long time, I felt...*free*," I told Juliet.

Now a professional patient, I helped myself to a cup of hot tea and shared that there were still some gray areas I had been coping with.

In May, about three months after I'd moved out, Bianca and I met up for dinner after a Galaxy game against the Sounders in Seattle, where Bianca was visiting her family. She had asked me to meet her at a restaurant by the stadium. She was still trying to make "us" work, but was treating me like a mother would a son, telling me who she had told and what her family thought about everything that was going on with us.

"I told my mom things aren't great, but I didn't have the stomach to share the news with my dad."

I couldn't help but think her dad wouldn't have been afraid to tell me what he really thought if she had chosen to confide in him. Ironically, I was no longer afraid to tell Bianca what I thought I needed to do either—the months away had helped me feel clearer about it all. I took a deep breath and told her what I felt in my heart: that I was pretty sure that I was done.

"Are you 'pretty sure' or are you 'sure'?"

"I'm pretty sure, I'm sure."

Bianca looked at me. I took a long sip of my water and committed.

"Bianca, I'm sure."

Now the words were out there. Bianca started tearing up. Then came more tears. But before I could say anything...

"I'm sorry to bother you—"

I turn around, and a handful of people are standing by our table, several still in their Galaxy gear.

"We're huge fans, Landon. Good game tonight! Would you sign this?"

They hand me a Sharpie and a Galaxy cap, and I sign it, then turn back to try and comfort my soon-to-be ex-wife.

Juliet shakes her head in disbelief.

"You are the reluctant superstar for a reason."

Funnily enough, sitting in Juliet's office, I did once again feel reluctant. Life after Bianca was a big unknown, but life with David needed to be addressed. Our meeting with Bruce would be uncomfortable. Our play together was never an issue—we meshed well on the field when we were both in form—but after two years as teammates it was clear we were never going to be buddies. It had nothing to do with differences in personality or even his advisers wanting him to wear the captain's armband. I was quite relieved that David had come in and taken some pressure off me.

What bothered me last year was the way I felt David approached the job when things went south. It didn't help that Ruud approached the Galaxy like a part-time job. When things really hit the fan—when more than anything we needed to work harder, pull together, and find some way out—Ruud failed us. And I felt like David was treating the L.A. Galaxy like we were beneath him. That isn't OK coming from any teammate, but especially not our captain.

I had seen what a model captain behaved like from my days in San Jose. There were times where Captain Agoos may have been too much of a hard-ass, but we knew it was coming from a good place. That wasn't the style of "MLS David." I knew he wanted to just fit in and be one of the guys, but he couldn't: He was too much of a global superstar and the rest of the team was a collection of ordinary guys grinding to make the league minimum and in constant fear of getting cut. Yet David was deeply empathetic to those guys, comfortable with the spotlight and driving media to our game.

Whatever the reasons, as the winless streak went on and the season fell apart, it felt like David was beginning to check out. It felt disrespectful. David had chosen to come here. He had made that commitment. But when shit got hard, I felt like it really impacted him. If you're going to be here, fully committed to us, make the sacrifices it takes to lead these men.

If you want me to surrender the captain's band to you, step up and be a captain.

Juliet was smiling one of her smiles.

"Who else does that sound like? Who else in your life wanted to take the credit without fully being available?"

Like a ton of bricks, it hit me.

Goddamn, Juliet. You're good at this therapy stuff.

I didn't feel like David was there at first. I didn't think David was providing for his team the way a captain should provide. I didn't believe David was holding up his end of the bargain. It felt like David—or whoever from his camp was calling the shots—was looking out for his own interests instead of the team's and not taking responsibility for his actions when it came to leading the Galaxy.

Just like my dad.

My dad not being there? My dad not providing like he should? My dad not holding up his end of the bargain? My dad looking out for his own interests? My dad not taking responsibility?

"This is what happens with trauma, Landon. When the needs of the parents supersede the needs of the children, when children feel they must forego their own needs, they stop feeling. Stop trusting. Stop talking. They shut off. They disappear into the background to keep the peace. You have exhibited this behavior with your dad, with David, and, yes, with Bianca."

I wasn't mad at David. I barely knew David. I was mad at how David's behavior reminded me of my dad's. But David's not my father. The scenarios might be similar in my mind, but they are very different. And if I'm viewing David's actions through my own perceptions of my dad's inadequacies... I'm not really viewing David's actions. I'm not even seeing David.

I was mad at myself for not having the strength to address David directly. Annoyed that I would tell a journalist what I thought instead of going straight to the source. What David said was right; it was unprofessional. If I had gone to him and told him what I thought, he could have addressed it—except I never gave him a chance to. David had uprooted his family, come to a new country, a new team, a new colossal challenge, and a new routine. He was expected not only to perform well on the field, but to elevate soccer across America. If anyone should have known the weight of trying to put soccer on the map in America, it was me.

It's also possible I was more upset than I let on about David accepting the L.A. Galaxy captain's band. As a compartmentalizer, it was second nature to bury my real feelings. In my heart, I didn't like the move, nor how it went down. I believed David was wearing the captain's band for MLS more than the L.A. Galaxy. Maybe I was more focused on what I'd lost than what he was stepping into. The result of all that? I had shown David no empathy. If we were going to make us work, I needed to make amends.

We arrived at the facility for our mandated session the next morning, and David and I joined Bruce in a claustrophobic, windowless meeting room, about as far from the press as you could get. We sat down as Bruce closed the door, then worked his way to his chair and sat, arms crossed, to kick off our little mediation.

"David, Landon. The only way we're going to have a chance to make this team better is if the three of us get along and agree. This place has been an absolute shitshow for—"

I cut Bruce off before he could get any deeper into a monologue.

"Bruce . . . let me start . . ."

I could feel my mouth drying up, but Bruce nodded; the room was mine for a moment of humility.

"David, I owe you an apology. It has been a really frustrating few years for me and I haven't been the best teammate. Instead of taking this to you and talking it out with you directly, I let out my frustrations with a reporter. That was really stupid of me. I want to apologize. I wish it hadn't happened that way and I'm sorry."

I could see David process this in real time, weighing what I was saying against his own thoughts and what I was quoted as saying in Grant's book.

Bruce chimed in.

"Look, I haven't read the book, nor do I intend to. But you have to remember, David, for Landon, the L.A. Galaxy are his Manchester United. He cares deeply about this club, like you care about Manchester United. If someone came in and there were some bad years, I think you would take it hard too."

Bruce was doing his best to facilitate this necessary conversation. He couldn't have his two best players fighting with each other.

David sat up and shared a few genuine and well-chosen words of his own.

"I appreciate the apology. I'm a good professional. We don't have to be the best of friends. But I am going to be a good teammate."

As what could have been a confrontation transformed into a conversation, David even took some ownership of the dysfunction of the past year and shared how frustrated he had been about the awful, trying stretch in his career. Neither of us liked losing. We dealt with it in different ways, but that didn't mean it wasn't affecting us.

Twenty minutes passed in that tiny sauna of an office. David and I had it out, shared all our frustrations, no holds barred. It was the best thing that could have happened, for both our relationship and our team. We all walked out a little lighter, Bruce included.

David and I were never going to be best friends. But from that moment on, playing with him became much more enjoyable. There was no question anymore about what we were committed to—we all wanted the same thing: to win and be successful. And we did. With Bruce in charge and David and me on the same page, we rarely found ourselves out of contention for championships. We put those first two years behind us, and the Galaxy soared because of it.

73' GOAL!

IF YOU TOOK the time to learn someone else's story, you'd have compassion for anyone.

My father was the oldest of five siblings. When he was 10, his parents filed for divorce. They ended up scattering all his brothers and sisters to other relatives across Canada. Separated from both his siblings and his parents, my dad landed with an uncle in Nova Scotia.

A year or so later, my grandparents got back together. They slowly gathered back all their kids. All of them except my dad. He was only 11.

I never did meet my grandmother, and I only met my grandfather once.

My dad is not a bad person; he just grew up in awful circumstances full of hurt. No wonder he's had problems with women; his mother abandoned him when he was 10. Coincidence? I believe my dad could never get along with any woman for too long because of his unresolved issues with his mom.

Dad's mom died from cancer when she was still relatively young. They never had a chance to face what needed to be faced.

History repeats itself, family history even more so. The rejection and abandonment that was handed down to my father was handed down to me. But where Dad lacked awareness, I was committed to breaking this cycle; the hurt will always perpetuate until we learn to heal it ourselves. I wasn't going to let the same thing happen between dad and me.

At the start of 2010—in my winter off-season from the Galaxy, and just before I began a loan to English Premier League–side Everton—I went again to visit Dad, who was now cancer-free and still living in Nashville. For years, nothing had been more important to him than ice hockey, and he had found his way back to his happy place. We had already gone on a little splurge for both of us at the sporting goods store. Hockey pads? Check. Stick? Check. Helmet? Check. Dad had practice that night, and I was ready to hit the ice with him. As we pulled into the complex with our hot new gear, there were about 30 or so men from his rec league team already on the ice or lacing up. You could tell that it was a proud dad moment as he introduced me to his teammates.

"This is my son, Landon."

It must have been 15 years since I had been on roller blades. Cleats were my shoe of choice, but my roller hockey memories with Adam instantly kicked in, and the next thing you know, I was zipping around Dad's hockey practice like I was back at Moore Middle School.

This is what it felt like to be seven years old having a sunny afternoon catch with my dad. This is me as a seven-year-old peeking out innocently from my 27-year-old shell.

As I raced around the ice with Dad and his teammates, I felt like I finally got my father-son fishing memory. There is so much I'd like to bury in my life about growing up without my father around. But happy memories like this brand deep into the psyche. We played for an hour or so, then went out for beers with his teammates.

Dad says he'll never forget that day. Neither will I. I've had some great days on the soccer field, achieved some amazing things. But if I'm ranking the top five moments in my life, you can put playing hockey with my dad right at the top.

74'

RICH AND I land in Liverpool and head straight to Goodison Park for Everton's FA Cup match against Carlisle. The FA Cup is the oldest national soccer competition in the world. As we pull up, you can feel its history; the energy and excitement of the fans pouring into the stadium this evening hits different. I notice the billboard just under the Everton shield: *Nil Satis Nisi Optimum.*

"Nothing but the best is good enough."

That resonates.

As a Californian in Liverpool in January, I'd come prepared for some brisk temperatures. I thought I was fairly unrecognizable all bundled up in multiple layers topped with a wool beanie.

No matter, Toffees fans were awaiting my arrival.

I learn fast that fandom is at an entirely different level here, as many of them—from all walks of life—not only recognize me but approach me as if I'm already a member of the fraternity before I've even played a single minute for their beloved club. It is welcoming. It is not remotely German.

Everton fans are like watchdogs, protective of their players. I recognize the opportunity before me: I can be one of them. As a guy who's always yearned to belong, I want to earn their adoration from the start. I can visualize what it would be like to bleed blue like the tens of thousands who've come to Goodison on this fine evening.

I know me. I do well when people respect me; it makes me want to go out and perform for the Toffees. This is the home of Everton since 1892, and I've been given an opportunity to be an Evertonian myself. To partake in the ravenous fabric and DNA of these passionate people.

Rich and I head up to the box, and you can feel the soul of the People's Club. A heady cocktail of loyalty and commitment from 39,000 maniacal Toffees. As I navigate the stadium as a spectator tonight, I make my own commitment to reach for greatness in every opportunity that presents itself over the next 10 weeks here.

Nil Satis Nisi Optimum.

The first day I showed up in the locker room, Captain Phil Neville asked me questions and helped me get acclimated. He mentioned he'd shared notes with Beckham, his old teammate from Manchester United, and that David told him I could run for days and cause tons of trouble for defenses down the right side. Coach David Moyes had done his homework on me too—he made me feel wanted straight out of the gate. And with Tim Howard here, I didn't come in cold—there was already someone here who knew what I'm capable of, someone I knew waiting to help me feel my way out. All of them made it easier for me to feel comfortable from the first day I had the honor to wear the royal blue and white.

I felt wanted.

I felt part of the family.

It made me yearn to perform for these fans.

Wearing #9, I would join the Merseyside club on the 10th day of the year—in '10—on a 10-week loan. You know I love my 10s. The fans were as dedicated as I was to the experiment, and I threw myself fully into every aspect of it—playing or supporting, it didn't matter. I had been curious about competing in the English Premier League ever since my almost-transfer when I ended up in L.A.; this was my chance.

David Moyes was not afraid to take a shot on American players. He'd previously brought in Brian McBride and now had Tim

Howard. I could feel right from the start that there was no convincing needed about my Americanness; I could let my game do the talking. During training, Moyes even suggested I take a few of the corner kicks. Absolutely. Whatever he needed from me, he was going to get. And it sounded like he was going to get it soon: Moyes told me I'd be starting my first game that first weekend.

I had only been part of the Blues for three training sessions, and they were ready to throw me smack into the fire: a game at Arsenal in front of 63,000 people. It was snowing and a blizzard was coming. But here I was, a kid from Los Angeles, still tanned, stepping in and ready to make my small dent. I felt nervous but confident. Twelve minutes in, I curled in a corner that Leon Osman hammered past Arsenal's keeper, earning my first assist in Everton colors. If not for a last-minute Arsenal goal, it would have been an away victory for us. The guys let me know this was our best performance of the season to date. It was a great way to start and helped build my confidence on the field and within the team.

I had come over to quench my curiosity. I wanted to know that I could play at this level. I didn't simply want to fit in—I wanted to show well and excel. So while I was at peace playing a supporting role, I challenged myself to be dominant down their right side. I had shored up a lot of the heaviness that had been weighing down my mind, and therefore my game, since Leverkusen. A confused Landon was an inconsistent player. That felt behind me now. I still had to prove it, but I was in the right place at Everton. Playing meaningful minutes for the club in games where we beat Manchester City, Manchester United, and Chelsea was nothing short of golden. And the experience of being part of this historic team and playing in front of its delirious fanbase made it truly special.

You could feel the love, support, and history in the narrow streets of Goodison Park on match day. The immense pride that linked old fans and young ones. You could feel the maniacal misfits. The bond was real between player and player. Between player and fan. Between fan and fan. It was family from the get-go.

Everything I had missed in Germany I found in Everton. Connection. Competition. Confidence.

When others believe in me, I can play at any level, with any player, in any circumstance. I believe that, but you don't know it until you go and do it. At Everton, I did it. I didn't allow the mental blocks and discomfort that came from my German experiences to hinder me here. I allowed myself to go in and deliver. And in Everton, I had a team that was willing to give me an honest and supportive chance; I give Moyes all the credit for giving me that opportunity.

My final Everton match was at home against Hull City, a team that hadn't won here since 1952. I allowed my mind to wonder what type of a sendoff I could achieve to give back to Everton's amazing fans. I would be coming off the bench for the game, and I shared with Phil Neville that I'd like to score one final goal if the opportunity presented itself.

Halfway through the second half, Moyes gave me the nod. I entered the match in the 70th minute, with us up 3-1. Twelve minutes later, I struck home my own thank-you to the sea of Blues. Four minutes after that, I was able to tee Jack Rodwell up for a goal of his own. Twenty minutes of play, a goal and an assist, and—most importantly—a 5-1 win. It felt like a proper way to honor and say goodbye to the fans. *Nil Satis Nisi Optimum.*

I had never experienced fans like that before—as ravenous about soccer as I was. After 12 glorious games, my tan had fully faded, and I was fortunate to have snagged two goals and three assists. After a draw at Birmingham City—and an embarrassing lap of honor at the request of my teammates—it was time to go home. My loan was up.

There was interest from both sides for me to stay. But I had promised Tim Leiweke and Bruce that I would come back in exchange for them letting me go in the first place. So I told Everton I would most definitely come back for another loan cycle if they'd have me. Fortunately for me, they would.

Back to America I went. Another World Cup cycle would soon be upon us, and I had unfinished business to tend to. Only this time, I was taking the well-earned confidence that I could play with the best in the world and the spirit of the Blues back with me to prepare for what would come in South Africa.

75′

SEATTLE HAD turned into quite the nemesis over the last year.

Not the Sounders—the city itself.

As I sat at LAX getting ready to board, I couldn't help but flash back to my last two trips to the northwest. It had been almost a year to the day since Bianca and I had that hard conversation up north. Since then, we had remained close and cordial, just not together.

A lot had changed in that year. Six months ago, I had returned to Seattle to play in the MLS Cup final against Real Salt Lake. Bruce's arrival had also brought back winning, although on that night, we ended up losing. Regulation ended in a 1–1 draw that sent us through a golden-goal overtime and finally to a shootout, where I missed a penalty that could have won it, then watched helplessly from the center circle as Real Salt Lake lifted the trophy.

We were now seconds from boarding and my mind was in two places at once. This would be my last MLS game before I departed for the final preparations for the 2010 World Cup in South Africa. For once, we had not drawn the Group of Death. Sure, we had England in our pool, but with Slovenia and Algeria also there, we felt primed to have a breakthrough tournament.

As the flight attendant was now green-lighting first-class passengers, I sauntered back to one of the younger players on the team who was standing with Todd Dunivant.

"Hey, Mikey—have fun up there."

I extended my first-class ticket to Mike Stephens, who would now be able to stretch his legs and relax in the front of the plane. This gesture triggered a ripple of excitement and joy across Mike's face as we swapped tickets.

Moments later, I followed Todd, Mike Magee, and Omar Gonzalez back into coach. Since the Bianca breakup, I'd graduated from living out of my car to locking down a place near these guys in Redondo Beach. The four of us had been spending more time as a foursome, but I remained a reluctant socializer. It was still soccer first, everything else second. This often clashed with the thinking of the affable social king Mike Magee. He was a natural extrovert with an uncanny ability for adapting to any social situation. In many ways, he and I had lived totally different lives. He was a Chicago "city kid" who was the life of the party, I was a Cali guy who preferred being alone or out in nature. He'd never had anything other than an amazing relationship with his parents, and, well, my parents could barely tolerate each other, even from afar.

Magee had joined our team as part of the Bruce rebuild, and the two of us had clashed a bit initially. He was often injured prior to joining the Galaxy, which led me to suggest he try taking better care of his body. There'd be mornings on the road where I was having my go-to breakfast—veggie omelet, no cheese, side of berries—and I'd notice Magee's plate was full of shit that weighed you down.

"Mo, you ever read *Fast Food Nation*?"

Magee, noshing on a cinnamon roll, rolled his eyes. "Here we go again."

I was serious.

"How about *The Omnivore's Dilemma*? You could be great, Mo, if you stopped eating crap and took better care of your body."

This had become a regular on-the-road conversation, although it was more like two monologues walking past each other. To Mike's credit, he mostly just wanted me to lighten up a little. I was so serious about my prehab, rehab, and other soccer habits—in my mind, there was very little time for life outside soccer. Mike was the opposite. He was easygoing and gregarious, and could often be found holding court and swapping stories in the training room. I'd regularly see him taking time and laughing with our teammates, while I rarely deviated from my routine.

This trip to Seattle ended up being considerably more pleasant than the last two, as we pummeled the Sounders in what is now known to us as the 4-0 Refund Game. It was a day game on a Saturday in front of a packed house. It was Seattle's second season in the league, and we were only five weeks into the season, but it was our third game of the week. We should have been tired but wanted to make a statement.

Twenty minutes in, Jovan Kirovski and I ran a little give-and-go and he ended up slipping one through the hands of Seattle goalie Kasey Keller. In the second half, we doubled our tally in the 52nd minute on a corner from my foot to Omar's head. It was a perfect set play, as he used a screen from Chris Klein to break free before rocketing his header. You could hear a pin drop 10 minutes later after I took a free kick that somehow skidded by a defender to Todd, who glanced it in with his head.

With that, Todd Dunivant has officially scored more goals than me so far this season—a grand total of one. It's the only time in our friendship where he's held a goal-scoring lead on me. It lasts 11 minutes: Edson puts a great ball behind the center back and I do the rest. 4-0.

When all is said and done, I was fortunate enough to contribute one goal and three assists. And the people of Seattle were fortunate enough to get their money back. We beat them so badly that the Sounders refunded all 50,000 bitter ticket holders. It cost them well over a million dollars.

Mike, Todd, and Omar were more than ready to head out on the town to relish the worst home defeat in Seattle Sounders history.

"Landon, come join us."

With the World Cup around the corner, I passed, and Magee had his own monologue to unleash on me.

"Landon, dude... it's OK to relax a little, man. We all know you are committed. But you aren't responsible for holding the entire weight of U.S. Soccer on your shoulders. If you don't lighten up a little, you're going to miss out. What's all this for if you can't enjoy it, anyway?"

I knew Magee wasn't coming at me—he only wanted me to enjoy the fruits of our success. I just wasn't in a place mentally to do so. So they went out and I went back to the hotel. I lay in bed, resting in that space between asleep and awake, thinking over the exchange and the day, like I was back on Juliet's couch.

I wanted to be let in by my teammates. I always feel like I'm just outside the inner circle, peeking in through the snow globe glass, saying, *Let me in.*

It's not a Galaxy team problem. It's an *every* team problem. Residency. Leverkusen. San Jose. The national team. It was a Team Bianca problem too.

Let me in.

When you're 17, you don't want to be a colleague. You want to be a friend. Not an acquaintance. Or a coworker. Maybe some saw me as a loner, or a prodigy. I saw myself as "left out."

Let me in.

Now I'm 26. I am friendly with my teammates, but I'm not really their friend. They're friendly with me, but they're not really my friends. We're teammates.

Let me in.

I hear Mike Magee's voice.

"Look, man. You're an amazing soccer player—probably the best we've ever produced. But if you don't lighten up, you're going to miss this. Come out with us."

All this loneliness, keeping myself apart, focused on nothing else but soccer—a child prodigy and a poster child, waiting to be let in. But to be let in, you must let others in first.

They're asking you to join them, Landon.

Let them *in.*

76'

THIS U.S. Men's National Team is a seasoned group—tried, tested, and up for the challenge that awaits in South Africa. We got the lay of the land a year earlier at the Confederations Cup, an eight-team tournament that served as South Africa's trial run for hosting the World Cup. Things didn't go well our first two games, losing to Brazil and drawing with Italy. Our third pool game was against Egypt, and we pushed like crazy and found a way to beat the Pharaohs handily. Our 3-0 victory sent us to the semifinals, where we would face the best team on the planet right now: Spain.

Spain came in on an unbelievable 35-game unbeaten streak. What they were doing was unheard of. Fortunately for us, though, we had played them in a 2008 friendly in Santander, Spain, and while we lost 1-0, it gave us confidence we could compete with them. At the Confederations Cup, we did more than just compete— we shocked the world's #1 team by taking them down 2-0, thanks to a full-team performance and goals by Jozy and Clint.

Waiting for us in the final: Brazil. In front of 50,000 fans and who knows how many people watching around the world, we started fast against the *Seleção* and held a 2-0 lead at halftime. Unfortunately, we couldn't hold on. In the second half, they scored three goals to win 3-2. It was an anticlimactic final 45 minutes and a disappointing final score, but it was, by any count, an incredible final.

This game included one of my personal favorite goals of all time: I received the ball on a counterattack shy of midfield with just me, Charlie Davies, and two Brazilian defenders sprinting down the field. I played the ball to Charlie on the left and ran past the defender marking me, and as Charlie returned it, I calmly controlled the ball with my right, cut left, and let my defender sail past me before burying it with my left. The full-field run, the control, the finish. It had everything you could want in a goal. I only wish we'd held on to win the game.

Games like that taught us something, though: When we were playing well, when the lights came on brightest, we could play with anyone. You don't beat Spain and go up 2–0 on Brazil because you aren't good. The nucleus that Bob had been nurturing for three and a half years was responsible for those performances. We were confident, and we liked each other. We were a group of guys who could be together for weeks on end without wearing on each other, and that's big when you're thrown together for 30 days on the road in a foreign country. We came into South Africa ready to show 2006 was a fluke.

Of course, when you give up a goal four minutes into your first game, you do worry if history's repeating itself. England's Steven Gerrard took a pass on the run at the top of the box and placed it past Tim Howard to put them up far too early.

I remember thinking to myself... *Here we go again.*

In 2006, our slow start was the stuff of nightmares—we'd given up a goal five minutes into our first game against the Czech Republic and here we were mirroring that most unwanted moment. That game had spun horribly out of control as we sleepwalked through it. We'd had four years to stew over that terrible opener. Could we respond better here?

In the 40th minute, we answer the question thanks to a bit of luck: Clint gets the ball about 35 yards out, makes a sharp series of spins to carry it to about 25 yards, and delivers a low, sharp left-footer at Robert Green, England's keeper. What should be a routine save turns into their horror and our great joy—the ball somehow rolls through Green's hands and straight across the goal line. And with that, it is a whole new game come halftime.

We each get our chances to go up in the second half. Tim Howard turns away solid opportunities from Emile Heskey and Shaun Wright-Phillips, and Green makes up for his misplay with a beautiful save on a Jozy Altidore shot that looks set to give us a lead. When the final whistle blows, we remain knotted at 1 and are set up for our second match against a Slovenia side we should handle.

Which makes it all the worse when we find ourselves 45 minutes from catastrophe—somehow down 2–0 at half to the smallest nation in the tournament.

We walk into our locker room, and there are no heads drooped low. No pessimistic banter. Like I said, this is a battle-tested bunch, and we aren't going down without a fight. We know we need to empty the tank now or risk flaming out. No one feels like we're going down to these guys. We've been here before; we believe we can fight back. Bob barks at us: "No way. We're not fucking going down, men. Let's go!"

Bob makes two tweaks at halftime: Maurice Edu is on for Jose Torres and Benny Feilhaber is on for Robbie Findley. We're not strangers to being behind in games, and we start the half aggressively. Two minutes in, Steve Cherundolo plays a long ball down the right side that surprisingly sneaks past Slovenia's left fullback. I run it down and find myself open in space, just outside the penalty area. It is eerily similar terrain to where I hesitated four years ago against Ghana.

Today, there is no hesitation as there's nothing between me and our first goal but 30 yards of green, a rapidly closing center back, and a keeper. I dart straight towards the goal from this slightly odd angle. I'm now a quarterback going through my progressions, both computing the different possibilities and reacting in real time.

Ninety-nine percent of the time the play is to summon the goalie off his line, then roll the ball into the center of the box.

Look to cross: Is there already someone there? No.

Another touch towards the goal.

Is anyone showing up across the goal mouth for a pass? No.

Another touch towards the goal.

Top of the box: Is someone arriving? No.

I'm still going full speed towards the keeper with no stop in sight and am now just eight yards away from him. And the option now is to just...

Shoot it as hard as you can at his face.

These are the words of LA goalie Brian Rowe. I had seen this exact scenario just five months earlier, in preseason with the Galaxy, with Rowe in goal. I had worked my muscle memory on this angle at his suggestion—he'd said this was a brutally tough spot for keepers to get their hands up—and roofed a goal by hitting it directly at his head, just like Rowe said I should.

Knowing what to do and executing it down 2-0 in the World Cup are two different things. Four years ago, against Ghana, I wouldn't have made this decision. I would have tried to roll the ball across the goal. But here? Odd angle. Three yards out. Just me and Slovenia's keeper. Do what I did in preseason: Shoot it as hard as you can at his face.

Keeper Samir Handanovic stands up from his crouch, more reacting to almost getting fully beaned than to stop the ball, and I have roofed it in the net near post. Hope returns—five minutes into the second half, we have cut the lead in half.

No way. We're not fucking going down, men. Let's go!

Thirty minutes later, we're still looking, when I find myself in almost the same place Cherundolo had when he'd sent his long ball down the line to me. This time, I clip a ball to Jozy at the top of the box. He goes up for it and heads it forward and into space for a streaking, freed-up Michael Bradley to run under. It takes one bounce... then another... and as it is coming up off the second bounce, a sprinting, sliding, toe-poking Bradley gets his toe on the ball and sends it high over the goalie's hands before dipping underneath the crossbar.

2–2!

Pandemonium ensues!

With momentum acting like our 12th man, we continue pressing forward, hoping for a winner we just feel will come. And when we earn a free kick outside the box, it feels like it is about to happen.

The fans are going nuts. Slovenia is on their heels, barely holding on. Our men in blue are lined up inside the box, jostling for position. I set up and send the cross in from the right, and Maurice Edu streaks clean past everyone to volley home the winner!

Bedlam!

3–2 *America!*

Edu is a hero!

I'm sprinting to leap on Maurice when we hear the whistle.

The referee is pointing as if there was a foul on the play. The goal that was a goal is now not a goal. Disallowed. Maurice Edu and Michael Bradley are steaming. No one can figure out what's just happened or why, and we're angry, but the call has been made and we're still stalemated at two.

I was on the corner away from the call, so I hustle back and assume the foul was a foul. I don't know what's happened, and it doesn't matter anyway—the call's been made. It wouldn't be until later that we'd look at the tape and see what the world had seen— that there was no foul whatsoever. If anything, a Slovenian defender had *his* arms wrapped around Bradley, keeping him from making a play. It's beyond frustrating to put so much into something and have it taken away with one bad call.

But the game's final moment fades away, the final whistle sounds and we have at least closed the gap on Slovenia. We have two draws to show for our two games. And while we should be in first with our disallowed goal—and a 3-2 win—we're instead sitting in third place in Group C with one game to go. We still like our chances to get through, as we approach a winnable—but now *must-win*—final group play game against Algeria.

87'

MAURICE EDU'S penalty kick goal will not be taken away. It is there for all to see, for the rest of time, residing in the score book on this historic, record-breaking day. No whistle will erase this one from history.

Maurice had stepped up to the stripe at the Home Depot Center and hammered home a penalty kick in the 86th minute to shatter the shutout for my Galaxy team. Just a few days earlier, the two of us had been teammates in camp up at Stanford, but Jurgen cut us both from his World Cup roster. So instead of being on our way to Brazil, we were competitors at the tail end of a 4–1 Galaxy victory over the Philadelphia Union in Los Angeles in front of an adoring Saturday crowd that included Mom, Tris, Rich, Randee, and Adam.

And while I would have much preferred to be playing World Cup tune-ups, I had experienced one of the most emotional moments of my Galaxy career just 38 minutes before Maurice marred our clean sheet.

I wasn't looking to score. I'd played a ball through to Robbie Keane. While Robbie's probably played with 50 guys like me in Europe, I've never played with anyone else who could see the field in such an advanced way as Robbie does. His vision and instinct are perfectly on display here, as Robbie brilliantly returns the favor with a pass across the goal to my feet just inside the mouth of the goal. My right foot taps it into the open net.

It is my 135th MLS goal. With it, I have become the all-time leading scorer in league history.

When that ball goes in, I have forgotten for a moment that it means I have broken Jeff Cunningham's record. All I know is that I am finally at the end of an awful 72 hours that started with me being cut from the World Cup team. As I peel away from the goal, I drop to my knees, throw my head back and scream, one massive release of all the toxic crap and shitty feelings mixed with the joy and exhilaration of scoring a milestone goal. The fans are roaring, and all I want now is to stop time for a second and soak it all in. As I come to, I see Robbie coming at me—the first to lift me up in an embrace—and then all my teammates join in.

The fans are going crazy and I'm so happy to be doing this right here in Los Angeles. The crowd feels like my family. Some of them are. It is an amazing swirl of emotions.

I add goal #136 in the 80th minute. Once again, it's Robbie who finds me front and center inside the box; this time, it is my left foot that does the rest.

Does it feel good?

Fuck yes.

Where the first celebration was more an exorcism of the last week, this one I can just enjoy. An emotional "you'll always relish this" moment, breaking the all-time MLS record on a Saturday afternoon in front of my beloved home fans.

When Maurice makes his PK to add the final number to that 4–1 score, I'm thinking about how three days ago, neither of us were supposed to be here. And then I'm thinking about that phantom call four years ago, the one that took away his game winner that would have put us atop Group C. How history would be different if Maurice was the hero of that game—as he should have been. We'd have entered that third group game against Algeria needing only a draw.

With no points from their first two games, the Algerians would have been already eliminated, playing only for national pride. I'm sure Bob would have started most of our same players, but our strategy would have certainly been different. Playing not to lose instead of pressing to win is a different game.

If Maurice's goal had held up against Slovenia, he might have come out of 2010 as the new face of U.S. Soccer. Scoring on a stage like that has a way of lifting you up. That moment should have been one of the greatest moments of his life—the goal that sent us through. Instead, we came in needing a win against Algeria. Instead, we faced a scoreless draw 90 minutes in, heading into extra time still desperately needing one goal to keep our hopes alive, and with almost no time left in which to do it. Instead, we had one of the greatest moments of *my* life—a moment that probably wouldn't have happened if Maurice got what was rightfully his.

At the end of this game in Los Angeles, Maurice and I connect on the pitch at midfield and commiserate over the opportunity taken away from us. Both of us wish we were somewhere else. We're both coping with being on the wrong side of someone else's subjective decision and the emotions that come with it. But both of us are here, playing for our club teams. The decision is out of our hands; the show must go on.

I take in the cheering from the stands and the fans' immense swell of support. For so many reasons, I will never forget this night.

Rich was right.

It feels good to get back on the field.

78'

I'VE NEVER *really* had an off button for soccer. And since I was 15 years old, I've never truly experienced an off-season. If I wasn't playing for my club team, I was proudly playing for America. If it wasn't a qualifier, friendly, or World Cup, it was the Olympics, the Pan American Games, or a Youth World Championship. If I wasn't suiting up in front of our American Outlaws, then I was on loan competing against the best players in Europe.

For the last 13 years, I've never had more than six weeks hiatus after any given season. Never had a true break for my game to fall out of shape. Never had an opportunity to look for the off button. But as we headed back to the locker rooms at Loftus Versfeld in Pretoria after narrowly escaping a 0–0 tie that would have seen us torn apart by the American media, I was ready to turn it off for one hell of a celebration.

For 90 minutes of a 90-minute game, 35,000 World Cup fanatics were treated to a combined zero goals as we attacked Algeria and they, largely, defended. And if it was frustrating to us to be stuck scoreless, at least it was about as entertaining as a 0–0 game can be, with near misses, clanged posts, and one questionable off-side call that waved off a would-be goal by Clint Dempsey.

For 90 minutes, the 2010 World Cup was poised to end no differently for America than 2006 had. A better show in the standings, but with us going just as far: three games and home.

Four minutes of stoppage time are added on after the 90. Algeria is on the attack—and every player on our team knows what's at stake, as well as their role. This leaves us light in the back because we need a goal or there's no tomorrow for us in South Africa. Jay DeMerit, Carlos Bocanegra, and DaMarcus do the best they can to defend the Algerian attack, but a ball comes clean across from out wide into the box. We're lucky their header from 12 yards out ends up in Howard's hands. And as he gathers it and immediately starts the break with a throw downfield in the 91st minute, those fans— the American ones anyway—are about to get their money's worth.

You can't possibly know which moment is the moment that leads to *the* moment. The half-field toss leaves Timmy's hands and I'm running under it with space—all those Algerians crashing our net have left gaps of open space behind them—and I've got Jozy, Clint, and Edson Buddle spread out right to left ahead of me, all running full speed towards the net. As I pass the ball forward and right ahead of Jozy, I'm surely not thinking, *Follow this and score.* I'm not thinking much outside of handing the keys to my body over to my intuition, allowing it to overtake all of me as it has done so many times before.

Jozy pulls one of the two defenders to him and taps it on to Clint, and now the keeper's closing in on him. Four potential scenarios flood my mind at the same time, and it's like visualizing four different futures concurrently, each with a different outcome.

Clint takes Jozy's cross, pounces on it, and scores himself. Redemption for the man who almost already won this thing on a called-back goal and another hit post.

Or Clint's shot redirects off the goalie and trickles out for a corner. We run to take the corner and try to keep our hopes alive.

Or the horror movie version, where Algeria's Rais M'Bolhi doesn't just charge and tap the ball but grabs it, smothering it with his body to kill the opportunity, which almost certainly would kill the game.

And with these three outcomes playing out at once in an overlay, I recognize in my mind where I need to be as an insurance policy for a fourth possible scenario. The tear-jerking, made-for-TV version where M'Bolhi dives and barely gets his hands on Dempsey's attempt, and the ball, somehow, miraculously, rolls its way back towards where I'm trailing the play. If these are the four scenarios, then there's a 25 percent chance the play will unfold the way it does. And thank god I'm bulldozing into the box towards that outcome, because as fate—or luck—would have it, the rebound arrives at my feet, and it will not stay there for long.

Hello, dear friend.

Four years of frustration, weight, and waiting about to be smashed into the net.

For a moment, it's as if I can hear Joshie asking me, *What's your dream in life? What do you want to accomplish?* And I answer the voice as emphatically as I can, kissing that ball back the direction I received it from, towards the gorgeous openness of the net.

This is my dream. This *is what I want to accomplish.*

Before the ball has stopped spinning at the back of the net, I am turning down the endline towards the corner flag—I know the next 30 seconds are about to unlock all the feelings I've been bottling inside my entire life. When I first lock eyes with Stu Holden, who is euphorically sprinting down the sideline with the full bench barreling towards me, I perform a perfect headfirst dive that soon leaves me on the bottom of an exuberant pile of teammates, a tidal wave of relief and joy crashing down upon me in the form of damn near everyone. Mass celebration is always a great idea in theory, yet less so in practice when you're the 5′8″, 160-pound guy now residing at the bottom of the dogpile.

Moments later, with the ball at my feet, the final whistle blows. I boot it high into the stands along with whatever residual anxiety I've been holding onto since the World Cup in Germany. I wish I had the type of personality where games like these didn't affect me, but I don't—my play in 2006 and the negative media around it had stayed with me. It was like walking around for four years with a 50-pound rock in my pocket. When the final whistle blows on Algeria—just a minute after the ball leaves Tim's hands, to my feet, to Jozy's cross, to Clint's shot, to my goal that helps send us through—that weight all drops away.

The USA has won Group C. Eight years later, America is advancing and back in the final 16.

I'm hugging everyone—Dempsey, Jozy, Beas, Bob—when Michael Kammarman bolts over with his own celebratory leap. Michael is the head of communications for U.S. Soccer, and he's always been my kind of guy. He's a carryover from the Bruce days; he'd have been in that human pileup near the corner flag a few minutes earlier if he was allowed on the field. But he is now reminding me that the media is waiting for me, so off I go through "the Zone" to face the world.

How do you find the right words when you've just avoided elimination, then put your country through to the elimination rounds with a goal in the waning seconds of a do-or-die match?

I'd dreamed of going to the World Cup since I was six. Of having that Air Jordan moment where you hit the game-winning shot. The difference in soccer is that moment only comes around every four years and you're lucky if you even get the opportunity to take a shot. But here I was, somehow on the other side of that moment. After all the hours and preparation. The prehab, the rehab, the running and travel and sacrifices. Getting back up after being knocked down by foreign opponents and domestic media four years ago. Here I was, in an interview of a lifetime with over 7 million people tuning in on ESPN back home and many more around the world.

Tears in my eyes, I went with my heart and sprinkled in a dash of what I needed to get off my mind.

"I've been on a long journey for four years. And I'm shocked. And so proud of our guys. It's unbelievable. People who know me

closest know how hard I worked for this moment. This is unbelievable. I know the people back home are watching. We're not done
yet. Thank you, guys."

Shirts are off. Music blasting compliments of DJ Stu Holden. Beers
popping.

My eyes adjust to the energy in the room, and I can't believe
how many people are in there. FIFA is usually a stickler for access,
but here is a full-fledged VIP function in progress. To my right is...
Reggie Bush? In South Africa? He's talking it up with Tim Howard
and a few others. On the other side of the room, Jay DeMerit has
his arm around former president Bill Clinton.

Secret Service agents are scattered around the locker-room
perimeter. We always have security, but this is an entirely different
level. They seem OK with Jay's invasion of the president's personal space—Jay is holding both Bill Clinton and court as if *he's* the
president. He holds up a Budweiser in the hand that's not around
Clinton and shouts, "This is the greatest victory of all time, and this
is the greatest moment of my life!"

Sunil—who isn't too far away—interrupts him:

"Jay, you just told me that qualifying for the second round was
the greatest moment of your life."

Without missing a beat, Jay snipes back, "That *was* the greatest
moment of my life. Now *this is* the greatest moment of my life. Mr.
President... it would be an honor if you shared a beer with us."

Without missing a beat, Bill Clinton slides off his blazer, rolls
up the cuffs of his button-down, and everyone inside our dressing
room goes bananas. You know how people talk about wanting a
president you can grab a beer with? Well, here we are doing that—a
private, celebratory beer with the former president of the United
States. I bet it's nice for him to have a moment away from the media
to just relax as one of the guys; that's how we feel too. Right now,
President Clinton is just another proud American in the room. He

approaches me with a handful of the U.S. soccer brass, shines a charismatic smile, and says, "That was such a great goal, Landon."

"Thank you, Mr. President."

At some point, *he* asks *me* if he can get a picture. When the president wants to get his picture with you, you say yes. I find myself in the middle of five suits, still wearing my game jersey (one that I was not trading away on this day or ever). I'm handed an American flag, and suddenly I'm surrounded by President Clinton, Sunil, MLS president Don Garber, Clinton's right-hand man Doug Band, and future president of U.S. Soccer Carlos Cordeiro, all right by my locker.

At the hotel, Bob surprises us with our families. We haven't seen much of our loved ones in South Africa. From our point of view, we've been in the thick of a highly focused business trip. But here, waiting for us as our bus pulls up, is everyone—for me, it's the rarest of nights where Mom, Paul, Tris, and Dad are all here together. I can't even think of many pinch-me scenarios where both my parents were in the same place at the same time with the same respectable demeanor. To the victors go the spoils. Bottles of champagne are passed around the lobby until the wee hours. It's an incredible night.

Back in my room, I'm fried and left alone with my thoughts, but they are unsurprisingly easy tonight. I don't check the internet, my phone, or the news; I just begin fading away into dreamland, thinking about this special group of guys who have been in almost every camp together. The feeling of being *united* in something. The sense of not letting down the guy next to you, of wanting so desperately to perform, for everybody watching, and for ourselves. It feels incredible. It feels like maybe, finally, we're putting U.S. Soccer on the global map—doing something bigger than anyone expected.

I open my eyes the next morning and wonder: *Did all that really happen? That wasn't just some wild visualization, right?* But I don't need to see the press reports to confirm what is fully seared into my brain.

Anyway, we're so far away from America that it's not until after breakfast that news from the USA starts trickling in.

I go to do Kammarman's show on the USMNT Facebook page (Studio 90) later that day, and when I get there, he tees up a YouTube video and asks me, "Landon... did you see this yet?"

He hits Play. Now I'm the spectator, watching packed bars of people on the edges of their seats, sipping pints and cheering us on. We roll through their emotions, feeling what they're feeling. From fear to tension to, at last, that jolt of magic in the dying moments of the 94th minute... While I don't see the goal or even a TV, I stare at what comes next from their jubilation. Fans go wild in a bar in Lincoln, Nebraska. U.S. Soccer jerseys bounce in a packed pavilion outdoors in Kansas City, Missouri. Strangers hug strangers in New York City. Beer-spilling Americans celebrate in Springfield, Missouri.

It's five minutes of fans strung together from different cities across America, all taking in the Algeria goal, all set to the *Rudy* soundtrack. Proud *USA! USA! USA!* chants in Covington, Kentucky, and Tucson, Arizona. Hugs, high-fives, and hand pounds in a Las Vegas Sportsbook at seven in the morning. Americans on the same team in California, Kentucky, New York, and South Africa.

It is beyond gratifying. You can see what it meant to people back home—a firsthand view of our World Cup win bringing joy to so many Americans. I didn't realize that my corner-slide dogpile included another 100 million Americans on top. For all the talk of red states and blue states, all I see in that video is people united from the Red, White, and Blue, all of whom had woken up early to pack in bars and take in the tension of our World Cup match as one nation.

I sit there with a big grin on my face. I had no idea the impact that moment had had on America.

I ask Kammarman to play the five-minute clip again. Even the second time through... *chills*. I look and it's already accumulated one million views. A million views for men's soccer in the U.S.? I feel like I'm watching a transformational shift in real time.

I power on my cell phone to an endless barrage of texts. Hundreds—*thousands*—of congratulatory, incoming messages. Coach Ellinger and Coach Hafley. Joshie and Adam. Rich and Randee. Magee, Dunivant, and Omar. Everyone. One thing is for certain—last night definitely happened.

And with that, my mind flips to our Round of 16 opponent. By winning our group, we've avoided facing the winner of Group D: Germany. Instead, we'll get the second-place finisher from Group D: Ghana. *Why do we always seem to get Ghana or Germany?*

No matter. With this team, we are confident we can do what needs to be done in the next round. Ghana is waiting for us and they're a good team.

And in three days' time, we have the chance to book a ticket to the quarterfinals. And when we take the pitch in Royal Bafokeng Stadium in Rustenburg, we won't be taking the pitch as 11. For the first time since I can remember, soccer's gone mainstream. We'll be walking out there with the full support of America behind us.

88′

————

GERMANY'S WORLD-CLASS keeper Manuel Neuer is not a small man. It's been 12 years since I peppered his predecessor with an arsenal of shots on the global stage and had him turn them away in every direction. I promised myself if my moment came today, I'd deliver for America.

We're trailing 0-1. I enter the match as a "super-sub," and it doesn't take long for us to click. Twenty minutes into the second half, we are now even with the Germans.

Five minutes later, I'm running behind the German backline with a defender glued to my hip. I'd experienced this same tactic for the first time 17 years ago at Leverkusen. Today, the weathered version of me is unaffected, and I tuck away the game winner on a field full of World Cup elites.

I'd spent countless hours visualizing myself scoring against Neuer in the summer of 2014. I just thought it was going to happen at the World Cup in Brazil, not at an MLS All-Star Game in Portland, Oregon. There is nothing I can do here to take away Neuer's World Cup victory—he's earned that feat—but I could still do something to help lift my 2014 MLS All-Stars over his Bayern Munich side.

The goal is initiated by Diego Valeri, playing on the right. I've seen some version of this Beckhamesque 50-yard ball a hundred times before now… most frequently courtesy of David's feathery touch. This one balloons from right midfield, then arcs beautifully to just inside the top of the box. I bring it down with my chest and, even with pressure on my back from two defenders and Neuer charging, settle the ball with my right foot before surgically slotting it home with the same foot.

It's a mic drop moment and instigates this super-sub now getting subbed himself. I soak in the ovation from the packed stands. As I walk to the bench, sharing love back to the fans, I'd be lying if I didn't think for a flash that this was how a manager could have used me last month in Brazil.

It's the last summer classic I would ever play, and I walk away MVP of the game. Final score: MLS All-Stars: 2–Bayern Munich: 1.

It's not the World Cup—it's not really even Germany, just their best club side—but it's still nice to get one on *some* Germans… even if it's a German team I actually mostly enjoyed playing for. Is this the moment I had yearned to deliver? No. I have put that life behind me. I no longer feel the need to prove to Leverkusen or Germany that they made any kind of mistake. If anything, they had their regimented way of doing things and I had my own—the two just didn't mesh.

As for now, I am content that my 14th consecutive all-star game is going to be my last. Tomorrow morning I'll let the world know what only Rich and I currently know is coming: I will retire from professional soccer at the end of this season.

The next day at a press conference in Los Angeles, my announcement catches the press off guard, but I feel fully at peace. It is only Bruce who catches me off guard by getting emotional and shedding a tear when I break the news.

In so many ways, Bruce has been like a father to me. I'd like to think I have also been like a son to him. We've been through so much together—he brought me to the national team, and then I helped bring him to Los Angeles. And while the end may be in sight, the two of us are not done yet. I've won five MLS Championships—same as Agoos. I've made good on catching my former captain; I can still make good on passing him. I've got one last opportunity to try.

79′

———

IT'S EASY to navigate the media zone when you win. But when you leave your guts on the field only to receive a Ghana sucker punch in extra time that sends you packing from the knockout rounds, getting thrown to the cameras by Kammarman is a true test of character. One of the mandates after World Cup games, win or lose, is flash interviews straight after the match. It comes with the job, even when I'm hurting and devastated.

In theory, we have no reason to hang our heads. But when you dream for more, sharing your tattered soul in a composed manner with 19 million Americans minutes after a Ghanese team put an end to your tournament is hard work. When you give up yet another absurdly early goal, then claw your way back to tie it up only to have it all snatched away in overtime by one fantastic individual play—it hurts. There's no shame in being knocked out 2-1 by a good Ghana side. It doesn't make it any easier to swallow the pain in the moment, though.

It isn't until I'm back in America that I learn our heartbreaker was the most watched men's soccer game in American television history. You've come a long way, USA.

We land back in the States 21 hours after taking off from South Africa, and new text messages land too. There's one from Ellinger congratulating me. Another from Frank Yallop doing the same. In the sea of new text chains there's also a fresh thread from my Galaxy teammates Mike Magee, Todd Dunivant, and Omar Gonzalez. I scroll through their exchange, and relive the soccer parts of South Africa through their running commentary.

I follow along, smiling, and keep coming back to three little words:

Let them in.

Only now it is followed by an idea. A single, spur-of-the-moment weekend word that even I am surprised I thought of. I need to blow off some serious pent-up steam. Thirteen years of it. And I've suddenly got an idea that is so *not me*, I don't even know if I should throw it out there.

Don't overthink it, Landon.

So I don't: I thumb out a one-word response and stare at it for a moment on my phone, just to be sure I'm really ready to put this in motion. And then I fire it off to the squad:

Vegas?

I don't know why it popped out.

I don't know how it popped out.

But now it was out there.

Magee pounces like the goal scorer he is. Within seconds, he chimes back: Vegas! Yesssssssssss!

Then Omar: VEEEEEEEGAS. Fuck Yesssssss!

And finally, Todd: VEGAS? Fuck You Guys.

Bruce has granted me a little rest after South Africa. Magee is currently banged up from an injury that's kept him from traveling to road games. Omar is suspended and missing the next game on account of yellow card accumulation. Only Todd has an obligation to head to the sauna of New England's stadium for a July summer soiree.

The goal was to take some of Magee's advice to heart. He'd been trying to get me out for a drink and some off-the-pitch fun for two years. What better way to overachieve than to suggest a two-day trip to Las Vegas?

Magee, of course, had a guy in Vegas. I should have known—he seems to have one in every city. As our Chief Fun Officer, we learn Magee has a buddy who works at Aria and takes care of guys like us. By the time we're wheels-down in Vegas, a limo is waiting.

We arrive at Aria, and it's the first time I truly experience the impact the Algeria goal had in America. I've not really been out in public yet, but here I am in gamble city and it's like a snowball of recognition rolling downhill. First there's people pointing. Then some catcalls. Then someone booming out, "Landon Donovan! USA! USA!" Then another. And next thing you know, we can't go 10 feet without getting mobbed. It becomes the theme of our next 48 hours. The young, old, clothed, and practically naked stopping us for a high-five, a picture, or an autograph of a shirt, hat, betting ticket, body part . . .

The first night, we enjoy a table tucked away from the madness at Social House for sushi. I usually shy away from this kind of attention, but living in the pressure-free moments of this trip and taking it all in through the eyes of the guys, I let it go and enjoy the acknowledgement.

The subject turns to soccer, Algeria specifically. Magee tells me, "I watched by myself and was losing my shit. I'm so fucking happy for you—one of the coolest things I've ever seen." Omar is 22 and in Vegas game-shape—he's conquering a Sapporo that looks as tall as he is.

We follow up sushi with a wild night at Haze in the Aria hotel before jumping over to the late-night scene at Drai's. Thirty minutes in, our table has become everyone's table. While it's epic to be hugging total strangers, the club decides it's best to get us out of direct sight and moves us upstairs away from the swarm. We find ourselves now at a closed-off table with Victor Drai himself, his business partner Michael Gruber, and the as-cool-as-advertised Mark Cuban. After a round of pleasantries and more vodka sodas, I take in what looks like 20,000 people raving below us.

Now, I'm a good teammate—I try never to miss a Galaxy game—but we've been a bit occupied this evening. So when I pull out my phone to check the score, it is a bit of a surprise to learn that the last-place Revolution has not only beaten us 2–0 but has snapped a 347-minute scoreless streak against Todd and our defense. I shout the news to Omar and Magee.

"They fucking lost tonight."

Magee holds up his phone.

"Well, we're winning tonight... I'll let Todd know."

Magee snaps a picture of me then shows me the text: Hey remember when we all went to Vegas and made it rain with 20,000 people while you were playing in front of 200—pretty much the same thing.

Three of us are texting one another from one foot away, and I realize there are now officially two different Landon Donovans: Landon BA (Landon Before Algeria) and Landon AA (Landon After Algeria).

Landon BA was always locked in because of soccer but also pretty locked up. There was always a lot of pressure that went with being that guy. Landon AA is taking in a party that even Dennis Rodman could appreciate. Landon AA has had the weight of the soccer world lifted from his shoulders. I'm pointing to people below who are waving back up at me—allowing myself to be open to things, to be more than just a soccer player.

Of course, Chief Fun Officer Magee makes sure we aren't at this table solo. A bachelorette party of 12 shows up in the club below, and before I know what Magee's done, a solid handful of them have become part of our table upstairs, including the incredibly beautiful bride-to-be. And as only the universe could manifest, I notice that the 12th and last to join our party is just as gorgeous as the sash-wearer herself.

And how could I make such a statement so confidently?

Because they are twins.

Of course they're twins.

As the night goes on, I'm talking it up with these twins while Omar, Gruber, Magee, and Cuban are multitasking, talking to our new friends while whispering to each other and watching me interact with my new friends. Everyone is hoping to partake in the afterparty after the afterparty. A few of us don't make it back to the room until four in the morning.

The next day is more of the same, only we start off considerably more beat up from day one.

We are welcomed to the pool at Liquid to chants of *USA! USA! USA!* from the afternoon crew of midday pool partiers. Sunglasses are my savior today, but this does not suck. We power through the hangovers with the help of bottle service, toggling back and forth between our cabana and the daybed.

Omar is passed out on the daybed, and Magee's reminiscing about the events of the day before. "I've been out with David before. But I've never seen anything like last night. People were hounding you like you were Justin Bieber."

I laugh. "I'm sure that's how it is for David in England."

I then realize the DJ is flagging me to join him up in his booth. Apparently, this is the new normal for me here.

Hey, Liquid! Guess what?! Landon Donovan is in the house! USA! USA! USA!

It feels like the entire place stops and turns, and now the pool crowd is joining in. *USA! USA! USA!* we all chant in unison. It's happiness in every direction for a full 48 hours. Like most soirees in Vegas, things get a little foggy near the end, but as we limp out of Nevada, one thing all three of us know for sure is that it was a legendary, once-in-a-lifetime weekend.

We get back to Los Angeles and immediately rally for a Kings of Leon concert, which Todd—now also back in L.A.—can join us for. We're recovering from Vegas, and he's recovering from missing it, not like he wasn't following our every move in the barrage of text messages documenting the weekend in real time.

Omar has somehow never heard of Kings of Leon, but he gets up to speed quickly when they invite us to join them backstage before their set. Turns out they're huge soccer fans. We're chatting, and they're in their element backstage waiting to go on.

We're having a totally relaxed conversation when Nathan Followill, the drummer, calmly tells us... "We're on in two minutes, but come hang after the show."

One grabs a water. Another, a guitar.

Seconds later, the lights go bright and they're on.

80'

THE THREE nonstop days of fun would spark three epic years of friendship. Todd, Omar, Mike, and I made a unique crew. Todd was the reliable one with the Stanford degree, Mike the extroverted social chair, Omar the happy-go-lucky rookie who was taking it all in. And then there was the newer, relaxed version of me that Juliet liked to call the Reluctant Superstar.

I was so focused on soccer as my all-important, all-consuming job before Algeria. I put so much stress and pressure on myself to perform and live up to the responsibilities and expectations. It was an unnecessary, heavy burden I didn't have to put on myself. I look back at those years, and I wish I could have enjoyed it all and appreciated it more in the moment. Algeria and Juliet and these guys made me realize that soccer didn't require that I carry that weight, and certainly not alone. I owe these guys for that. And with them, I was going to make up for lost time.

That Vegas blowout aside, we all preferred the low-key beach life. After that weekend, we'd spend endless carefree nights after games at the two-floor dive bar Beaches near the Manhattan Beach pier. We'd take over the downstairs while Trish, the bartender, dished out drinks. On the road, we'd almost always grab dinner together, talking sports, life, or anything else that caught our attention. We were all there the night Todd met his now-wife, Caroline, on a road trip in Chicago. The assist for that one goes to Omar... or really to Omar's wife, Erica, who had brought her friend—the future Mrs. Dunivant—with her that evening.

I eased up a little on my monk-like training and started joining the guys for their day-after-the-game, day-off "rehab," which was anything but. Landon AA finally gave into curiosity and let himself play around a little. A moment in time where I could finally enjoy some of the fruits of my success. It was good practice for letting other people in, and if nothing else, I now had a few stories of my own to share with my teammates on recovery days.

But the best part was that for the first time in my career, not only did I feel like a reliable teammate, but I felt like a reliable friend. I discovered that I could have fun off the field and still dominate on it. It even helped make the game a game again.

It wasn't all smooth sailing. After a good season in 2010, the Galaxy got bulldozed in the playoffs, but we all felt like we were building in the right direction and were primed to make a run in 2011. Or, as Mike, Todd, Omar, and I like to call it: the Year of Louis XIII.

It was late at night after our second home game of the season, and we'd pitched a 1-0 shutout against Philadelphia. We were at Magee's place, and he pulled out a bottle of Louis XIII cognac that his father had shipped him—it's $2,000 per bottle, and there was about an inch left. We decided to split it among the four of us and have a toast when Omar had an idea:

"Hey... what if we all chip in and buy a bottle of this? Every home game we win— no matter what we have going on that night—we come here first and take a victory shot."

Any idea sounds good when you're drinking that kind of booze, so we all sign on. It's a deal.

This pact would be a good thing. As the high of the 2010 World Cup was waning, I was yearning to get the Galaxy going. We'd been competitive since Bruce had taken over—we'd made it to one final and lost and been back in the playoffs last year—but it had been a while since we'd won it all. Bruce and Chris Klein, who was now president, had put together a formidable team, and this little side tradition seemed like an ideal way to keep a team within the team focused, rewarded, and inspired.

The next home game, I scored twice in a 3-0 win against Portland. We stayed true to the pact: The bottle is for wins only. Back to Magee's we went to hit the bottle.

And in 2011, there were a lot of wins. From March through November, we scored goals, kept clean sheets, and most of all, collected lots of wins. We didn't drop a single game at home. We barely dropped one on the road: From April to August, we lost only a single game in 20. There were many nights when the final whistle signified the start of a celebratory double header… the second game kicking off at Magee's and carrying on to a second half at Beaches.

Was it that Louis XIII bottle? Was it the fact that Bruce had finally pulled together a roster capable of playing up to his expectations? Was it that David and I had moved past the issues we'd had his first two years and were getting along on and off the pitch? Was it that Todd had settled down with a family and I had found World Cup solace? Maybe it was a little bit of all of that. Whatever it was, add it all up and we came out the other side back in the finals.

We win the Supporters' Shield, awarded to the team that has the most points on the year. It's a perfectly fine honor, but what we truly desire is the MLS Cup. On November 20, we have our chance. Playing against Houston in front of a record crowd of 30,000 fans, we know this is not only a home game but a Louis XIII game. We control the majority of the final with ample opportunities to take the lead in the first half but can't find the breakthrough. It's more of the same to start the second half, as Robbie Keane strikes a shot inches wide of the far post. We should be up 3-0. But we remain deadlocked and scoreless.

Then in the 72nd minute, it all comes together. Beckham receives a ball from our backline and flicks it on with his head to

Keane. Keane slips a pass into daylight. I run onto it in the box and make the most of my first touch: a right-foot poke that Houston's keeper gets a hand on, but not enough to keep it from finding its way into the side of the net. The Galaxy's big three combine to put us up in the most important game of our Galaxy careers, what we have all come here to do.

The place erupts, and I do too.

When the final whistle blows 20 minutes later, I jump into David Beckham's arms to celebrate our 1-0 championship victory. We have been through so much together. For years we struggled to get it done. Finally, at long last, everything we have worked for has paid off.

It is my fourth MLS Championship.

The following year, we defend our cup, defeating Houston again, this time 3-1. Repeating as winners in 2012 is the perfect way to send David off in style. We've been teammates for five years now. He leaves as a two-time MLS champion. He is one of the best I've ever played with, and I'm honored to have been his teammate. David will go on to play a few months for Paris Saint-Germain, but this is effectively his final ride. He came to America to help raise the profile of the game here and to win championships. He's done that, and no one can ever take that away from him. With our repeat, I notch my fifth MLS Championship, tying my old friend Jeff Agoos as the all-time MLS Cup leader.

As much as I want to break his record, I can feel that now familiar pull to do something else. I'm six months past my 30th birthday. From the time I earned my first contract to now, I've never really had a break. There are weeks where soccer no longer feels like freedom; it feels like a chore. When I'm sleeping in a random road hotel for the fourth time in a week. Or having another dinner interrupted by a request to sign an autograph. Or going an entire month without seeing someone I care about who isn't on my team.

It was a decade of being tugged and pulled and told where to be at what time for what game ... or what flight ... or what practice ... or what training session.

For half my life I've been on someone else's schedule. Coaches dictating my time. Team executives telling me when my car is picking me up. Publicists telling me when the photoshoot is. U.S. Soccer telling me where to show up for an interview. For 15 years, every move I've made has been because someone told me what to do, where to go, and when to be there.

I've won five MLS Championships.

I've played in three World Cups.

I've gone overseas and conquered demons.

What do I have left to prove in soccer?

I am happy with my career. But I am also tired, and bruised, and more than a little burnt out. And I am severely depressed.

I've been wanting to do it for years now.

Perhaps it's time I finally took some time.

Ahead of the 2010 World Cup, my third—
I scored three goals in four games but the
loss to Ghana in the round of 16 really hurt

FACING PAGE, TOP: After scoring the extra-time winner against Algeria in 2010, my greatest World Cup and USMNT moment
Kevork Djansezian, Getty Images courtesy U.S. Soccer

FACING PAGE, BOTTOM: Playing for Everton in 2010, leaving Manchester United's Darren Fletcher and Gary Neville in my wake

Celebrating with the Galaxy in 2011: winning the MLS Cup (ABOVE) and the Western Conference (LEFT)
courtesy the LA Galaxy

ABOVE: With David Beckham at the White House to celebrate the Galaxy's 2011 MLS Cup with President Barack Obama
courtesy the LA Galaxy

RIGHT: A letter from President Obama on my first retirement from MLS... I would come back and play nine games for the Galaxy in 2016

THE WHITE HOUSE
WASHINGTON

March 10, 2015

Mr. Landon Donovan
Los Angeles Galaxy
Carson, California

Dear Landon:

I send my warmest congratulations on your retirement from Major League Soccer.

Your career has been defined both by your achievements on the field and by all you have done to promote the Beautiful Game throughout our country. As one of the greatest players in America's history, you have raised the sport to new levels, and the spirit and style with which you played will echo in the accomplishments of athletes for years to come.

As you begin this new chapter, I wish you the very best.

Sincerely,

LEFT: Ticket from the Galaxy's 2014 home opener

BELOW: Celebrating with fans on October 10, 2014, after my final national team game—my 157th
Jim Rogash, Getty Images · courtesy U.S. Soccer

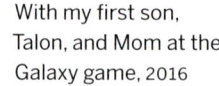

With my first son,
Talon, and Mom at the
Galaxy game, 2016

ABOVE: Inducted into the National Soccer Hall of Fame, May 6, 2023, left to right: Joshie, Mom, Tris, me, Hannah, Randee, Rich

Richard Rodriguez, USSF, Getty Images courtesy U.S. Soccer

LEFT: At home with Hannah and our three kids, celebrating Slate's third birthday

One of the best days of my life: playing hockey with my old man

81′

I'D BEEN LIVING the single life for five years now and had enjoyed the benefits of being a famous athlete. The free and easy life was fun but began to feel hollow and empty. This really hit me at Todd Dunivant's wedding in 2013. Flying home the next morning, after attending the ceremony solo, I felt empty.

While I had some thoughts about next steps on the dating front, I first needed to address my professional life.

Bruce Arena and L.A. Galaxy president Chris Klein were meeting Rich and me for dinner at Mangiamo's in Manhattan Beach, and Rich got down to business immediately: "Thanks for making the trek down here tonight. Landon has some news he wants to share with you in person. It's not a rash decision by any means, but I'll let him tell you directly."

Four straight years of playing nonstop soccer—deep into the playoffs plus U.S. Soccer and international loans—had me feeling mentally, physically, and emotionally spent. It was time. I was on empty. "Guys... I'm exhausted. I need a break. I don't know if it's going to be a week, a month, five months, or a year. I just know I'm mentally shot. I need to step away for a bit and, at the very least, I'm not coming into preseason."

The guys took it in, and Bruce was the first to respond: "Landon, you need to go do what you need to do. Take care of yourself—we'll be here. How long do you really think you'll be out for? I just need to plan for it either way. If you're coming back or not coming back."

"I'm thinking six months."

Bruce nodded, processing my answer. "OK. How about you keep me apprised of what you want to do? In the meantime, go—take some time off. Can we agree on three months for now and we'll reconvene before the beginning of the season to see where we are?"

Bruce gets me. I didn't know if I'd be ready in three months—I didn't even know if I'd be ready in six months or ever again—but this was a plan. It worked for me. By the time we left the restaurant, we had an agreement in principle. Chris and Bruce took off in one direction; Rich stayed back with me.

"Well, Pibe, you're a free man. That's what you wanted, right?"

It was exactly what I wanted. It almost didn't feel real. It got more real over the next few days, as the other ramifications came trickling in. For one thing, the Galaxy informed us they would not be paying my salary for the three months I was out. I was a bit less excited about that part. You'd think that giving my all for eight years, helping them win three championships and make tens of millions of dollars while being the face of the franchise, would be enough to earn me some paid vacation time. But I understood it wasn't about me; they're running a business and couldn't set a precedent of continuing to pay my salary in case the situation presented itself with someone else in the future.

I was making $4 million annually, meaning I'd be walking away from more than $300,000 a month for three successive months. But some things are more important than money.

I was ecstatic to take some real time off. It would be about a month before we'd share the news with the media, but I knew I would be spending that time with Mom, Tris, and Tris's husband Mark in Yucaipa, California. They were excited to have me come home for an extended stay. I'd been gone so much for so long. I also splurged on a Super Bowl trip to New Orleans with Adam, Coach Hafley, and his oldest child, compliments of Gatorade.

And while I was excited to reconnect with family and old friends, I was set on having some serious *me* time. I refresh myself and gain energy by being alone. I wanted to finally have my *Into the Wild* moment—to make like Chris McCandless and go on an adventure. I already had my assistant Jen looking into where I could go to really get away—preferably somewhere exotic in Asia or the South Pacific.

Jen surprised me the next time we chatted, though—she hadn't found a *where* that she liked, she'd found a *who*.

Jen had been introduced to Hannah Bartell by my real estate agent, who must have felt that homemaking extended to match-making. Jen often vets people for me to confirm they aren't absolute loons. Having to set up speed bumps before meeting new people is sad but part of life in the public eye; Jen makes sure I don't walk into a bad or unsafe situation. She had talked to Hannah, liked her, and thought we should connect.

Hannah and I started small. We spoke on the phone, and I could tell right away that she was cool, confident, and intelligent. She was a tennis player who knew nothing about soccer, which I liked—she wasn't interested in what I did on the field; she was interested in what was going on in my mind. We filled the next three weeks with texts, phone calls, and pictures before meeting in real life.

Jen was pleased that we were off to a good start. Meanwhile, I had found an adventure to a place on the other side of the world that she thought I'd really love. It was a luxurious, secluded boutique resort called Song Saa just off the coast of Cambodia on two private islands connected by an arcing wooden bridge. I came across the website and was greeted by sheer beauty at the edge of the planet—20 or so intimate wood-and-straw bungalows on two islands surrounded by tropical blue water. It looked perfectly remote in the best way—a place I could escape to where nobody would know me.

My gut was telling me to go. I had such a visceral response to it, I had basically made the decision already—I wanted to see this place for myself. Twenty-four hours after looking at the website, I had booked my trip to the island.

Back in Manhattan Beach, I was preparing to go on my first in-person date with Hannah. It had been so long since I'd been on a real date, I felt like I needed an online class to remind me what I was supposed to do. I'd also been purging a lot of the fancier things I'd previously surrounded myself with, so I found myself pulling up outside Hannah's house in my newly purchased used gray Ford Escape, with a sad question floating across my mind that affirmed just how entitled I had become: *Should I honk the horn and wait for her to come out? Or do I go knock on the door?*

Fortunately, I go with TRTTD. Her sister opens the door, and I see Hannah for the first time—she's descending a staircase and has the biggest, most genuine smile on her face. It is an image seared into my memory. We head to Terranea Resort on the coast in Palos Verdes.

We clicked right away. She is from Rancho Santa Fe in California but had gone to college at Boston University. She is the oldest of three sisters. Her dad is in the hotel business, so she has seen a few things. But she seemed grounded and down to earth. It became clear that she really did know very little about soccer, which was a huge victory in my book.

Hannah was funny. I liked that she could care less about being in the limelight or social media. I learned about how close she was with her sisters and her family. I shared with her what life was like as a twin and my journey through sports and therapy. Hannah was very curious about my experience with Juliet. We had a lot of fun talking and were off to a good start.

I ended up spending the night that night... and no, we didn't do anything. I could tell there was something here, and I wanted to go on another date with Hannah. We had a great time connecting.

I could tell she had a strong personality but was also quite chill. She had a good sense of who she was and seemed at peace with that person. Ironically, I was about to go 8,000 miles away to try and be at peace with *my*self.

It wasn't like I was journeying to Cambodia for three months. I would be there for only 10 days. I packed light—just me and my carry-on. A few pairs of shorts. Two swimsuits. A handful of shirts. My toothbrush and floss. Just the essentials.

Getting to Song Saa is not easy. I board at LAX and land 14 hours later in Taipei, Taiwan. From there it's a comparatively quick flight west to Phnom Penh, Cambodia's capital, followed by a three-hour ride down a series of rugged, dirt roads. Cambodia doesn't crack the top 140 of wealthiest nations on the planet, and I feel more than a little uncomfortable seeing that kind of poverty through the window of a Mercedes. For three hours, we're passing raggedy bikes, motorized tuk-tuks, dusted-up goats, dogs, and cows, and all manner of humanity. We finally reach the western edge of Cambodia, where I'm greeted by a private boat for the final 30-minute ride to Song Saa. I'm jet-lagged, dazed, and tired, but it sure feels like I've pulled into Fantasy Island off the coast of Koh Rong. Welcome to Paradise.

Song Saa is as advertised: two tiny islands connected by a beautiful crescent walkway bridge. On one island are the luxury thatched-roof bungalows and facilities; on the other side rests a more uninhabited space ripe for exploration and meditation, as well as their spa.

And while it is luxurious, Song Saa isn't snooty or pretentious; it's a flip-flops type of place.

It's late in the afternoon when I arrive at my villa, and it's nothing short of extraordinary. An elevated bed faces out my room's open terrace. The bed is soft and fluffy. My villa's balcony hovers off a cliff, a long way down into a sparkling, deep blue sea below. I can walk outside for a dip in my own private pool, and I do, floating and watching as the sun slips behind the horizon in breathtaking fashion below the sapphire Gulf of Thailand. The price of admission has already been met.

It's a place to sleep in, wake up, and fall into the water. To escape the hustle and bustle and put the clock, the internet, and stardom away. As the fresh first morning shows itself, I walk freely around Song Saa, so happy to be there without having to be "Landon Donovan." I feel liberated and anonymous being just me, whoever that is. I've brought my journal at Juliet's suggestion to try and work through that mystery. While I might not always write rampantly about my life, I know I want to document what I experience on this trip.

I'm feeling in a light and exploratory mood, so I pack a book and head off to see what the island offers. I take a kayak across to the uninhabited island and hang out with my thoughts on the beach. It's a peaceful day of reading, writing, sitting, and eating the lunch the staff has packed me. It's stunning to be somewhere where there are no cars, and in the first few days I'm here, I barely even see other guests. I stroll this pristine five-mile stretch of white, sandy beach and feel it: This is it, my Chris McCandless moment. I have finally gotten away from it all.

I met a staff member named Jelena when I first arrived, a Bosnian who manages Song Saa's Diving & Water Sports Center. She is an avid diver, and I could tell she was a kind and curious soul. Like most of the island staff, Jelena spoke stellar English. I'd never been scuba diving before. Jelena asked if I'd ever meditated, and I shared that I knew a thing or two about that: breathing and being aware of your breath. Jelena said that scuba diving is nothing more than submersing yourself fully underwater and looking at beauty in all directions while you focus on your breathing.

That was enough to sign me up. I had to do a bit of training first, but then the two of us and the captain could head out. I can feel my heart racing nervously as we zip out to the middle of the vast gulf.

When the captain slows the boat, Jelena gives me the cue and we take the plunge.

It is like being lowered down through an invisible little door into a silent new world of peaceful, freeing stillness: purple soft coral reefs, swimming turtles, and breathtaking marine life, including miniature seahorses. Many of the bigger underwater creatures aren't visible today, but Jelena's right—it is a meditative experience. I can see her out of the corner of my eye and feel the connection between us. With no words underwater, communication shifts to gestures and mind-to-mind. We occasionally share something in this blissful language as we take in the calm beauty of the underwater universe. I can see why Jelena enjoys doing this for a living.

The next afternoon, Jelena takes me to the local island where all 120 of Song Saa's staff live, about a half-mile boat ride away from the resort. She has planned an adventure on foot. Jelena fills me in on the background of Song Saa as she leads me away from the staff camp. She tells me that the guest's gourmet meals are all made from locally sourced foods. That the resort assists the local community with its conservation, education, and waste management programs. That Song Saa is a model for sustainable development in Cambodia. We approach what she wants me to see: a village called Prek Svay, where a group of the locals still live. From a purely material stand-point, they are the poorest people I have ever seen.

There are wood huts with tin roofs, right on the edge of the water. Kids with no shoes. There's no running water, no electricity, no showers or modern toilets. It's as basic a lifestyle as you can imagine. But as hard as their lives must be, they look truly happy. Jelena takes me to a little school and it's more kids with big smiles and happy faces. They don't know what they don't have, only what they do have. I'm reminded that everyone has the potential to be happy, from the filthy rich to the poorest of poor. If you're happy, you're happy.

I play soccer with the kids, who have no idea who I am. Playing with these kids in a muddy field, seeing this level of poverty, I'm in awe of them. What could just one month of my held-up salary do for this community? Then again, I've never seen people living with less seem this fulfilled. Everywhere I look, people are enjoying themselves. Parents and children are smiling. They seem to have nothing but space to roam in, but judging by their energy, you'd think they had everything. I think of the times I've had everything but felt I had nothing.

I know a lot of unhappy famous people, and a lot of people who suffer from depression. Some go to therapy; many can't get past their egos and do not. I still think about these Prek Svay kids a lot: They have very little but time, space in which to play, and their community, but they seem so much happier than so many wealthy Americans. It makes me wonder if the pressure of modern civilization is worth it. It is not beyond me to think that these kids—many of whom have never experienced a warm shower—are in some ways far ahead.

I spend time with Jelena whenever she's not working. I spend time with her even when she is—acting like a staff member, helping and hanging out at her water sports shed. There aren't very many guests at Song Saa, and Jelena tells me staff members are encouraged to connect on a deeper level with the guests if the guests are interested. And we're having fun together, so we spend our days talking, connecting, getting to understand one another.

We watch her favorite movie at my villa one night, and Jelena tells me more about her life before her time at Song Saa. She's 36— the same age as Bianca.

"I knew I wanted to be a fashion designer since I was six years old. I loved it. I had a plan. When I was 18, my family paid for my studies and got me a flat in Florence. This was 300 miles away from home and I ended up becoming a fashion designer in Italy until I was 30. Quite successful too—I had 'made it.' But what did I really make? I had reached my goal, but I wasn't happy. So I dropped everything and started following the ocean. I had been diving and was liking it more and more. I left my job and became a diving instructor. Now I had no plan. I just wanted to travel. I started in Croatia. Then Egypt for two years. Then the Andaman Islands in India for eight months. Then back to Croatia. Then here to Cambodia."

I am in awe. Jelena is the opposite of me; she is free.

Some of this is not just knowing who you are but being OK with who you are. You can't accept who you are on the surface until you accept who you are on the inside. The goal is to find your peace. But where to look? I too had traveled the world searching for it. Germany. New Zealand. Liverpool. Australia. South Korea. South Africa. San Jose. Los Angeles. I went searching for it everywhere only to realize that I really needed to be looking inside. I've taken this amazing journey across the world—8,000 miles to two isolated islands, by planes, boats, and cars—just to circle back to where I started: myself.

The trip has been a huge success. One filled with connection, laughter, thinking, journaling, and perspective. I've had a truly wonderful time.

On one of my final afternoons, I head to Jelena's. She's hanging out with her best friend at the resort, a woman who runs the resort's food and beverage needs. Jelena's room is a tiny spot in the middle of the jungle equipped with air conditioning, cable television, and a hot shower. We're all sitting snug in her room when one of them asks me if I smoke pot. I tell them not only do I not smoke pot— I've never smoked *anything* before in my life.

I'm not a fan of putting anything in my body that could impede my game. But... curiosity is calling. I'm not going to be playing for a while. There's no drug test in my near future.

"Let's do it."

As they pass me a joint, I have no idea what I'm doing. *Am I doing this right?* I don't know, but they're excited to be taking part in something so clearly illicit to me. They share that they got it from the mainland, which means nothing to me, but it leaves me in a chill and pensive state. I can't remember the last time I felt this relaxed.

The next morning, I wake up thinking about the night before. I ask them if they want to smoke again that evening. They swing by my room just when the sun does its beautiful dip below the water, accompanied by a bunch of joints. We smoke a lot more than the previous night, but this time, I'm not really feeling anything. They leave around 8 p.m. I walk them to the door, wish them goodnight, and then head to the bathroom to brush my teeth.

I grab my toothbrush and apply toothpaste—but when I open wide I am shocked to see worms in my mouth.

In the sink, I see frogs.

On the ground squirm more scattered worms.

Holy shit. What is going on?

Everywhere I look now I'm seeing something. I try to take a shower, but I panic and decide it would be best to lie down. I've never gone through anything like this before and I'm starting to really freak out. I try calling Jelena, but I can't get a hold of her. I lie down and close my eyes. That makes it worse.

I start seeing sparks and flickers and flashes of bright white lights. It's like a portal into some corridor in my own mind I didn't know existed. Do I trust it? Do I go there? Do I not? Before I can answer, a decision is made for me: A vivid world of weird spills out across my room. An uncontrollable mass of worms and frogs.

Is this real? It can't be.

The weed—or whatever might be with it—is taking over. And my thoughts are racing in crazy directions.

I am Landon.

Not Landon Donovan.

Forget Landon Donovan.

I'm a 10-year-old boy named Landon from Redlands. I'm racing to get through my homework at school so I can go outside and play when I get home. What will we play today? It could be soccer. Roller hockey. Whatever. I am happy. I am free.

I jolt back to Song Saa. I am Landon Donovan. I am shackled by success. I am alone. No one knows the real me ... *I don't know the* real me. Gravity is winning and my chest is heavy. I want to go back to the lighter, freer version of me.

I press and race back to the past again.

It's summertime. We're in a pool. Playing basketball. Joshie and I are rushing through dinner to get back outside to relish the last few hours of daylight.

I slingshot back to Song Saa. I am hallucinating Landon Donovan. I am scared. I am out of control. I like control and this is not control. I don't know what to do. My heart is pounding a million beats per minute.

Back to little Landon. The violin. Ms. Goding. Dinosaur diorama box. Cal Heat. One day I was just playing a game, and the next the weight of being a professional took over. Play got beaten out of me. I want to hold onto *this* play version of me. I can't.

Back to Landon Donovan. Heaviness. Hurt. An eternity away from that little boy. Something else is here. Maybe it's someone else. This feels like something I haven't experienced before, in the worst way. There is something here I have to confront. The intensity is deafening.

Is this real?

Am I hallucinating?

I am hallucinating.

I want to get the fuck out of here.

I want this to end.

What exactly is this?

A trip?

An episode?

A complicated life?

I should be full, but I am alone.

I cannot turn it off.

Too many thoughts flood my head.

They flicker and flash through my mind.

I don't know what to do.

Who am I?

Landon, the boy?

Landon Donovan, the disgruntled man?

Not just right now? Always?

Who the fuck am I?

I see someone coming. The answer.

This must be my dad. But it's not my dad.

It's someone smaller.

A boy walking towards me.

It's me. I'm walking towards me.

Ten-year-old me smiles at grown-up me, who is sitting in my car at Home Depot Stadium.

I understand.

I nod. I cry.

I say I'm sorry.

Ten-year-old me looks at me in the most comforting way.

I blink.

Now 10-year-old me is just playing soccer—just smiling—one of those happy Cambodian boys.

I understand.

I see him. I smile.

That's me.

Ten-year-old me turns and walks away.

I see Juliet approaching. She is smiling.

Walking me off the ledge.

Peace is coming.

I follow this path.

The happiest moments of my childhood flood my mind. Joshie. Hafley. Hockey. Adam.

I am just a simple kid from Redlands.

This is who I always was.

I was happier with less.

At the core, that's who I am.

That's where I find my joy.

I was young and there was joy.

Then it was less and further between.

My joy became my job.

My mind is on overload. I want it to stop. I need it to stop.

Suicidal thoughts flood my mind.

Should I do it? Should I not?

The coldness and fear of these words. My mind nudging me to go jump into the ocean and make it stop. Every 20 seconds, my mind is visualizing myself jumping over the edge to stop the frogs and worms and feelings and thoughts. I get up and go to the door... then talk myself back down.

My mind is racing.

Get back in bed.

Every time I open my eyes I'm hallucinating. Every time I close my eyes, my mind's telling me to end it, find a way out.

I don't hate life. But to stop this hallucination, I need to jump off the cliff. This is not going to end. But if I go over the ledge, my life is over. If I go over, nothing is going to bring me back up.

It keeps intensifying. I walk to the edge. Back to the bed. Over to the pool. Back to the bed. Then to the brick wall. Back to the bed. It's getting worse.

How do I turn these fucking frogs off?

Run... jump...

No... focus, Landon.

I park my thoughts. An elevator in my mind lowers me slowly down to the base of my nose. My thoughts are not here. It's just my breath. The rest fades away... for now.

Stay in my nose. Breathe. Just breathe. Don't judge yourself. Just observe it.

The breath slowly begins to quiet my mind.

OK. OK. I'm aware of it. Come back to the breath.

The thoughts rumble again. I slide back down to my breath. Something clicks.

I move my mind to a more consistent meditation. I find my breath and keep coming back to my breath. A peaceful battle to escape my brain. Waves of it for hours until the sun comes up. I stay with my breath for what seems like eternity, channeling what Juliet's taught me.

Finally it passes.

I fall asleep.

My eyes open to stillness. Looking straight up at the straw roof above me.

I'm here, right? I'm not dead?

I breathe. I can hear my breath.

I'm not dead.

It's crisp outside. Trepidation turns to relief. Morning is here. I'm supposed to partake in some one-on-one yoga but forget that. I need to reach Juliet. I find my phone. The plan was to not turn on my phone at all while I was here, but I turn it on. I call Juliet and, luckily, she picks up. I share it all.

"What was it that you smoked?"

"I don't know."

"Was it laced?"

"I don't know."

"So, you decided to get high in a foreign country, buying weed off the black market in a place known for its opioids?"

"I guess so."

Silence may fill the air, but I can clearly hear what Juliet isn't saying. I continue.

"One of the girls here thought I should go see someone in Bangkok."

Juliet snaps. "Do not get on a plane. That's the worst thing you can do. That's throwing gasoline on the fire. What's going on is biochemical. Do not get on the plane until this thing has subsided. Do you have anyone over there that you trust?"

"Yes. The people here are great. They are so down to earth."

"OK. Don't go out. Have a drink or something that will make you relax. For now, stay put for 48 hours and surround yourself with your friends. Ask them to bring you food. After that see how you feel. I believe it will go away. Got it?"

"OK."

"The day you come back, I want to see you. If there's a need for medication, we'll cross that bridge."

I hang up and I feel better.

I need to find Jelena. I need to not be alone with my thoughts.

I slowly sit up. The frogs, worms, and fuzziness from last night are gone but a not-so-distant memory. The voice telling me to jump the wall was real. This is not good. *I need people.*

I trudge to the Diving & Water Sports Center, hoping Jelena is working.

Knock! Knock! Knock!

I still don't know what the fuck is going on. I'm raw. But Jelena opens the door, and I tell her what happened. That the high never really happened and then the lowest of lows took over.

Jelena sets me up on this colossal bean bag that I don't dare inch from for the next four hours. Gravity is laughing at me, pushing me down while I try to make sense of the night before. I'm out of it but still in trouble at the same time.

I already have a propensity for depression. I can feel the heaviness of it creeping in. I'm in survival mode and still have three days to go on the island. Seventy-two hours of deep, dark depression where Paradise Island becomes problematic. When Jelena can't get away, I lie on the beach and try to stay near people. I feel physically unable to do anything. I just lie down and can barely get myself up off the sand.

I think about leaving Song Saa but Juliet's right—there's no way I'm in the headspace to fly. I feel like a failure. Thankfully, Jelena is there to keep me sane and safe. She spends so much time with me over the final three days. She hangs out in my room. Comforts me. Nurtures me.

By the third day, I finally feel stable enough to leave Cambodia. I have one last evening and I ask Jelena to stay in my room. She has been lonely on the island and this request makes her smile. Over the course of the week, we had continuously confided in each other. On that bed, that last night, we might as well have been underwater—though it was less mind-to-mind and now more heart-to-heart. It was innocent, siblingesque, and beautiful. After 31 years of chaos, I'd gone halfway across the earth to find this sympathetic moment of care. I saw so many people in Jelena. I saw Jelena for who she was. In her sweet, kind, and caring side I saw Tris and my mom. I saw the potential of me as the guy I always wanted to be—free. All of us in there, mashed up inside one open and loving soul.

When it was finally time to go home, I was ready. I took one last trek to Jelena's jungle room and wrote on a yellow sticky note "… this too shall pass." Then I placed my journal on her chair and the sticky note smack in the center of her television.

Song Saa felt very different when I left from when I arrived. With my carry-on bag over my shoulder, I stepped onto the boat back to the mainland, and thought of Chris McCandless again. I'd had my adventure. I'd gone much further into the wild than I'd expected. Chris never made it back. Would I?

The boat pushed out to sea, and a thought played across my fatigued mind:

HAPPINESS ONLY REAL WHEN SHARED.

I knew why I hadn't jumped in Song Saa. And what I wanted to do next. I couldn't wait to get back to America to see Hannah.

83'

————

IT FELT GOOD to be back in California. I had seen enough in Cambodia—some real, some not—and I was sharing it with Juliet, who had wanted to see me as soon as I arrived home. The weight of it all had left me feeling heavily depressed. And while I was considerably better now, I was concerned that those feelings might come back.

"It might be a lifelong bout, Landon. Depression isn't one note, and it shows up differently in different people; many people cope with some form of depression for the duration of their lives."

Juliet was back to being my "mind coach," explaining the different forms and symptoms that come with these tiers of sadness. She explained that depression was a mood disorder that causes a nagging, constant feeling of sadness that often leads to a profound loss of interest in the things that bring you pleasure. Such as... soccer.

Ironically, despite the lingering scars of my Cambodia sojourn, I had started back with the Galaxy, and I was quite happy to have returned to the field with the guys. The end of my break almost killed me, but the rest of the time off had truly served me well. I came out the other side rested, refreshed, and ready to go. Soccer was back to being a job, but there was real comfort in the routine; after my near-death experience, I welcomed punching in and punching out on the field and hanging out with the team. And the

2014 World Cup was around the corner, so I was getting my legs under me and making sure my game was sharp. Jurgen had been considerably less receptive to my sabbatical than Bruce was, but he'd given me the green light to play on the Gold Cup team later this summer, and I was happy to be rejoining the national team for the stretch run to Brazil.

I still wanted to learn about those different types of depression, though. Which shade of depression was … *mine*?

Juliet approached the question like she was breaking down game tape of the most common forms of depression. There was Clinical Depression—a major depressive disorder that's chronic and constant. That didn't sound like me. Seasonal Depression, where people might suffer through winter but be perfectly fine in spring. While Germany could be chalked up as my perpetual winter, living in Los Angeles felt like it eliminated this form of depression from my lens, though it felt more recognizable. Neither Bipolar nor Postpartum seemed particularly on point for me. The one that felt the most like me is one Juliet calls Situational Depression, which speaks for itself—being depressed because of a traumatic event.

I thought about the issues I'd had with Dad and the feelings I had going through my divorce, and I could see how I might fit into her description of this variety. There were times in my marriage when I would become fully closed off from Bianca and other people. I'd remove the human part of me and any semblance of joy or ability to show love or affection.

Or maybe a better way to explain it is to say that I tucked these thoughts and feelings so deep inside that I couldn't feel them, to a point where I had lost myself in me.

The heaviness of this type of depression has only happened a few times in my life; the immediate aftermath of Cambodia was one of them. But I saw enough of a small opening of opportunity, and I've always trusted my intuition, so I ran through it.

This too shall pass.

And it did. And while it might come back... that's OK. I would now have the tools, training, and support to deal with it.

I was still curious to try and make sense of the lizards, worms, and frogs I saw on that long night in Cambodia. And while I'm certain I didn't want to jump off any ledges or end my life, any time a thought like that floats to your conscious surface, you must take it seriously.

I was feeling so much better in the weeks since I'd returned to Los Angeles. Being back at work with the Galaxy had taken my mind off that evening at Song Saa. And things were progressing well with Hannah—the joy and excitement of a new, real relationship was helping. But occasionally, I'd go back to that scary scene and think about the urge to do *something* to shut off the hallucinations. I would be driving in my car and that night would appear out of nowhere.

"What did you do when these thoughts came into your mind, Landon?"

"I'd usually call Tris or Hannah, just to have someone comfort me."

Juliet nodded in approval. "Good, good."

While her head was nodding, I had something I needed to get off my chest. "Juliet... is having this thought normal in any way, shape, or form?"

"Quite normal, yes."

I was more curious about why the thought had come about and if it was out of the ordinary.

I don't think most of us ordinarily question what's ordinary.

I think that has been the largest win of my sessions in therapy: I might not be abnormally normal—but I *am* normal. I know that now. These thoughts we have in our heads that we don't often share make us feel alone, but we are not alone in having them. We are all more alike than we know.

I think about my goals in therapy, and that makes me smile. I was no longer that old heavy cup being weighed down by ChapStick, a remote control, and everything else.

As my time with Juliet nears completion—both today and more regularly—the conversation turns lighter. I have the awareness now to know this is a clear sign that we're coming out the other side. Juliet asks how things are going with Hannah, and I share that she's now sitting with my family at Galaxy games.

Our time is up. I stand to leave and take one final look around Juliet's office. It dawns on me that not much has changed about this place since I first stepped foot in here a few years ago. And yet, as I say goodbye to Juliet and walk out her door, I realize that almost everything about me has.

89′

IF YOU ASK any of my teammates or any member of my family, they will tell you the following truth: Landon Donovan is a bad liar. And I'd be lying if I said I hadn't contemplated not shaking Jurgen's hand as I walked off the field for the last time in a U.S. Soccer jersey in 2014 on, naturally, the 10th day of the 10th month.

But I took the high road.

There was no question that it was also the hard road, but I sucked it up and shook the man's hand. I didn't need to send any bitter messages today. Today was about celebrating the games I had gotten to play for America, not about the ones I hadn't.

Sunil Gulati, the president of U.S. Soccer who I'd known since I was 16, had generously agreed to charter a private plane to fly my family from the West Coast to East Hartford for a friendly against Ecuador. And so, 15 of my loved ones—including Mom, Dad, Adam, Rich, Randee, Eden, and Hannah—watched from a box as I sported a #10 U.S. Men's National Team jersey for the last time. I walked onto the field holding the hands of Rich's twins, Eli and Sammy.

This sendoff game had Sunil's fingerprints all over it. It would be my 157th time playing for America—the second most caps in U.S. men's soccer history, behind only my former Galaxy teammate, the legendary Cobi Jones. The plan was to go out for 30 minutes—a little under one final half, wearing the captain's armband for the

Red, White, and Blue. I blew a kiss to my loved ones up in the box as the national anthem rang out with me on the pitch for Team USA one final time, then hugged the boys tightly before one last hoorah with all my teammates.

I was hoping I could reward U.S. Soccer's kind gesture with a goal. I got as close as you can in the 25th minute, clanging one off the post on a beautiful set-up from Jozy when we were already up 1–0. While the plan was to go for 30 minutes, Jurgen ended up leaving me on for another 10.

Another 10.

What success looks like to me is another #10—someone who pushes American soccer further than I could ever take it. I hope I can witness it live—to see another #10 break the U.S. goal record that Clint Dempsey and I share at 57. I love that this is a moment— one record that shall also pass one day—that I share with Clint, my frequent USMNT partner who had a fire and killer instinct like no other teammate, to go with my more killer intuition and technical approach. I hope we can celebrate together when another #10 blows past us to take our crown. Maybe it will be another #10 who surpasses my all-time U.S. assist record and joins me as the only other American to hit both the 50-goal and 50-assist mark. And maybe it will be another #10 who carries America's team deeper into a World Cup—maybe even wins it. Nothing could please me more than to see someone take America up those podium steps to hoist a trophy I only dreamed of winning.

While there will most certainly be another #10 for me to support and cheer for, I get to wear my lucky number one more time tonight. And when Jurgen finally waves me over to exit near the end of the first half, I leave to an emotional standing ovation from the crowd, and I thank America as America is thanking me.

The walk to the sideline triggers a mental movie trailer of U.S. Soccer memories. The standing ovation goes silent while flickering moments from my soccer life race through my mind. Making the national team at the Cocoa Expo. Pushing to the semifinals in New Zealand with my teammates at the U-17 World Cup. Shocking Portugal in 2002. Snapping Spain's 35-game unbeaten run at the Confederations Cup. The ever-sweet, ever-familiar *Dos a Cero* victories over Mexico. Battling alongside legends like Howard, Beasley, McBride, and Dempsey. Learning under father figures like Ellinger, Bradley, and Arena. And of course, the goal against Algeria, the wild celebration with my brothers, and the beers that followed with President Clinton.

My part of the race now done, I slip off the captain's band and pass the baton to Jozy with a hug. For such a light piece of fabric, carrying U.S. Soccer can be a heavy burden. I hope whoever gets to wear it next makes it look far easier than it sometimes felt to me.

I embrace my teammates.

Soak in the love from our devoted fans.

Send one last kiss up to my emotional family in the box.

And, for the final time, donning the #10, step off the field.

90'

_____

IF MY 14-year career in MLS is a story, then I wanted a storybook ending and championship bookends to go with it. But we opened the 2014 playoffs by posting a 0-0 tie with Real Salt Lake in the first leg of the Western Conference semis, and that could have been the end of it all.

When we come back to L.A. for the second leg on November 9 against RSL, we need a win to move on. I put the first one on the scoreboard 10 minutes in: a header off a floating cross from A.J. DeLaGarza. We're not just playing to extend my career—we're all playing for A.J. too. His newborn son Luca tragically passed away in September from a rare heart defect one week after he was born. The further we go, the more we can keep playing for Luca and help give the DeLaGarza family something else to think about. Ten minutes later, I slide a ball across the goalmouth to Robbie Keane, who slides in our second. Up 2-0, we're now rolling.

In the 54th minute, Keane guides a pass my way behind their backline. What I learned from Ellinger's Brazil tape 15 years ago gets put to practice once again, as I blaze ahead of two defenders. I bear down on Nick Rimando and it's just like old times. I wait for him to cement his feet... go past him... and... left-footer into the open net. 3-0 Galaxy.

Marcelo Sarvas adds another nine minutes later, and in the 71st, Keane chips a beauty over the back line, and I guide it into the corner

304

of the net for my third before the ball ever touches the ground. I race to the bench and give my teammates some love, including a high-five to the gregarious Alan Gordon, who has returned to the Galaxy in a mid-season trade. Alan and I had been teammates for six years, but he left in 2010 and missed out on the championships. I'm so happy he's back with a chance to win it all now. After today, we're one step closer, into the conference finals with an aggregate win of 5-0. And it turns out it had been 15 years since the last playoff hat trick; not bad for an old guy on the edge of retirement.

There'll be no storybook ending if we don't beat the Sounders. Now standing in the way of me prolonging my career are the Gatorade green jerseys, legendary coach Sigi Schmid and Clint Dempsey. It would take 50 minutes before the lone goal, via an ugly deflection off Marcelo Sarvas after halftime, but it's enough to give us Game 1; a 1-0 win at home sending us up to Seattle with some confidence.

That would all fade away early in Game 2 on a frigid northwestern night in Seattle. They come out strong, scoring two goals in the first half, with Clint nabbing the second one.

Down 2-0 in a chilly second half in Seattle, we need a goal to pull even on aggregate and get to MLS Cup final. I send a corner kick into the box in the 54th minute that drops and bounces past everyone, coming to rest at the feet of my Brazilian teammate Juninho just outside the box. Juninho's scored exactly zero goals so far in 2014, but he rectifies that with the only goal he needs, silencing 45,000 Seattle fans with a long-range blast off the post and in. We are still down 2-1 in the game, but he has tied the score in aggregate, and it is the lone away goal of the series—the tiebreaker that can send us through. There are no more goals, and it's just enough for us to squeak by and into the finals.

It's a picture-perfect Southern California day on the morning of the MLS Cup Championship game. We will be playing in front of 27,000 home fans at the newly renamed StubHub Center. You know you've been in the league a long time when you see your stadium change its name. Standing in our way are the New England Revolution. They've been to four championship games before but never won it.

I think about New England and how many times they've been here and never had the ball bounce their way. I think about them breaking their streak against us all those years ago, with Todd playing in the rain in New England while the rest of us were in Las Vegas. I think about Magee's text message: Hey Todd, remember the time we all won in Vegas while you lost in the rain in Foxboro? That text never gets old, but it reminds me that we do. Beckham retired from MLS after the championship game two years ago. I'm retiring after this one.

So many people have passed through my life and my teams in those 14 years. Gordon is back. Chris Klein has gone from veteran teammate to boss as president of the Galaxy. Even my cognac crew has scattered—Omar and Todd are still chugging along with me, but Magee is now in Chicago. He had the chance to go back home and play in front of his family in 2013, and couldn't pass up the opportunity. He ended up scoring 21 goals—second in the league—and was named MVP of MLS in 2013. Happy as that made me, I still missed my friend. It would have made me even happier if the Galaxy Four could all take the pitch one final time together against New England and gather for a shot of Louis XIII afterwards.

I believe that the world is happening the way it's supposed to. 2014 has been a trying year filled with ups, downs, and in-betweens, but I've truly come to believe that things played out as they should have. Of course I wanted to represent America at the World Cup, but there were lessons I now embrace from getting let go, like Kyle Beckerman coming into that bathroom stall and consoling me after I found out I'd been cut from the team.

Since we were 16, starting at the IMG Academy, Kyle and I had played together all over the world. Yet Kyle had to wait over half his life to finally get the nod to go to a World Cup. Here I was, a guy who had never been cut in his life, facing rejection for the first time. And who is sitting right next to me when he should be out there celebrating with his new teammates? Kyle. That level of compassion is unprecedented, though it took me a few weeks before I could truly appreciate the selflessness Kyle showed. I have started thinking about life after soccer and wondering about coaching. Just about everyone in life gets cut and I really haven't, not since the age of eight. Now? I'm no different. See, I think to myself, *this* is normal.

Getting cut and Kyle's kindness are two memories I store away. This is where empathy is made. I know something I didn't before, and if I do go into coaching, I will remember these vivid moments that will surely help me relate to my players.

My focus comes back to the opportunity to finish my career here in front of my home fans by hoisting my sixth MLS Cup. I remember winning my third cup in 2005 and joking with Todd that I was coming for Agoos. It took six grueling years of becoming a better teammate and a better person to get on the same page with David and win cups #4 and 5. Here I am today with the opportunity to achieve that absurd goal.

I think back to my first Quakes team with Captain Agoos, what feels like an eternity ago. When I started in Major League Soccer, the league was holding on for dear life. There were only 12 teams. There were barely any soccer-specific stadiums, little mainstream TV coverage, and plenty of empty stands. There are 19 teams today with more coming, soccer-specific stadiums built or planned in most MLS cities, and full stands with supporters' sections. I think of all the star power I've been able to share the league with, players like David Beckham, Robbie Keane, Tim Howard, Clint Dempsey, Jozy Altidore, and Michael Bradley. It makes me smile.

And of course, I've had the honor of playing for the two greatest U.S. Soccer coaches to ever manage the national team: Bruce Arena and Bob Bradley. The fact that I get to take the field today still being managed by Bruce is nothing short of spectacular. Fourteen years ago, Bruce trusted some cocky, undersized 20-year-old kid to come off the bench against Mexico; his faith in me put me on the road to being the player I've become.

We take the field in our all-whites, New England in dark blue. I walk out holding hands with my goddaughter Eden. She looks up at me as we walk out into the bright lights and says, "Don't be nervous, Landon. Just have fun." Leave it to her to try and make *me* feel relaxed. I do feel relaxed but focused. Whatever happens today, I'm happy with the career I've had and the things I've achieved. But I still want to win that sixth trophy.

The game starts, and we catch New England off guard in the first minute. I send a quick through-ball into Robbie Rogers, who takes it and cuts straight into the six-yard box. He shoots—it's deflected and bouncing towards the goal, but a New England defender somehow plucks the ball off the goal line and clears it, just robbing us of the fast start we've craved. New England settles in, and the rest of the half is two disciplined defenses holding each other's offense in check. We head into the break still tied at 0.

In the locker room, I can't help but look around and think this is the last time I'm going to be in here as a player. I think about David again and his joy in going out a champion two years back. If we can score, I'm 45 minutes away from doing the same. My bookend championships—winning it all in 2001 in my first season and winning a final one in my last—are in reach.

We up the level at the start of the second half, stringing together a few higher-quality passes to create some chances. And it pays off in the 51st minute when hometown kid Gyasi Zardes makes the most of a winding cross to the corner of the six-yard box, taking on two defenders and burying a hard-angle left-footer just inside the far post. I run in just in case to clean it up and get the best view in the house as it goes in.

I feel a huge burst of relief. 1–0 Galaxy. Forty minutes to go.

We're still clinging to a lead with just 12 minutes left when New England's Patrick Mullins finds some space deep down our left side. He takes the ball all the way to the end line, pulling Omar with him, before playing it back up top to a streaking Chris Tierney, who touches it once around our last defender and on his second touch makes us pay.

It's a new ballgame, but the momentum is all theirs. Five minutes later, they almost get the game winner when Teal Bunbury mishits a left-footed cross that clears our keeper, hits the crossbar, and rebounds away.

We hold on to take the game to extra time. It's more of the same in the first session—New England controlling play and getting opportunities. They look fresher and in the 102nd minute Patrick Mullins runs past a line of four Galaxy defenders to take a ball that comes in from over the top, then hammers a shot from the left side. If not for an exceptional diving save by Jaime Penedo, Mullins would have put the Revolution ahead.

But in the second session, we flip the script. Marcelo Sarvas plays a ballooning long ball over the top of the Revolution's defense, and this time it's Robbie Keane running under it. Robbie sends a beautiful right-footed shot back across the mouth of the goal that the New England keeper has no chance of stopping. As the ball finds its way into the net, Keane cartwheels towards the fans in the southeast corner of the stadium, and pandemonium ensues.

Keane is mobbed in the corner. There are nine minutes to go, but New England aren't coming back from this. Running from the other side of the field, I'm no longer the first one there—the speed isn't fully gone yet, but it's downshifted a little. I get to Robbie and hug him—we grab each other's heads and know it's almost done.

New England sends everyone forward now—they must—and while they give themselves an opportunity to get it even, they fail to score. We kill off the minutes... nine, then four minutes more.

The whistle blows.

It's over.

The Galaxy are the first MLS team to win five championships.

I am the first player to win six.

I am no longer a professional soccer player.

The pandemonium of winning a trophy. The pictures. The confetti. The fans. Lifting that massive chalice up above your head. Robbie gets the honors—it's really his team now, and it should be. Hugs from absolutely everyone. Before I leave the field, I take it all in. I send kisses to the stands—they are ecstatic and electric. I sign autographs for giddy kids. I send love to the three rock-solid women of my life: Hannah, Mom, and Tris.

I conduct a few interviews for the final time, and everyone wants to talk, so I'm one of the last into the locker room. Sure, I'm now on the wrong side of 30, but it's nice to know I'm still the last to leave the field on this final day of my career. This time, when I get to the locker room, all the guys are waiting for me with bottles of champagne. We uncork them, and for one last time, a championship party ensues. I drink from the cup and get emotional about everything.

I take in these final precious locker-room moments with Bruce, Todd, Omar, Robbie, and all the young guys, champagne matting the hair I have left. I think about all the games I've played in and the championships I've won. I think about how amazing it feels to win a sixth cup. To do it in front of my home crowd, my family, and my friends. I can't believe it's over . . . but I smile, because I know it isn't over yet. I've still got a couple hours left to celebrate with my teammates.

90'+1' EXTRA TIME

IT'S BEEN 20 years since I first scored in a World Cup match against Mexico. It's been 12 years since we sent America into a frenzy with a 91st-minute goal against Algeria. It's been eight years since I took home my sixth and final MLS Championship. And it's been seven years now since Hannah and I said, "I do." Those seven years have been filled with their own twists and turns, a ton of wonderful memories, and a hat trick of little Donovans.

Today, we're having a family adventure exploring the acres of lemon trees that call our backyard home. It's a long way from the 900 square feet of my own childhood. Our middle child, Slate, holds Hannah's hand and curiously examines a ripe lemon on the ground while Talon—our oldest at six—emerges from behind one of the trees. It seems like just a blink ago he was a tiny bowling ball of a boy resting in my arms.

Charging towards me in a full fearless sprint is Raven, our youngest. My dad tells anyone who'll listen that he thinks she has the making of a future Olympic athlete. Like me, Raven figured out the whole walking thing eerily fast; she was cruising around on her own two feet at nine months. And she has her two older brothers as measuring sticks. No matter where life takes them, it makes me happy to think about the adventures these three will have together.

I think about my own adventures and my own life.

For most of that life, some part of me has been rattling around in there pondering the big question.

When I didn't have a dad...

When I didn't have a wife...

When I strip away soccer...

Who am I?

It always came back to this question.

Now I know the answer.

I am Mom's survival gene.

I am Dad's intensity.

I am Tris's selflessness.

I am Joshie's competitiveness.

I am Frank's ability to make you believe.

I am Coach Ellinger's ability to make men out of boys.

I am Coach Hafley's positivity.

I am Bruce's talent for maximizing talent.

I am Bob's knack for setting the tone.

I am Rich's TRTTD.

I am Bianca's curiosity.

I am Magee, Dunivant, and Omar's work harder / play harder.

I am Juliet's lasting teachings.

I am Hannah's knowing confidence.

I am my three kids' protector and role model.

Only when you assemble this collection of people—and the experiences we had together—does the mosaic of "me" present itself. Like Juliet said, we're just walking through life as cups and all that sticks to us. This collection of special people are the magnetized coins, mints, and lip balms on my life's cup.

Raven races up and proudly shows me a lemon in her hands. I relish this moment, enjoying the freedom I couldn't have as a player to make memories on my own terms, with my own family, on my very own time.

Becoming a dad has changed me for the better. I soak up the luxury of being there for my kids. The greatest present I can give them is being present. I love that I can give them an intact family. They are growing up as part of a team.

I look to my left and there's Slate and Talon playing among the rows of lemon trees on our property. When life gives you lemons, you just want to squeeze and hug them for all that they're worth.

Hannah and I start to pack up our things. As we do, I think of my dad sitting under that old tree just off our property in Ontario, waiting for me.

We gather the kids and their clothes and head back to the house.

I don't know if they will remember hanging out on this timeless afternoon, but hopefully the feeling of being wanted and together will stay with them forever.

LIVING WITH
DEPRESSION

I'VE HAD three major bouts of depression in my life: the first after the 2006 World Cup, the second after my divorce from Bianca, and the third after my unfortunate hallucinogenic experience in Cambodia.

Where does depression come from?

What exactly is it?

Depression is a mental health disorder characterized by persistent feelings of sadness, hopelessness, or emptiness, causing significant impairment in daily life. Possible causes include a mix of biological, psychological, and social sources of distress.

My story may have started out as a personal quest to be the best at soccer, but along the way it shifted to a quest to just be the best version of myself. That meant trying to understand what I could do to make myself feel both happy and happier about myself. No matter how fast I was on the field, I could never run away from myself.

It took me decades to realize that peace was possible only when I understood the difference between "Landon Donovan" the soccer player and "Landon" the person. Stripping out what I did—and why I did it—from who I was became a necessary step that allowed me to better deal with the pressures of life as a professional soccer player and experience joy and friendship in my personal life.

Landon Donovan is fiery and competitive.

The real Landon is sensitive.

Landon Donovan is driven.

The real Landon is content.

Landon Donovan forces himself to be a force around thousands of people.

The real Landon gains energy from being alone.

Landon Donovan knows exactly what he needs to be.

The real Landon is learning who he is.

Landon Donovan attacks whatever is in his way.

The real Landon likes setting up other people.

Landon Donovan blocks out distractions and plays like a machine.

The real Landon is curious and welcomes human connection.

Landon Donovan is a superstar.

The real Landon is reluctant in the spotlight.

Once I knew who I was, I was able to let others in. Depression doesn't just go away, but when I let others into my life and allowed myself to really connect with people, I gave myself the tools I needed to confront it and find my peace.

I owe so many people for helping me with my growth. Perhaps no one is more deserving than Juliet, for guiding me to myself and my happiness.

There is no shame in seeking and accepting help.

The Donovans are a pro-therapy family.

We invite you to be the same.

POSTGAME

———

THERE'S A quote I've always liked that may have originated with John Lennon:

"When I was five years old, my mother always told me that happiness was the key to life. When I went to school, they asked me what I wanted to be when I grew up. I wrote down 'happy.' They told me I didn't understand the assignment. I told them they didn't understand life."

You can love anybody if you take the time to learn their story. When I really tried to understand my father's past, I was able to find compassion for him and empathize with his behavior. Doing that allowed me to forgive him. Today we have an incredible relationship that I cherish greatly.

My dad is kind, thoughtful, and interested in the real me. I'm far from perfect and I embrace the flaws that have come from my life of adventure. I hope a few of the people that I may have failed from time to time—people like Bianca, David Beckham, and perhaps even Joshie—will forgive me for any hurt caused by our collisions on this planet. Now that you know my story, I hope some of "me" makes sense.

I judge myself less now by what I've done and more by who I've become. I have come a long way from the kid looking for a way out. It turns out that the only way out was to find a way *in*. To get out from the closed-off person I had become, I had to go inside: inside my mind, inside myself, and inside my truth. And I had to learn to let others in to help me.

I see myself today as a man, as a husband, as a present dad, as a coach, as a teammate, and as a human being at least as much as I see myself as a soccer player. I am all those things; each is a part of me developed little by little over decades thanks to the help of so many others.

My journey began with feelings of anger and anxiety due to my fatherless upbringing; I recognize that I am hardly alone in that. According to the U.S. census, almost 25 million American children are growing up without their biological fathers in the house. That's one out of every three kids. When you break it down by ethnicity, the numbers are even starker: While only one out of every five White kids lives without their biological fathers, one out of every three Hispanic kids and one out of every two Black kids are growing up fatherless. Fatherlessness and all its effects is one of the largest epidemics our country faces, one we have yet to really acknowledge. And that doesn't count the millions more with emotionally vacant fathers—physically present, but too occupied with their own issues to be there for the other people in their household.

If you are one of those kids and you are reading this book, take a deep breath, and please know this: My story really *can* be your story. I came from thrift clothes and Spam dinners, from an effectively fatherless childhood and a loving but overworked mother, and I was able to move beyond it to something better—not just by succeeding as a soccer player, but by growing as a person. I hope you can find it in your heart to keep going and to *believe in yourself*.

Through therapy, I was able to confront and mend my relationship with my father. I found the compassion I needed to understand the complexities of his life, and that helped bring us back together. I understand that not everyone can be so lucky and that there are relationships that cannot—even some that should not—be mended.

But if you are a parent who would like to work through a difficult relationship with your son or daughter, and you haven't yet done so, I hope you will consider giving it a shot. If you are a son or daughter who would like to improve your relationship with a parent, perhaps start by sharing this story with them.

And if you have a stepparent who you took for granted in your life, perhaps it's time to extend an olive branch. Paul... this branch is for you. Thank you for all you did for my mom, for Tris, and for me. You became so much more than just "the Magician" to me a long, long time ago.

If you feel like you could benefit from talking to a therapist, I'm here to tell you that you can. No matter our age, deep down inside we are all little children trapped in the shells of our adult bodies. Confronting what needs to be confronted can be the most liberating feeling on the planet. While you cannot control how others respond to you, coming to terms with yourself can give you the freedom to move on.

My story is a story about what's possible when you don't allow circumstances that are out of your control to control you. With hard work, you can do anything.

If I can do it, you can too.

I hope you believe that to be true, and remember:

How you do anything is how you do everything.

LANDON

ACKNOWLEDGEMENTS

TO THE PAGE TWO TEAM,

Thank you for your guidance, support, and patience throughout this process. Jesse, your leadership was vital and I am incredibly grateful. Rony, Leslie, Viktoria, Rachel, and Felicia—it was a pleasure to work together.

MOM,

Now that I have children, I don't know how you did it. You were a single mother with three children, working full-time as a special ed teacher while struggling to make ends meet. And I never ever heard you complain once. You are an angel. Thank you for being the wind beneath my wings.

DAD,

While I wish my childhood would have been different, I am incredibly grateful for the past decade we've had together. You've become an amazing father and grandfather. Remember, work hard and play smart!

BOSS,

Thank you, Rich, for being the father figure I so desperately needed. You're the best soccer agent in this country, but, much more than that, you're an incredible human being. Thank you for your unconditional love and support.

TRIS,

We were in the womb together! You have always been my guiding light and kept me humble whenever my ego got the best of me. Thank you for always supporting me and my dreams, even when they brought you pain. I love you so much.

JOSHIE,

The greatest joys of my childhood revolve around us playing together. Thank you for being the best brother a boy could ever ask for.

RYAN,

What a journey this has been! Thank you for your patience through all the hard work and challenges. I know it hasn't been easy, but you've handled it with grace and compassion. Thank you for embodying *How you do anything is how you do everything*!

TO MY ANGEL,

I never thought I would get married again. That all changed when I met you. Thank you for supporting me through all my crazy endeavors and believing in me. I love you so much.

CHEETAH,

You challenge me in so many amazing ways I never thought possible. I love your kind heart, big brain, and desire to always push the limits.

SLATEY,

I never thought I would have a child that was more obsessed with soccer than me! I love your contagious laugh, patient soul, and calm wisdom.

YAY YAY,

You are truly one of a kind. Thank you for bringing me joy every day. I love your bubbly spirit, the way you roll your eyes at me, and your gentle kindness.

ABOUT THE AUTHOR

LANDON DONOVAN is a U.S. soccer icon, a six-time MLS Cup champion, and the all-time joint-leading scorer for the U.S. Men's National Team. He's also the namesake of Major League Soccer's MVP award. After a career that spanned stints with Bayer Leverkusen, Everton, and L.A. Galaxy, Donovan transitioned into media. His podcast with Tim Howard, *Unfiltered Soccer*, offers candid insights into the world of soccer. A Southern California native, Landon lives in San Diego with his wife and their three kids.

ABOUT THE WRITER

RYAN BERMAN is a best-selling author, keynote speaker, and the host of *The Courageous Podcast*. He's also the founder of Courageous—a fear-fighting courage company that helps organizations install courage where (and when) they need it most. A lifelong U.S. soccer fan, Ryan still believes the beautiful game can help "Unite" the States. He lives in Southern California and loves his wife, his two kids, and this courageous story. He thanks his brilliant brother Matt for all his editorial contributions to enhancing this important memoir.